Creative Justice

Creative Justice

Cultural Industries, Work and Inequality

Mark Banks

ROWMAN &
LITTLEFIELD
INTERNATIONAL

London • New York

Published by Rowman & Littlefield International, Ltd.
Unit A, Whitacre Mews, 26-34 Stannary Street, London SE11 4AB
www.rowmaninternational.com

Rowman & Littlefield International, Ltd. is an affiliate of Rowman & Littlefield
4501 Forbes Boulevard, Suite 200, Lanham, Maryland 20706, USA
With additional offices in Boulder, New York, Toronto (Canada), and Plymouth (UK)
www.rowman.com

British Library Cataloguing in Publication Data
A catalogue record for this book is available from the British Library

ISBN HB 978-1-7866-0128-5
      PB 978-1-7866-0129-2

Library of Congress Cataloging-in-Publication Data is Available

ISBN 978-1-78660-128-5 (cloth: alk. paper)
ISBN 978-1-78660-129-2 (pbk: alk. paper)
ISBN 978-1-78660-130-8 (electronic)

∞ ™ The paper used in this publication meets the minimum requirements of American
National Standard for Information Sciences—Permanence of Paper for Printed Library
Materials, ANSI/NISO Z39.48-1992.

Printed in the United States of America

Contents

List of Tables

Acknowledgements

Justice is about acknowledging debts and paying dues. So I want to give thanks to all those people who have variously helped me to think about, talk about and (eventually) write about the ideas contained in this book: Daniel Allington, Heidi Ashton, Sarah Brouillette, Richard Collins, Bridget Conor, Mark Doffman, John Downey, Byron Dueck, Doris Ruth Eikhof, Kirsten Forkert, Melissa Gregg, Alison Harvey, David Hesmondhalgh, Marjana Johansson, Tim Jordan, Jilly Boyce Kay, Austin Li, Paul Long, Sara MacKian, Vicki Mayer, Liz McFall, Jack Newsinger, Kate Oakley, Justin O'Connor, Stevphen Shukaitis, Martyna Sliwa, Catherine Tackley, Dan Webster, Helen Wood, Kath Woodward and Natalie Wreyford.

Special thanks must go to Jason Toynbee – a just critic and a true friend.

Thanks also to Martina O'Sullivan at Rowman and Littlefield International for her great support in commissioning and developing the book.

Chapter 3 is partly based on a previously published article:

• Banks, Mark, 2012. 'MacIntyre, Bourdieu and the Practice of Jazz.' *Popular Music* 31 4: 69–86.

I am grateful to Cambridge Journals for permission to reproduce extracts from it here.

This book is dedicated to my daughters, Ellie and Pip – two of the fiercest critics of injustice I know.

Chapter 1

Introduction

Cultural Work and Justice

Social justice, we might say, is about both giving and receiving. To give or *do* justice is to offer respect and due consideration – to attribute appropriate weighting to specific qualities, and to treat fairly and reasonably in the light of those qualities. To *receive* justice is to be evaluated equitably and given our due, or to be appraised and administered in accordance with our legitimate rights, entitlements or needs. It is a tautology – but an important and meaningful one – to say we must be treated justly in order for justice to be done. In this book I want to focus on both the giving and the receiving of justice in the contexts of work and education in the cultural industries.[1]

Initially, the first kind of justice I want to give is to culture itself. This might seem a strange point of departure, but is meant to divert attention towards something I think we are in danger of losing sight of in our determination to relativize value and reify the 'creative economy[2]' – a sense of the objective qualities of culture and the aesthetic. At first reading this might appear a reactionary move, a prelude to advocating some return to idealism and veneration for the 'pure' work of art – but it's not meant to be. Instead it's an effort to connect with a valuable and long-standing (though now somewhat unfashionable) concern with the goods of 'things in themselves' – or, to put this in more academic terms, how cultural value might be better understood through a non-relativist sociological aesthetics. Less abstractly, just as Andrew Ross so ably demonstrates in *Real Love: In Pursuit of Cultural Justice* (1998), it is an attempt to 'pay respect' and do justice to culture, which first involves trying to take it seriously on something like its own terms:

> While culture may be viewed as a vehicle for rights or political claims, part of my purpose is to show that justice must also be done to culture itself. Doing justice to culture, for example, includes respect for the rules and law of a genre.[3]
> (Ross, 1998, p. 4)

In *Real Love*, Ross seeks to combine this sense of justice for cultural forms, with evaluation of the values and claims that culture is invested with, as well as the capacity of culture to help manifest and enact different kinds of social action. While I'm not especially concerned here with particular genres, this full and inclusive respect for cultural industry objects (appraised within their appropriate social context) foreshadows something of my own approach in this book.

Secondly, I want to think about how justice might be given to cultural work[4] itself. Again, to clarify, this is not meant to idealise or romanticise labour, or to ignore its deleterious effects, but simply to recognise the standing of cultural work as a specific kind of *practice* (Keat, 2000; MacIntyre, 1981; Muirhead, 2004). Such an approach focuses explicitly on exploring the plural value(s) of work – the range of qualities or benefits (and disbenefits) we might attribute or obtain through its undertaking. This involves consideration of cultural work as a source of (not just) an economic value, but also a social value, as well as an aesthetic one, underwritten by different kinds of political sensibilities. Doing justice to cultural work therefore means respecting the 'internal' goods and qualities of work as a practice – but without discounting the 'external' structures and pressures that tend to make such work somewhat less than appealing, and often deeply unfair and unjust.

Thirdly, I want to consider how different institutions – such as art schools, universities, firms and organisations – distribute their resources and favours in more or less fair or equal ways. More specifically, I am concerned with *distributive justice*[5] in terms of who receives the most prestigious cultural education, the highest pay and the best (or indeed any) kind of cultural industry job. Critical social science, workers' organisations and journalists have begun to draw attention to patterns of discrimination and disadvantage here, mainly couched in terms of class, gender and ethnicity, as well as age and disability. I will review some of this evidence, firstly in relation to arts and cultural education, secondly in terms of employment opportunities and thirdly in respect of pay and income. In doing so, I consistently adopt the view that a more even distribution of positions and rewards in the cultural industries is defensible on grounds of economic opportunity (everyone who wishes to should have a fair chance to enter, participate in and earn a living from cultural work), on cultural grounds (in cultural work, people should have similar opportunities to obtain recognition, and to express themselves and their interests, within certain limits[6]) and in terms of enhancing the democratic polity (a pluralist, multivocal society that permits cultural dialogue between different democratically inclined parties and interests is better than one that does not). These are some of the foundations on which arguments for *creative justice* might be built.

Such an approach assumes the prerequisite of accepting *equality* and *equity* as social goods and inequality and inequity as social bads. I take equality in this case to mean that people are able to be treated as dignified beings of equivalent human worth who have the right to seek education and employment on an equal basis with others[7]. Additionally, thereafter, I suggest that any differences in the way positions and rewards are socially distributed should be *equitable* – that is, the result of a fair and just process[8], one whose outcomes are sufficient to minimise or offset undue disparities in opportunities, incomes or social statuses. While equality and equity are not the only possible principles for justice, they are foundationally important in the cultural industries, where primary concerns lay with (a) economic resourc ing, (b) cultural expression and recognition and (c) political participation. It might be argued that if the economic resources that circulate in the cultural industries are unequally (or inequitably) distributed[9], then opportunities to make a living in cultural work are unlikely to extend to the fullest range of the population. Unfair privileges and the hoarding of wealth undermine the capacities of the less privileged to participate and contribute as social equals. Similarly, if only certain persons or social groups are recognised as legitimate cultural workers, then other populations who might wish to make contributions may not be afforded equal opportunities to do so. This not only has consequences for the particular populations involved, but creates a broader democratic deficit, since the range of voices and perspectives that circulate in the cultural arena is diminished. Thus, in economic, cultural and political terms, a limiting of wealth, access and opportunity leads to an underdevelopment of individual (and social) potential. This is to the detriment of society as judged from an equalitarian and equitable perspective.

A TIME FOR JUSTICE?

Why should we be concerned with issues of 'creative justice' at this particular moment? I think there are at least three compelling reasons:

- Firstly, in social science, there is an apparent 'crisis' of cultural value – partly evidenced in efforts to challenge the idea that cultural *objects* (and the cultural *work* that manifests them) might contain their own objective value. Certainly, in sociology especially, claims that cultural objects might contain their own 'intrinsic' value have come to be regarded as partial, elitist or otherwise politically suspect – and much less significant than theorising either the social origins of value judgement, or the (non-aesthetic) economic or social benefits that culture might usefully provide. As I will argue, while I have many sympathies with this approach (not least because it can expose injustices and inequalities), it has its own limitations, in terms of being (a) sociologically reductive and (b) having a tendency to overlook both objective value and the social necessity of normative judgement[10]. In terms of work, as the commercial imperative has become more central to the cultural (or 'creative') industries, so *other* kinds of values or motivations to work have come to be regarded as less significant (in commercial and policy terms) and much less vital (in political or socio-logical terms). Culture, therefore, (whether located in 'object' or 'work') has not only become routinely (and reductively) cast as an instrument of power, but increasingly decoupled from its potential to offer meaningful, non-commercial experiences, including progressive elements of social or political *critique*. Both of these developments fail to do justice to the full potential (and actuality) of culture (and cultural work), in my view.

• Secondly, we need to challenge some of the more extravagant claims being made about the economic value and social benefits of the so-called 'creative economy'. While governments have tended to present evidence of rapid and expansive growth in cultural and creative education, jobs, incomes and revenue, with benefits presumed for all, research from critical social science, public policy and the third sector has offered a quite differ-ent perspective. Indeed, beneath the official statistics and the eye-catching headlines, such research has revealed a more complex and troubled pic-ture – one where, for the majority, the best kinds of creative education remain elusive and good jobs in culture are becoming harder to obtain. Additionally, in low-status and entry-level work, wages seem to be rapidly depreciating or disappearing, opportunities for promotion diminishing and conditions of work becoming more oppressive and unmanageable, espe-cially when compared with the conditions enjoyed by some of the more established industry elites.

• Thirdly, we should be concerned because it's no longer sufficient to say that working lives in the cultural industries are unknown to us. The last decade or so has seen a huge turn towards studies of cultural and creative labour in the social sciences (and beyond[11]) – and its well known that the allegedly universal benefits of the creative economy are proving elusive for the majority and tending mainly to accrue to the privileged few. The empirical case demonstrating problems of (say) exploitation, discrimina-tion and misrecognition is now more firmly established, informing calls for reform that have become more vocal and more pressing. Thus, while new empirical work remains vital, scholars have begun to pose questions that seek to move us beyond the particularities of specific cases and speak more generally to the formation of normative principles for action. These ques-tions include: What kinds of values or actions might underpin a fairer or more just cultural work? What kinds of better working lives do we want to imagine or help create? This book aims to suggest (at least some) tentative answers to these vital enquiries.

Such questions are not necessarily new of course, but they do seem to have become more resonant for practitioners and academics alike, and scholars have approached them from a variety of disciplinary perspectives. However, I think it is sociology, media and cultural studies that have offered the most sustained and fruitful engagement with such questions, and it is mainly within their parameters that I frame the intellectual concerns of this book. Throughout, I will draw variously on three (quite loosely defined) perspectives that I think best interrogate the questions and dilemmas suggested by the idea of creative justice:

- The first is a 'critical' or 'critical theory' approach, which I use in a deliberately broad sense, seeking to incorporate a diverse group of scholars working in various strands of sociology, political economy, feminism and media and cultural studies. This includes research on cultural work by recognised experts such as Andrew Ross, Angela McRobbie and David Hesmondhalgh, work on artistic labour by Janet Wolff, but also culturally literate research with a slightly different (and more philosophical) focus such as that undertaken by Nancy Fraser, Russell Keat, Alasdair MacIntyre and Andrew Sayer. All this research shares the virtue of being especially eloquent on issues of economic and cultural injustice. Mostly, it tends to be quite openly normative[12] and much concerned with prospects and potentials for the reform of (cultural) work and the structural or institutional conditions that shape it.
- The second approach is more specifically informed by the sociology of Pierre Bourdieu. This is less explicitly work-focused, tending instead to concentrate on the ways in which value is socially defined in the 'field of cultural production', as well as the ways in which education (and work) are based on systems of cultural misrecognition that help reproduce established patterns of inequality (e.g. Bourdieu and Passeron, 1977). It also focuses on how cultural producers compete with one another to secure various capitals that can aid in the securing of social prestige and status (e.g. see Kirschbaum, 2007; Faulkner et al, 2008; Pinheiro and Dowd, 2009). While this approach is similarly 'critical', it tends to be less explicitly normative and much less concerned with making statements about justice or social reform per se than the first kind of approach, though such statements are not entirely absent from it (e.g. see Bourdieu, 1998).
- Finally (and featuring much less prominently in the book) is a 'pragmatist' perspective that tends to favour emphasising the more specific and contingent aspects of cultural valuation and organisation and the ways in which these might be exposed through deep(er) forms of empirical inquiry. Research in this vein tends to align with critical anthropology, actor-network theory or the new 'sociology of critique' (e.g. see Hennion, 2007;

Stark, 2009; Fox, 2015; Entwistle and Slater, 2014) and is often marked by an agnostic (or occasionally hostile) attitude towards normative social science. I also make reference to others, such as Georgina Born (2010), who has attempted to assemble a more integrative ('post-positivist') approach that combines both pragmatic empiricism, with elements of critique drawn from Bourdieu, and critical theory.

As I'll show, each approach has something to offer, though (as will become clear) one is perhaps better equipped than the others, both to theorise and help more fully realise the kind of creative justice that I'm inclined to favour. So while the main purposes of this book are, firstly, to do justice to the qualities and values of objects and work; secondly, to concretely identify examples of distributive injustice and inequality *in* cultural work; and thirdly to outline some of the ideas and strategies that are (or might be) used to tackle such injustices, its further ambition is to consider these concerns within the context of different ways of thinking about cultural work. Or, to put this slightly differently, this book seeks to identify the kinds of social science understandings that might provide the best or most congenial underpinnings for a theory of creative justice.

THE CHAPTERS

In chapter 2, I begin this exploration of creative justice by making a case for the more objective valuation of cultural objects. If this seems an unusual place to begin a book that is predominantly about cultural *work*, it ought to be noted that discussion of the products of cultural labour – cultural goods themselves – must be foundational to any account of creative justice; they are, after all, much the motivating reason why anyone chooses to work in culture in the first place. Yet, that we take cultural objects seriously – in their own right – runs counter to much contemporary socio-cultural analysis, which, in a mainly constructionist vein, has tended to look on cultural goods as having a value that is entirely subjective and largely determined by the status and power of those making an evaluation. Taking the work of Pierre Bourdieu as exemplary, the chapter outlines how recent sociology has undermined the idea of objective cultural value and so sidelined a set of contrasting and well-established concerns about aesthetics and the specific qualities of cultural goods. Using the work of some of Bourdieu's critics – such as Janet Wolff, Simon Stewart, Georgina Born and Antoine Hennion – I outline a case for a sociological aesthetics that takes both subjective apprehension *and* objective qualities as being component parts of the value of cultural industry goods. In this way, I propose we can do better justice to the objects that lie at the heart of the cultural industries production process – and so more fully recognise their value and potential.

Chapter 3 continues the theme of objectivity (and Bourdieu critique) by focusing on the idea of cultural work as a socially embedded and ethical *practice*. This is an effort to do justice to the fullest qualities of cultural work itself – and the native reasons why anyone might choose to partake in it. While the production of art and culture – at least in Bourdieu's terms – is principally an exercise in social competition, status seeking and self-interest (however consciously or unconsciously this is deemed to proceed), in the terms I present it (drawing on the work of neo-Aristotelian philosopher, Alastair MacIntyre), it's *also* an activity driven by intrinsic rewards, objective standards and ethical concerns for the community. Cultural work is presented as an undertaking that produces both 'internal' and 'external' goods – the former being specific rewards that can derive only from immersion in the demands of the practice in question; the latter being rewards such as money, prestige and power that stand in a contingent, rather than dependent, relation to the practice. Yet, practices of professional cultural work – let's say in dancing, journalism or music – require *both* internal and external goods if they are to develop and flourish, and it's the interplay between the two that shapes the form and character of the activity. Foregrounded here is a sense that cultural work is a locus of objective relations – a place where concern for the qualities and properties of a real activity (let's say the objective standards of dancing a jive, writing an editorial or drumming in a rock band) – relate to an articulated sense that the practice is itself good in terms of supporting and extending 'human powers' and our personal and social needs for self-expression, recognition and reciprocity. It just so happens that, at the same time, external considerations are also in play. These include (as Bourdieu shows us) struggles to define what is culturally legitimate, since the objective standards and hierarchies of value exhibited in cultural practices are also partly arbitrary, and contested, in the sense of being strongly shaped by histories of socialisation and partial, politicised judgements. Thus, as in the previous chapter, chapter 3 attempts to offer a more qualified objectivist (as well as subjectivist) understanding of cultural work in order to do the fullest justice to the qualities of work itself.

By way of contrast, chapter 4 focuses somewhat more on the social construction of the creative economy by offering a sympathetic reading (and application) of Bourdieu's work on educational selection. Here we move into the discussion of how resources and positions are socially *distributed* and how cultural value is recognised and judged. The focus here is on 'talent' – that most precious and abiding value in the cultural industries. While, once again, the approach I take presupposes some kind of objective basis for talent (in the sense that people have physical and mental capacities they are in some way capable of expressing), the chapter focuses more specifically on the ways in which talent is socially defined and attributed in the cultural industries. It is shown how, even if we accept that ordinary people might possess their own particular creative qualities or capacities (whether we believe these to be predominantly inborn or socially ascribed), there is no guarantee that such attributes will be recognised or given opportunities to become cultivated or flourish – because entrenched patterns of social and workplace inequality tend not to permit it. I explore how the discourse of talent serves also to cast a convenient veil over some exclusive and unequal systems of cultural and creative industry education – ones based on inequitable selections that favour the favoured and so pervasively undermine the very egalitarian structures they claim to support. As is discussed, institutions such as art schools, conservatoires and elite academies are revealed to be much less guilty of elevating and rewarding the naturally 'gifted and talented' than reproducing established prejudices and patterns of social advantage.

The issue of cultural work access and opportunity – and its social distribution – is taken up in chapter 5. The UK cultural industries have long been regarded as exemplary meritocracies, places where ordinary people can carve out careers based solely on their talent and application. However, some recent evidence has started to challenge the assumption of a creative meritocracy, and there are now serious concerns that the cultural sector is far from the level-playing field that many assert it to be. Much of this evidence points convincingly to accelerated inequalities in cultural work and so a contradiction of claims that arts and culture offer full participation opportunities for both ordinary or minority social groups. But before reviewing this contemporary evidence, the chapter poses a more foundational query: Have the cultural industries *ever* been meritocratic? To try and answer this, I return to the middle part of the twentieth century, the period of the economic 'long boom' that began in the 1950s, where the cultural industries were rapidly expanding, and where a meritocratic discourse based on access and opportunity began to achieve social currency. By exploring some historical patterns of work and employment, I show how – far from being a contemporary phenomenon – inequity and inequality have *always* been present in cultural work, to some greater or lesser degree. However, the chapter then goes on to reveal that the relative lack of data about these historical inequalities may also have helped to negate serious discussion of some of the problems of the *contemporary* cultural workplace.

Chapter 6 continues the theme of distributive injustice by exploring the ways in which pay, wages and income have been socially shared. The chapter begins with a general assessment of the endemic problem of low pay across all arts and cultural work, before moving to look more closely at income differentials within discrete cultural industries. Here, one of the more persuasive arguments made to explain the prevalence of low pay amongst artists and cultural workers is that 'the market decides' – in accordance with the laws of supply and demand. In this formulation, low wages merely reflect an 'over-supply' of workers, and pay is being further diminished by the widespread collapse of established cultural industry business models and income streams, and additionally undermined by the public's increased expectations that they should pay less (or sometimes nothing) for access to art and cultural goods. Yet, as is discussed, what this argument overlooks is the significant *disparities* in the distribution of income between the elites and the majority, and how these inequalities are just as fundamental in explaining patterns of (mostly low) pay in arts and culture. The elite 'economy of superstars' – whether these be artists, managers or executives – are being increasingly rewarded at the *expense* of the ordinary worker – suggesting a further (socially unjust) closing down of opportunity for the majority of cultural industry aspirants.

Chapter 7 brings the book to a conclusion by outlining, in provisional fashion, some concepts and principles that might help effect a greater creative justice, tied to particular recommendations for action. While these concepts are propositional and somewhat abstract, attention then turns to how they might *already* be informing strategies currently being used to bring justice to cultural work, including some of the concrete interventions currently being made by workers, campaigners and organisations. In such contexts, while the more general prospects appear inimical to creative justice, we find the hope and possibility of fairer and more equalitarian cultural workplaces emerging. Yet, it is also being recognised that the problems of cultural work – and the economies that contain them – are serious and systemic and pose some significant challenges for establishing *any* kind of egalitarian justice.

Finally, one or two caveats. While this book is concerned with social justice in the cultural industries, I cannot claim that it offers any comprehensive or definitive account; indeed, it remains quite open as to what justice might even *mean* in this context. As Andrew Ross has noted, 'When it comes to cultural justice, nothing is very formalized' (1998, p. 3) and I keep in mind Michael Walzer's observation that justice is a 'human construction, and it is doubtful that it can be made in only one way' (Walzer, 1983, p. 5). So, while I want to take this opportunity to propose my own ideas, 'creative justice' is first offered as a provocation and point of departure that invites others to speculate on its wider potentials and possibilities. Mainly, however, I use the term as a signal to draw attention to what I consider to be a most important issue – the need to raise consciousness of *in*justice and to help connect the creative economy – and the cultural work it contains – to some normative principles that might make work more progressive and equalitarian, as well as fairer and more just.

NOTES

1. Cultural industries are defined here as those activities involved in the production of goods whose economic value is primarily derived from their aesthetic, expressive or symbolic value. The alternative term 'creative industries' – now more widely used in the United Kingdom, Western Europe, China, South East Asia, Australia and beyond – refers to much the same activities (e.g. film, television, the visual and performing arts, music, fashion, design, writing and journalism, the media industries more generally) but is a more pragmatic, economistic and policy-oriented locution that carries much less connection to critical aspects of politics and culture that have always been implicated in the undertaking of these activities and that remain vital to theorise and value (see Oakley and O'Connor, 2015). For this reason, cultural industries is my preferred term, though creative industries is at times deployed in the book to reflect or account for its usage by others in different and specific contexts.

2. The 'creative economy' is officially defined (in the United Kingdom at least) as all the people employed in the officially designated 'creative industries' (whether these people have creative jobs or not) plus all the people working in creative occupations employed in 'non-creative' industries. The creative economy was estimated to be worth around 133 billion to the UK economy in 2014, comprising around 8.2% of the economy as a whole. This is a highly prestigious and desirable sector that employs over 2.5 million people (see Nesta, 2013; Department of Culture, Media and Sport [DCMS], 2016). Yet, while the creative economy is routinely offered as a productive space where people with talents and imagination are at liberty to pursue their interests in environments marked by openness and equal opportunity, the reality, as we will see, is quite different. 'Creativity' and the 'creative economy' are better understood as part of a prevailing economic doctrine that aggressively promotes the virtues of free markets, entrepreneurship and competitive individualism, while ignoring (and so deepening) problems of inequity and inequality (see Schlesinger, 2007 for an effective critique).

3. And not simply respect for genres, but for the work involved in making them; the labour and the performance of culture demands our respect. As Ross outlines in relation to the case of rap, the work involved is considerable, and 'genre justice…is [significantly] learned at the microphone' (1998, p. 67).

4. By cultural work, I tend to mean activities of artistic, creative or aesthetic production that take place in the contexts of the cultural industries (see endnote 1 above). This mainly includes the labour of artists, designers, musicians, authors, etc. – those primarily responsible for the production of symbolic goods and commodities, and whose labour is taken to be exemplary in that it is imagined to be meaningful and creative, and to contain freedoms and potentials unavailable to other kinds of (non-cultural) worker. While the 'specialness' of cultural work is contestable (e.g. see Stahl, 2013; Toynbee, 2013) and the grounds for its idealisation is open to dispute, it *is* suggested here that culturemaking has a particular (if not exclusively held) value as the kind of work that *might* allow for both economic provisioning *and* the meaningful (personal and shared) examination of life. One premise of this book, therefore, is that given this potential, and its standing as 'good' work (Hesmondhalgh and Baker, 2011), opportunities for cultural work ought to be made more available and more equally and equitably shared. However, the problems of cultural work are

not overlooked, and neither are the *other* kinds of work that, in significant part, make possible the labour of the artist or author. From time to time I will make reference to other kinds of work and worker that exists in the cultural industries (for example in chapter 5), though it should be clear that the primary focus does tend to be on the 'artistic' worker (for want of a better term) throughout.

5. Distributive justice is concerned with 'comparative allotment' (Frankena, 1962, p. 9) – the ways in which material or social goods, conditions, opportunities, incomes and roles are dispersed to, and received by, different populations (see also Walzer, 1983).

6. Freedom of expression is not an absolute – and there are more or less desirable forms of it; most obviously, designated forms of 'hate speech' are regarded by many states as an indefensible and illegal, for example.

7. My understanding of equality here borrows from Martha Nussbaum's more well-known formulation that underpins her work on 'capabilities' (e.g. see Nussbaum, 2003, 2011).

8. If equality is concerned with justice through *sameness* or *equivalence*, then equity is concerned with *fairness* or *justice in proportion* – the idea that each person gets his or her due or what he or she deserves. In the case of cultural work, this means that people's capacities, achievements and contributions, as well as their social advantages and disadvantages, should be justly accounted for in the allotment and distribution of social positions and rewards. Thus, it's worth noting that to be treated equitably is not necessary to be treated the same as someone else – since we might want to make an adjustment in our allocation to 'take into account' social background, for example, or we might feel that someone deserves a differential reward as a compensation for greater effort or attainment. We can therefore have equity without equality – and vice versa. However, as we'll see, the two ideas are also quite closely related. It is often because people in cultural work are treated *in*equitably that inequalities tend to ensue – when black people are not treated fairly (by being racially discriminated against in job interviews, for example) then there tends to be a resultant inequality in the way positions and rewards are socially distributed.

9. Again, this draws our attention to the difference between equality and equity; we can aim for a more equal distribution or a more equitable one; we might want sameness or fairness, in other words. Often these aims are incompatible, or difficult to reconcile, but we might also argue that a more equal distribution can also be a more equitable one, since we might regard the moral worth of human beings as the primary criterion for selection or allocation, and that to treat equally *is* to treat fairly, regardless of other kinds of differential contribution. For example, in the United Kingdom, the adult right to reproduce, or to vote, are both equal *and* equitable, on these terms. In respect of cultural work, we might argue that a more even distribution is also a more equitable one, since a belief that people (as culture-making beings) should have a fair opportunity to participate in cultural work, should they choose to do so, might incline us towards a more equalitarian provision of resources sufficient that the maximum number of participants have the wherewithal to enter and maintain cultural work careers; equality therefore helps furnish the equity (or fairness) that comes with guaranteeing maximal participation for the largest number of potential entrants.

10. Human life is normative life – thereby inherently *evaluative*, that is, always concerned with value and weighing the difference between what *is* and what *could* or *ought* to be, as Andrew Sayer (2011) has persuasively argued. As John Fekete has also put it, 'No aspect of human life is unrelated to values, validations and validations' (Fekete, 1988, p. i), and as Steven Connor further argues, 'The play of value is bound up intimately with motivation and purpose of every kind' (1993, p. 31). For John Frow, value organises 'every aspect of daily life' and there can be 'no escape from the discourse of value' (Frow, 1995, p. 134). Making judgements (and acting upon them) is simply what human beings do – and not just in social science (see Stewart, 2013).

11. For example (and simply from the Anglophone literature on cultural work), see: Ashton and Noonan (2013), Banks (2007), Banks, Gill and Taylor (2013), Brouillette (2014), Caldwell (2008), Cohen (2012), Conor (2014), Conor, Gill and Taylor (2013), Deuze (2010), Eikhof and Warhurst (2013), Forkert, (2014), Gill and Pratt (2008); Hesmondhalgh and Baker (2011), Luckman (2012), Mayer, Banks and Caldwell (2009), McKinlay and Smith (2009), McRobbie (2002; 2016), Ross (2003), Taylor and Littleton (2012). This list barely scratches the surface of the vast array of work that has been produced, globally, in the last decade.

12. It's worth further clarifying what is meant here. Conventionally, of course, social science has been suspicious of 'normativity'; a term often used pejoratively to infer the suspect presence of ethnocentrism, ideology or 'bias'. It was once widely held that in order to be objective (in the sense of 'neutral' or 'value-free'), social science should disavow any normative claims. But the idea of a non-normative social science is not only impossible, it is self-contradicting, in that it uses a normative position ('normativity is wrong or bad') in order to disavow normativity (see Connor, 1993; Sayer, 2011). I would argue that any critical social science worthy of the name *must* be in some way normative – it must adopt an orientation of evaluation and judgement in order to be effective *as* critique; that is, to be able to say why some things are better or worse than others, or indeed to argue for any kind of position, since even a principled non-prescription is itself based on a normative claim. This does not mean that such normative claims are always right or infallible – often they can be wrong – but it is a requirement of critique that it seeks to evaluate and then to posit a *fallible alternative to the actual*, otherwise it can only ever merely describe what already exists, and by doing so exclude the possibility of theorising any kind of progressive or emancipatory change (Horkheimer, 1982; Diken, 2015; Fenton, 2016). The importance of this will be reiterated later in the book.

Chapter 2

Justice for Cultural Objects

How can we do justice to cultural objects? I suggest partly by treating them with respect, on their own terms, and according to their own objective qualities. But this is not so easy to do, at least from a sociological perspective. Here, what is termed 'cultural value' tends to be regarded as subjective and arbitrary, and without objective foundation. Worse, it's commonly argued that cultural value tends to act mostly as an instrument of social domination or oppression. In this respect, what is good and what is prized have little to do with objective quality and much more to do with the self-serving hierarchies established and maintained by more prestigious and powerful social groups.

In fact, within sociology, treating cultural objects[1] as possessing their own inherent qualities has come to be seen as deeply problematic. Pierre Bourdieu remains the most celebrated scourge of such 'idealist' theories of art and culture. His work has proved devastatingly effective in exposing the social basis of taste and dismantling claims for the autonomy of the aesthetic. However, from what we might term a more 'objectivist' (or perhaps in this case 'aesthetically realist') point of view, the characteristic feature of any entity is that it *does* possesses objective[2] qualities that render it sensible as a certain kind of thing, and as one distinct from others – a view I'll explore in this chapter.

The suggestion here is that by insisting on the arbitrary and power-laden foundations of aesthetic judgement, some writers (of which Bourdieu is exemplary) have undermined the possibility of evaluating cultural objects through anything other than currently dominant sociological criteria. In this vein of writing, as Janet Wolff has argued, the unyielding critique of the idea of an autonomous aesthetic appears to 'leave little room for an innocent enjoyment of the encounter with the object' (2008, p. 71) since spontaneous pleasures always appear contaminated by the interests that prefigure them. But while the idea of a 'pure' aesthetic encounter might not survive even the most cursory intellectual scrutiny, it remains the case that a particular kind of injustice is rendered when the qualities of cultural objects are reduced to their role as expressions of some extrinsic sociological properties – and not regarded as *also* having their own objective qualities that might shape their efficacy as valuable and meaningful cultural phenomena. The underlying argument of this chapter, therefore, is that while we must do justice to those sociological contexts (and subjects) implicated in acts of aesthetic evaluation, so we must also respect the cultural objects that are being valued.

The *purpose* of such an argument is to help underpin a critique of how cultural objects have come to be regarded in the creative economy. This is necessary for two reasons:

- Firstly, critical discussions about the *value* of cultural objects, especially in the contexts of the post-Global Financial Crisis (post-GFC) arts and creative economy, have become increasingly reluctant to foreground discussion of the fundamental significance of what is often (idealistically) termed 'intrinsic' value. Partly, as I've suggested, this is because of the quite proper recognition that the attribution of such value has tended to be linked with exclusivity and the imposition of social power. Yet this disinclination has tended to undercut reasoned discussion of *any* of the objective qualities that might inform aesthetic value – usually regarded by practitioners and enthusiasts as being of primary significance in art and cultural production. As a consequence, cultural workers, artists and their supporters now more commonly point to other, complementary or contrasting notions of value, quite often to justify different kinds of funding, recognition or support. This is not necessarily a problem per se, given the wide range of uses to which art and culture might be put, but limiting discussion of this foundational value risks undermining the legitimacy of the sphere of aesthetic judgement, which – whether we like it or not – many people still tend to regard as a primary motivation and interest for making and engaging with art and culture. In the creative economy context, it should still be possible (and is indeed beneficial and necessary) to talk about aesthetic value and the objective qualities of art and culture – not least to better account for why they might actually *matter* to those who produce and consume them.
- Secondly, relatedly, critical attacks on the status of aesthetic expertise (as 'partial', 'oppressive' or 'elite'[3]) and the emergence of non-judgemental and relativist approaches to aesthetic judgement have somewhat conveniently corresponded with growth of a more intensive focus on measuring the value of culture as commodity, especially in the commercial creative industries. As goods to be sold in the creative economy marketplace, whether they are public or private in origin, objects are now valued somewhat less for their aesthetic or (other) cultural properties and rather more

for their commercial potential. Clearly, for some commodities, both values can happily pertain and co-exist[4]. However, in many cases, the cultural value of an object seems damaged or compromised when it is subordinated to – or made to appear commensurate with – an economic value. But while most cultural goods are produced for some kind of market, and would not exist otherwise, to regard them *only* as commodities is to do violence to one half of the dialectic that renders them recognisable as cultural objects in the first place – their aesthetic, symbolic and otherwise meaningful character (Ryan, 1992; Ross, 1998). In short, *politically*, we need to hang on to the idea that there is more to cultural objects than the commercial values they can expediently generate – evidenced not least in their capacities to objectively shape peoples' efforts to understand and live their own lives, and to live with others.

Therefore, I think it's important to retain some sense that – for cultural industry producers and consumers alike – cultural objects retain a value in themselves, which is *partly* derived from their objective properties (some of which are aesthetic), and not simply reducible to an expression of social interests or commodity status. Given this, the realm of culture and the aesthetic judgement it contains is also imagined to provide a political context where different, progressive and egalitarian social futures might still be theorised and imagined, which, however partial or compromised, seems an idea worth preserving – and is a foundational position for the kind of creative economy critique being proposed in this book.

But on what grounds might we support such a position, *sociologically*? In the following sections, following some initial discussion of Bourdieu, I address how four writers have attempted to value cultural objects in ways that are clearly sociological, but not necessarily sociologically *reductive*; writers who have sought to develop what Georgina Born has called a 'non-idealist, non-essentialist theory of aesthetic experience' (Born, 2010, p. 175). It is a difficult enough job. But it is in these writers' work we can begin to identify a more holistic effort to do justice to historical context, subjective apprehension *and* objective aesthetic value in evaluating cultural (and cultural industry) objects and goods.

BOURDIEU: ACCOUNTING FOR TASTE?

The pre-eminent sociologist of cultural value remains (the late) Pierre Bourdieu, whose work has proved enormously influential in shaping the ways in which we understand cultural taste and the aesthetic. His approach – an object lesson in comprehensive sociological analysis – aimed to make visible that which had been previously hidden, namely the social basis of individual taste and the grounds upon which societies attribute value to different cultural objects and forms.

Bourdieu's writings on art and culture are a relentless exercise in demystification. The supposedly natural and essential qualities of 'great art' are revealed, under Bourdieu's unsparing view, to be an illusion – the product of the judgement of those who have a specific interest in judging, and the outcome of a trained perspective that is open only to those sufficiently schooled in the techniques of its execution. In contrast to the notion of a immanent and transcendental aesthetic, most famously attributed to Immanuel Kant in *Critique of Judgement* (1801), Bourdieu argues that artistic beauty is of social manufacture, brought into being by experts and connoisseurs whose elevated social positions rely on being able to express themselves as 'lovers of art' capable of identifying an essential beauty that is invisible to others. Bourdieu's analysis is therefore effective in exposing not only the fallacies of aesthetic idealism but also the ways in which such 'disinterested' aesthetic judgement helps to both manifest and maintain deeply entrenched social divisions and inequalities. The codification of 'high' or 'serious' art, and the classification of 'refined' and 'exquisite' tastes, are revealed as arbitrary judgements, whose principal function is not to allow their bearers access to superior aesthetic experiences, but to distance dominant groups from their social subordinates and cultural inferiors.

At the centre of Bourdieu's analysis is an account of the emergence of the idea of aesthetic *autonomy*. His work traces how the idea of a 'pure gaze' (that through which the innate essence of an art object might be revealed to the spectator) takes root in early-modern and emergently bourgeois societies, where an independent and autonomous artistic 'field' first begins to emerge, distinct from the patronage of church or court. The field is the arena in which social struggles over the definition and meaning of art take place – the social (and economic) context in which artistic practices are realised and where artists compete for prestige and legitimacy. For Bourdieu the rise of such a field – populated not just by artists, but newly formed markets, institutions, critics, galleries, suppliers and so forth – both creates and demands the conditions under which the idea of an autonomous aesthetic gaze can flourish:

> Although it appears to itself like a gift of nature, the eye of the ... art lover is the product of history. ... The pure gaze capable of apprehending the work of art as it demands to be apprehended (in itself and for itself, as form and not as function) is inseparable from the appearance of producers motivated by a pure artistic intention, itself indissociable from the emergence of an autonomous artistic field capable or posing and imposing its own goals in the face of external demands; and it is also inseparable from the corresponding appearance of a

population of 'amateurs' and 'connoisseurs' capable of applying to the works thus produced the 'pure' gaze which they call for. (Bourdieu, 1996, p. 288)

The desire to create an internally directed field of art, with its own practices and logic, distinct from other (more earthly) fields of endeavour, arises in counterpoint to the logic of post-Enlightenment societies where progress is measured in the application of human rationality to unruly natures. Art is a refuge for artists: special beings who see nature and the world differently, and who use distinct and different means to encounter them – most notably, the romantic, aesthetic gaze. Yet this aesthetic separation is also an economic separation. The pure gaze is central to an aesthetic posture which publicly disavows instrumentality and commerce, inverting the hierarchies of value to establish some apparently independent criteria of legitimacy. The world of art is in Bourdieu's well-known phrase 'the economic world reversed' since in this symbolic economy, participants vie for prestige, and all the trappings of consecration, and disavow the 'heteronomous' principles of money accumulation and wealth. But while an investment in the artistic field appears designed to generate a symbolic rather than financial profit, this is *also* seen (crucially) by Bourdieu as convertible or exchangeable, in time, to other kinds of capital, including more conventional economic rewards.

Principally, then, the field of cultural production is one of a number of relatively autonomous but intersecting fields ('the field of power', 'the economic field', etc.) where struggles for social status and position are routinely played out. At stake in these fields are precisely the various kinds of 'capital' which include not just economic capital but also cultural capital (credentials, qualifications) and social capital (networks, contacts), all fundamental resources that allow for the accumulation and transfer of power and advantage and the attendant subordination of others. This is revealed in the practices of art dealers, curators, museums, galleries, academies and schools, critics and commentators, with their history of canonised movements, vital institutions, favoured practitioners and the endlessly changing roll call of the consecrated, vilified or disclaimed. For Bourdieu, it is precisely this 'permanent struggle between possessors of specific capital and those who are deprived of it' that constitutes 'the motor of an incessant transformation of the supply of symbolic products' (1996, p. 127).

While the cultural field is relatively autonomous and durable, as well as inward-looking, the capacity for aesthetic judgement, to see art as it 'really is', is not without an external purpose and consequence, since to be able to appreciate the canon of great and serious works is to distinguish oneself as a person of cultivated taste, manifestly superior to those who lack such a quality. The possession of what appears to be an ease and familiarity with art is a marker of social (class) distinction; one that is not only suggestive of

intelligence but of a 'refined' background that values a committed and disci-
plined attentiveness to the demands of an aesthetic education. Often, people
who seem to lack the capacity for aesthetic judgement will feel peripheral
and uneasy when confronted by art. Shamed by their ignorance, or perhaps
conscious of their social disadvantage, the unschooled spectator can feel the
weight of their inferiority – though some might seek to challenge their subordination by either questioning the value of particular art or by dismissing
the need for art itself. Yet, for Bourdieu, those who reject art ('refusing what
is refused' as he would term it) serve only to reinforce the (class) boundaries
that secure privilege for those already privileged, since the tenets and arrangements of the art world – not to mention the personnel – remain undisturbed,
and indeed further legitimised, by this perpetual disjuncture and antagonism
between the art world and 'external' tastes and values.

The field of cultural production is therefore a social construction that
serves a dual purpose, firstly of providing a legitimate context for the expression of an autonomous aesthetic disposition (and all the struggles therein)
and, secondly, for distinguishing its participants as 'cultivated' and compe-
tent spectators and practitioners, relative to external and unqualified others.
It is however unfortunate that in this matrix Bourdieu tends to understand the
work of art itself as largely an *expression* of these struggles; that is, as the
reification of those extra-aesthetic social structures and histories that have
(in his view) determinately contributed to the naming and recognition of an
object as 'art':

> Given that works of art exist as symbolic objects only if they are known and
> recognised ... the sociology of art and literature has to take as its object not
> only the material production but also the symbolic production of the work, i.e.
> the production of the value of the work or, which amounts to the same thing,
> of belief in the value of the work. ... In short, it is a question of understanding
> works of art as a *manifestation* [Bourdieu's emphasis] of the field as whole, in
> which all the powers of the field, and all the determinisms inherent in its struc-
> ture and functioning, are concentrated. (Bourdieu, 1993, p. 37)

The great value of Bourdieu's work is to shatter the illusion of aesthetic
idealism and to disabuse us of the romantic myth of art[5]. To bring history
and sociology to bear on the aesthetic is to render it open to a different kind
of judgement – a more disenchanted, rational dismantling of the artistic aura
and the fetishised art object. Here, the 'work of art' is exposed, not as a self-
revealing entity produced by genius under conditions of ineffable indeterminacy but a specific crystallisation of time and social relations, where meaning
is not intrinsic but linked to social structures and the habits and histories of
those effecting a 'disinterested' judgement. This has been hugely valuable,

creating something of a paradigm shift in both academic and popular under-standings of art worlds, and in the social bases of cultural tastes and distinc-tions. But it has its limits – not least in its inability to recognise and give credence to evaluative criteria that lie beyond the compass of sociologically determined interests.

THE DISAPPEARING OBJECT

While Bourdieu is an exceptionally effective critic, within his work the cul-tural object (a.k.a. the elusive 'thing itself') has a tendency to disappear. This is because, as we've seen, the qualities of art depend on the socio-historical context in which art is defined, and evaluation or appreciation undertaken. In such a scheme, it becomes difficult (perhaps impossible) to offer an expla-nation or analysis of any particular cultural object that takes into account the objective features it might be said to possess, under any specifically aesthetic criteria. Since aesthetics is regarded as unable to fully account for that which it claims as its own, the objective qualities of art, it is left to the sociologists to contextualise (i.e. relativise) this objectivity and by doing so drive out any remnants of that which people tend most strongly to associate with art – such as its capacities to enrich and intensify our senses of beauty, ugliness, tran-scendence, transformation or magic, for example.

No doubt a Bourdieusian perspective offers a necessary antidote to essen-tialism and romantic fallacy – but it does struggle to account for how objects might be valued for non-instrumental purposes or even for their own specific sake. Let me illustrate with a personal example. A theory of habitus and field might appear to adequately explain my own love of David Bowie's music. It is consistent with Bourdieu's theory that someone of my age and social background would express a preference for an artist whose own social origins and trajectory resonated with, and strongly exemplified, the aesthetic aspira-tions of a large number of those born into the mid-to-late twentieth-century British white working and lower-middle class, who, when first presented with and then immersed in popular music and wider popular culture, were offered both compensation and aspiration, and models of personal transformation and social mobility that appeared both urgent and possible. The musical and aesthetic innovations of Bowie exhibited a clear continuity with the estab-lished stylistic norms of popular music, while extending them in new ways. They especially resonated with demands of audiences (like me) for a puta-tively new aesthetic and a model of expressive individualism that could fuel desires for transgression and self-making, while remaining recognisably fixed within a popular and collective form that I (and many thousands of others) consciously shared and (less consciously) helped to reproduce. In this way, mine and many others' taste for Bowie is a mere 'historical quintessence' (Bourdieu 1996, p. xviii; see also Stewart, 2013), amenable to explanation through duly informed sociological analysis. Yet what is not explained is how we might evaluate David Bowie's music, socially *and* aesthetically, in more *qualified* objective (as well as subjective) terms. This might be conceived of in the following ways:

• Firstly in terms of the music's own *structural properties and powers* – in crude terms 'the sound of music itself'. From an aesthetically realist perspective, we might first say that Bowie's music is a physical (material) entity that has its own constitutive properties; objective sonic attributes that are existentially separate to their subjective contemplation or apprehension, since they exist in the real world regardless of what I or anyone else might care to think about them (Sayer, 2000)[6]. While present, these objective properties and powers may or may not become activated, or made apparent, in any particular encounter with human subjects – as listeners bring their own interpretive resources and social histories to the reception context. But, more significantly perhaps, Bowie's music is also a set of sonic arrangements – partly made from physical resources and partly through social convention – that tend to suggest particular meanings, atmospheres or auras. While these are subjectively apprehended, and socially constructed, they are *also*, at the same time, objective – not simply because they too have an existence that is independent of the discourses used to describe them – but because they represent one of the inherent features of music; namely, that it is an entity that innately contains *aesthetic codes*. We might therefore say that the universal presence of aesthetic codes, whatever they happen to be specifically, is one of the objective properties of music (or art) itself. These are not *merely* discursive and ideational, or the pre-valued expressions of a recognised social interest, but objective entities in their own right – and, so too, have their own structures, powers and potentials.
• Secondly, one might also argue that Bourdieu's approach fails to account for the coming together of the objective features of music and the subjective *experience of listening*, or rather the co-productive happenstance of me, and the combined material properties and aesthetic coding of the Bowie music form, in a specific context, and the sensations, cognitions, meanings and bodily actions therein produced – what we might term the full and resonant spectrum of the generative musical encounter (see Frith, 1996; DeNora, 2000; Hennion, 2007). Taken together, we might propose that it is the (objective) physical and aesthetically coded qualities of Bowie's music that combine with apprehending subjects in differing social contexts to help create distinctive patterns of reception, which – while exhibiting some social regularity – also open up spaces of aesthetic indeterminacy,

or a relational 'emergent' situation[7], that is somewhat more open-ended and unpredictable in its outcomes and effects than conventional sociology currently allows for.

- Thirdly, relatedly, nor might such an approach fully explain why certain Bowie recordings have the aesthetic capacity to bring out emotions and feelings, or even bodily movements and physical reactions that *matter*, in the sense of making and remaking one's experience of being alive in a world of others, and that contribute to a sense of self-reflection, well-being, awareness or pleasure (or something opposite or other). Crucially, such effects are not merely socially conditioned, nor straightforwardly predictable, but also emergent in and through my own, and others', subjective engagement with the recordings. This engagement is itself not merely 'subjective' in the sense of simply referring to what I or other individuals might happen to think or feel about Bowie's music, but may be (at least partly) linked to the existence of some *objective* needs that are common to all human subjects – such as the need for care, our social dependencies and the necessity of addressing the various kinds of lack, want and desire associated with our capacities as humans to flourish or suffer[8] (see Keat, 2000; Mohanty, 2001; Sayer 2011; Hesmondhalgh, 2013).

These dimensions help to create and enrich our understanding of the social conditions under which aesthetic judgements about the quality of David Bowie's work are able to be made, both within his *oeuvre* and in respect to others. Bourdieu's theory on its own cannot easily account for these aspects, since it's inclined to regard them as epiphenomena that will express – and tend not to disrupt – the established patterns of social inheritance and norms of reproduction. But while Bourdieu's theory might plausibly reveal why I, or others with my social history, might tend to *like* Bowie's music, or even why I might prefer *Low* to *Ziggy Stardust*, what it can't satisfactorily reveal is the specific objective properties (in the sense I understand them, above), experiential engagements and meaningful effects, that are not simply histori-cal givens, nor, indeed, entirely predictable, but in part arise through specific in situ encounters with the properties of the works themselves; works whose value derives not only from what is socially shaped or inherited but also from the object's own aesthetic properties. To do justice to the cultural object, one has to take seriously not only its social origins but also its objective quali-ties – even if, of course, one does not always agree what they are – since to do otherwise is to presume it has *no* qualities outside of those identified in discourse, or designated arbitrarily through social convention.

Yet, of course, not all sociologists agree with Bourdieu that cultural value is a mere 'historical quintessence' or only an outcome of power struggles in the field of cultural production. In fact, various efforts have been made to reclaim some sense of the objective aesthetic qualities of art and culture, and to argue for why these are as important to consider as more subjectivist or conventionalist aspects in helping us to understand the value of art and culture (see Harrington, 2004 and Prior, 2015 for valuable work in this respect). So before I also try to defend art and culture in similar terms, it's necessary to consider others who have more fully explored this well-trodden – but perhaps not yet fully traversed – conceptual terrain.

THE AESTHETICS OF UNCERTAINTY

As a key figure in the sociology of art and culture, Janet Wolff has spent a long career exploring the idea of a sociological aesthetics. As she has it, 'in reading cultural products, we need to understand their [social] logic of construction and the particular aesthetic codes involved in their formation' (Wolff, 1993, p. 65) – but how might this work in practice?

In *The Aesthetics of Uncertainty* (2008), Wolff provides one example by focusing on evaluations of the work of the early twentieth-century Welsh painters (and siblings), Gwen and Augustus John. The early work of Gwen John – a painter of figurative art, comprising mainly subtle, intimate portraits of solitary women, often captured in domestic settings – met initially with success. With critical patronage, she emerged as an internationally respected artist whose work was displayed at the *Armory Show* (1913), the *Salon d'Automne* (1919) and was championed by the Tate, but which later fell out of favour and became overshadowed by that of her brother, a rather more strident and colourful (though now widely regarded as somewhat less accomplished) artist and personality. Later 'rediscovered', mainly through revisionist critiques offered by feminist scholars, and by a more general renewal of interest in high-modern figurative painting, she became once again recognised as an artist of rare quality. Wolff traces how the changing social contexts for art criticism of the twentieth century might provide frames for understanding shifts in the attribution of value of Gwen John's work. She notes how the conditions of appraisal waxed and waned according to the interests of critics, proposing that certain ingrained suppositions about women and women's art, dispositions towards figurative painting and broader shifts in aesthetic regimes and their associated schools of criticism and connoisseurship, played a significant role in patterns of valuation and revaluation of John's painting. Yet what she also notes is a thread of consistency running through this history of evaluation, some evident 'continuities of judgment' (2008, p. 42) related to the formal criteria of evaluation (the subtlety of brush work, use of shading and colour, composition, etc.) but also the quality of skill and technique used in John's intangible conveyances of intimacy, 'interior' feelings and so on – all of which lead Wolff to suggest that aesthetic criteria can display something of a quasi-autonomous or cross-contextual durability, that might flourish co-independently of the immediate interests of the critic and the social contexts of evaluation. In such a way, Wolff claims that cultural value appears to arise through specific conjunctures of the sociological and the aesthetic:

> The question of whether it is 'any good' is unavoidably a question of consider-ing past and present aesthetic judgments and their context, as much as it is a matter of composition, form and originality. ... In practice aesthetic judgments often mix the purely formal with referential criteria that, though not directly expressions of interest, may be traced to social or political values. (Wolff, 2008, p. 44 and p. 50)

Aesthetic judgement is therefore valid in its own right, but the extent to which formal aesthetic criteria are, as Wolff then claims, 'distinct from ques-tions of interest and use' (ibid., p. 50) remains contestable, and at the heart of what remains at stake in sociological perspectives on art and culture[9]. Nonetheless, even if that particular view remains controversial, there is some evident benefit in an approach that refuses to discount the aesthetic qual-ity of art objects – as if this were somehow an entirely irrelevant feature of their worth – and instead tries to bring them into consideration, using (in an appropriately reflexive 'post-critical' manner) the language and techniques of non-sociological evaluation. For Wolff, the truly vital question is not really whether judgements are able to explicated as either purely 'formal' or 'refer-ential' (that is, as more or less autonomous or socially shaped) but whether one has striven to make 'transparent the grounds for judgment' (ibid., p. 50) – to illuminate the conditions under which value is being attributed (by scholar as much as by spectator or critic) in both sociological *and* non-sociological terms.

In this respect, Wolff has consolidated her interests in the idea of aesthetic value as being 'community-grounded'; that is, neither existing in the prov-ince of universalism or relativism, but situated in the context of shared, democratically accomplished criteria of evaluation. In her view, 'a genuinely principled ethics [and aesthetics] emerges from the negotiation of values in dialogue' (ibid., p. 37). In this respect, aesthetic values are neither fictive or arbitrary, nor entirely socially formatted, but both provisional *and* objec-tive – inherently social and unstable, yet capable of achieving a 'context-transcending legitimation' as arguments in favour of certain ways of valuing particular objects or genres take hold or achieve wider currency. The idea of 'community' might suggest closure or a benign harmony, and may appear to gloss over vital inequalities and differences, but Wolff argues that in a post-idealist context, all ethical and aesthetical claims must proceed not from a position of closure but one of 'uncertainty'. That is, the possibility of making rationally defensible and justifiable claims about value is retained, yet must suspend on a shared recognition that they are conceived in open-ended dialogue, as positions of principle that should not be regarded as infallible or absolute, but as always open to refinement in the light of argument and democratic challenge. Indeed, in ideal form, that is what democracy *is* – the institutionalisation of uncertainty – since its very essence presumes instability and the possible of perfectible change. Wolff is therefore arguing for a more modest and provisional notion of cultural value – a more 'knowing' knowledge, suitably sensitive (after the fall of 'pure' aesthetics) to the dangers of ethnocentricism and the material inequalities (and other forms of violence) that might foreshadow and arise from the application of cultural judgement. Yet as to whether (or how) in these kind of dialogical community contexts 'the criteria for judgment would [or could] be made explicit' (ibid., p. 38) in ways that avoid reproducing existing inequalities and established social hierarchies is perhaps not (yet) fully explained.

THE DYNAMICS OF EVALUATION

Wolff's inquiries remain extremely valuable, but perhaps lack a concrete sense of what might happen in situ, at the moment of encounter with the object. In contrast, the sociologist Simon Stewart has more recently suggested a more mobile frame for capturing what he terms the 'dynamics of the evaluative moment' (2012, p. 153) – the point at which aesthetic or cultural value is attributed or made manifest.

Like Wolff, Stewart acknowledges that while social forces shape aesthetic evaluations (through sedimented class structures, inherited and entrenched systems of ethnic prejudice, gender discrimination and so on), such judgements are not regarded as reducible to these considerations, nor the efficacy of them entirely refuted by their social attribution. Stewart reaffirms the argument made in the introduction to this chapter – challenging the claim that any kind of evaluative, rationally based cultural judgement is arbitrary or merely 'subjective', and thereby divorced of innate relation to the qualities of the object under consideration. Stewart argues that while the broadly constructionist turn in social science has been (quite justifiably) motivated by opposition to some of the more elitist and ethnocentric elements of modernist thought, the common assumption that evaluative judgement is impossible, or rather, always fatally compromised by its hidden interests, is deeply problematic. Such a view not only disqualifies the possibility of one cultural object being regarded as any better or worse than any other, but it also runs counter to the kinds of necessary judgements that are a routine part of everyday life, as he suggests:

> If it isn't possible to form any rational judgement so as to distinguish one cultural object from another, it would not be possible for academics to assess students' work, for publishers to assess the relative merits of the literature submitted to them, for galleries to choose the work of one artist over another, for music colleges to award qualifications to their students. (Stewart, 2012, p. 159)

Developing an objectivist approach, Stewart quite rightly argues that judgement is an intrinsic part of the social and an unavoidable aspect of any kind of associative life that would seek to identify what is better or worse for individuals or society as a whole, in a given circumstance (see also O'Connor, 1993, Sayer, 2011; and chapter 1). While judgement always carries some kind of social risk, the more threatening danger here is that in abandoning the grounds for aesthetic judgement, value is reduced either to that determined by the market (what is good is what sells), or an abject cultural relativism pervades, whereby aesthetic or cultural value is simply what people say it is, irrespective of considerations of form and content, or even of the social and political consequences that might arise from an attitude of 'anything goes', with the implied disqualification of any legitimate intervention in cultural practices or the administration of cultural affairs.

Since judgement is both a practical requirement and a social and political necessity, the question arises of precisely *how* to exercise normative aesthetic judgement in a post-critical era, where structural factors are known to taint even the 'purest' of gazes and where an unbridled subjectivism is discounted as a hopelessly inadequate basis for evaluation and action. Stewart's approach is to try and focus his lens between these two extremes, accounting for both the crystallised power of social inheritance and the concrete sensibilities of taste:

> To zoom in on the dynamics of the evaluative moment means also to keep the cultural object in sight. It means, therefore, to be aware of the properties of cultural objects as well as the sensibilities and dispositions that enable their appreciation. (2013, n.p.)

For Stewart, the value is revealed through 'dynamic moments of evaluation' – in specific encounters with cultural objects. The role of the sociologist (or other critic) is to take these into account in their assessments of how people attribute value to culture. These dynamics are various but include: levels of pre-existing knowledge or experience, the influence of other people present at the moment of evaluation, the individuals and crowds that inform and shape our judgement; the 'level of engagement' with the object, in terms of the intensity of exposure, or the attention (or lack of it) paid; the particular methods through which we engage, the rites, performances and rituals, plans and procedures for encountering; the significance of place and location, where we are when we meet the object; and finally there is – in objective terms – the 'sensuous material qualities of the cultural object' (2012, p. 165), its formal, abstract or concrete properties, as well as its more corporeal, emotive or intangible effects. Stewart's aim is that this micro-social perspective might help better account for the specific value afforded cultural works as property-laden objects, *without* ignoring the socially contextualised and historicised structures that are brought to bear on such objects, and in acts of evaluating them. While he doesn't propose specifically *how* this unity might be achieved, and if there is a danger here of a somewhat messy pile-up of empirical evaluations and a difficulty of explicating aesthetic value specifically, he retains (like Wolff) belief in the prospect of developing a more balanced or intermediate view of the ways in which cultural judgements are founded and formulated.

EMPIRICAL HORIZONS OF VALUE

Further building on Wolff's approach is Georgina Born (2010), who has drawn widely on anthropology, sociology and musicology in her efforts to elaborate a 'post-positivist empiricism' dedicated to exposing the dynamic relations between cultural objects and social worlds. At first, Born's approach – like that of Wolff and Stewart – appears to represent a further search for some fertile middle ground between idealist and social readings of art in which to cultivate a 'non-reductive' account of cultural value, as she reveals:

> To be non-reductive such an account must take on the formative historical power of such aesthetic systems, their substantive artistic significance, coherence and differentiation; and this must be reconnected to an analysis of the interrelations between such formative systems and other social, political and economic dynamics. (2010, p. 188)

However, Born argues that previous efforts to theorise a sociological aesthetics (including Wolff's) have stalled at the problem of how to offer a *fully* critical interpretation of objects, mainly because they've paid insufficient attention to what she terms the 'analytics of mediation'. This refers to the sense in which cultural objects might be studied not merely as 'reflecting' existing social relations, or as possessing universal essences, but as generative entities that sit within (and help to constitute) the regimes of aesthetic value in which they're embedded. Objects are not therefore regarded as inert or static or fixed in value, but as productive and mutable, which, as they move, tend to both mediate and become mediated – providing a focus for, and helping to constitute new social relationships and different kinds of value. In this way, cultural value is linked to what she terms the 'productivity' (rather than passivity, or self-evidency) of the aesthetic – with artistic meaning and value being generated through context, mobility and active use. In support of this view, Born cites approvingly the work of cultural anthropologist Alfred Gell and his particular idea that

> cultural objects (or 'indexes') that result from creative agency condense and mediate the social relations entailed in their production, and ... do so by spinning forms of connectedness across space and time. Through the circulation of these objects the social relations are distributed both spatially and temporally, and in the process the social relations are transformed, as are the objects themselves. (Born 2010, p. 183)

Born recommends a mode of deep empirical inquiry attentive to the distinctiveness of the object and its aesthetic properties, but expressive also of the way in which such an object exists as an 'assemblage of mediations' (ibid., 183) – loosely defined as the complex coming together and movement of social histories, aesthetic conventions, institutional contexts, technologies and persons in and around the entity in question. In this complex, the cultural object is both a kind of distillation *and* an enabling force with its own emergent properties. It invites, through its distinctive properties, cultural producers (and consumers) to orient themselves to particular kinds of evaluation and action.

Born applies such thinking to her own previous and celebrated ethnographic work with IRCAM[10] (an institute of scientific and electronic music research, linked to the Pompidou Centre in Paris) and the British Broadcasting Corporation (BBC) (see Born, 1995; 2005). She outlines, in the former case, the distinctive approach to music (Pierre Boulez-ism) favoured by IRCAM, as it emerged through conjunctures of institutional goals, different authorial intentions and creative practices, yet situated in the wider and unfolding history of an avant-garde committed to musical experimentalism through technological innovation. But by analysing the multiple temporalities at work, Born uncovered how the apparently radical desire to both innovate within (and so revivify) modernism through collaborations between musicians and computer scientists, both expressed and helped manufacture a kind of *anti*-invention. She observed that the overriding value of IRCAM was to establish its credentials and position within the *longue durée* of a 'modernist ontology of cultural-historical time' (Born 2010, p. 197). This led to some conservative policing of aesthetic boundaries, a hostility to change and the installing of institutional protections that were deemed necessary to repel perceived threats from external agents, including other musical forms. In the case of the BBC, Born shows how the introduction during the 1990s of a more bureaucratic and managerialist regime, driven by efficiency targets and accountability measures, led to the production of cheaper, populist productions, and less aesthetic risk-taking and experimentation, but did not necessarily do so uniformly across all departments and genres. This was partly because at any particular juncture, different patterns of aesthetic creativity, inventiveness and redundancy tended to pertain, as much driven by the objective judgements and actions of artists and producers themselves, as by the broader institutional condition and context. Further, because Born argues cultural objects are themselves productive, and generative of social relationships, the composition and recognition of aesthetic value was in part determined by the extent to which the temporal phase of a text or genre was either 'propitious and generative, or unpropitious and in decline' (ibid., p. 193) at different moments. Thus, in the BBC, even under 'Birtism'[11], certain genres flourished and obtained aesthetic currency (post-social-realist dramas, more 'reflexive' and 'authored' documentary and reality formats) while others fell into decline (traditional realist dramas, conventional format documentaries), for both structural-organisational, agentic *and* aesthetic reasons.

In both of her case studies, Born advocates the importance of taking into account the full range of factors that might explain the ways in which cultural value is made manifest or ascribed. There is an effort to do justice not just to the physical and material quality of objects, but the contingent influences brought to bear on them in the 'assemblage' – structures and institutions, agency and subjectivity, time and space and questions of aesthetic quality and judgement. In her work, the issue of normative evaluation, or whether any *particular* work has a tangible, objective value in the sense of being 'good' or 'bad' is perhaps less important than offering a broader conceptual framework within which any works might theoretically be judged. What *is* signalled clearly is that the cultural object plays its own prominent role in informing the ongoing 'analytics of mediation' – a ceaseless process of motile and movable evaluation where the 'thing itself' (whatever objective form it might take) retains significant influence on matters of taste and judgement.

FEELING THE FEELING: PRAGMATICS OF TASTE

Finally, while Wolff, Stewart and Born are sympathetic to some idea of respecting and valuing cultural objects in terms of their own properties, none of them makes particular effort to engage with the materiality and sensuousness of them as *things* – in contrast to the approach of Antoine Hennion. His work has long been focused on revealing the specific qualities of cultural experience, whereby cultural goods, on their own account, 'present themselves' for taste and judgement by persons that possess singular and reflexive minds, as well as receptive and transformative bodies that can both sense and make sense.

If the conventional sociological way to evaluate cultural objects is to reduce them to manifestations of the production of belief, then Hennion shows another more 'reflexive' way of accounting for such faith:

> A reflexive conception of *amateur's* activities leads to a view that is respectful both of amateur's own understandings of their tastes as well as of the practices they undertake to reveal these tastes to themselves. In fact '*amateurs*' do not *believe* things have taste. To the contrary, they bring themselves to detect the taste of things through a continuous elaboration of procedures that put taste to the test. In testing tastes, *amateurs* rely as much on the properties of objects – which, far from being given, have to be deployed in order to be perceived – as on the abilities and sensibilities one needs to train to perceive them. (2007, p. 98)

An analysis of how an object is 'deployed' – and so given to reveal its innate qualities – is offered here through the (somewhat oblique) example of rock climbing:

> What climbing shows is not that the geological rock is a social construction, but that it is a reservoir of differences that can be brought into being. The climber makes the rock as the rock makes the climber. The differences are indeed in the rock, and not [only] in the 'gaze' that is brought to it. (2007, pp. 100–101)

More generally, for Hennion, cultural taste and the encounter with cultural objects is less a story of social determinations *or* essential quality, and rather more a kind of co-generated 'attainment' – a pragmatic accomplishment whereby what he terms an 'amateur' (a consumer, equivalent to a 'fan' or 'enthusiast'), fashioned by history but also generative and reflexive, deploys his or her capacities to judge the qualities of an object, which presents itself with formal properties but also as a mutable 'reservoir of differences' or 'possibilities' (ibid., pp. 100–101). This is so, because while it is possessed of particular characteristics, the qualities of an object are only really made manifest in the 'tasting' (literally or figuratively) undertaken by actors, in specific situations and contexts, who possess both shared and singular capacities and orientations to the object in question. In this respect, taste in culture, is a 'situated activity' (ibid., 101) a moment of coming together between

histories, objects and persons, aided by technologies and qualities of place
and moment, that induce specific sensations which are neither pre-determined
nor entirely individualistic, but emergent. As a pragmatist, Hennion is concerned with the sociology of *situations*, what happens in circumstances where
people do not submit blindly to the endowments of an historical social structure, or unthinkingly make the choices of necessity, but instead co-produce
moments of both determinism and spontaneity in engaging with objects.
What is at stake here is knowledge of;

> the heterogeneity of a real event, not only the masterpiece and the listener, or
> a wine and a drinker, but of bodies, of devices and dispositions, of duration,
> an ungraspable object, an instant that passes, states that emerge. (2007, p. 106)

Here, then, Hennion is proposing a (qualified) objectivist theory of
taste – one that first refuses to reduce encounters of any kind to a pre-
formatted expression of habitus or dispositional logic. The critique of Bourdieu is couched here in explicit terms:

> What *are* social determinants in the literature, by the way? They are blind forces
> that grip you and of which you are ignorant. You think you love things, when
> no, it is your milieu, your origin, your formation that makes you appreciate
> them. Or even more, *a la* Bourdieu, it is the very mechanism of this illusion that
> forms the preference. (ibid., p. 102)

For Bourdieu, it is the *illusio*, or belief in the necessity of the game of cultural production, that binds us to the love we claim as disinterested judgement.
Yet there is, Hennion insists, a 'way of making oneself sensible to things
through the things themselves' (ibid., 102), partly independent of habitus
and history and the mere reproduction of belief. More closely than Bourdieu,
Hennion offers an account of tasting as an *activity*, in which an object with its
own specific properties meets the sensory affordances of the body, in specific
contexts that are to some extent socially shaped, but are never merely the
expression of some exterior power or force. The activity of tasting lies somewhere 'between-the-two' (ibid., p. 101) and is itself generative of sensations
and experiences that are somehow shared and regular, yet are also unique
for each person tasting. Why we value different cultural goods, enjoy certain
sounds, paintings or games is somehow both settled yet wholly indeterminate – accountable in advance, yet spontaneous and made in the moment of
encounter. Hennion's work strives therefore to retain a sense of justice for the
object itself, its productive and propulsive agency and effects, and an intrinsic
value for it in a world of nested and interlocking associations and schemes
of worth. The object is a critical variable in what he terms the 'conditioned

performativity' of the moment of encounter; and this, for him, is partly what must be respected if we are to do justice to cultural worlds.

IMPLICATIONS FOR CREATIVE ECONOMY CRITIQUE

What have these critics told us about the objective qualities of cultural value? To recap: Wolff has offered a sustained critique of the social production of art that nonetheless retains a conviction that the (formal) aesthetic character of objects is both real and significant, and vital for shaping qualities of human experience. Stewart proposes a hypothetical scheme for the dynamic evaluation of cultural goods that are assumed to have their own objective qualities, while also being socially shaped. Born captures the complex enactment of cultural value in contingent settings, historically structured by wider social forces, yet also open and amenable to influence by agents and the object itself. Hennion proposes a sensual and situated pragmatics of taste, one that offers an irreverent challenge to the conventional sociologies of culture with their rigid and overdetermined accounts of socio-historical structure. In their own way, each has alluded explicitly to some (if not all) of the qualities of the cultural object, the sensational and generative aspects of encountering or tasting, and the plurality of possible consequences that might arise from personal and social engagements with such objects – all versions or variations of that which I earlier referred to (using my Bowie example) as the objective (and subjective) world of culture's *properties and powers, experiences* and *matterings*.

What does it mean to think of cultural objects in this way? The first thing to say is that it doesn't rule out any broad agreement with Bourdieu: the values attributed to art and culture remain as expressions of power and products of history. Yet, at the same time, a more qualified approach argues that cultural objects are not *merely* distillations of social convention and interest[12]. They also have their own objective properties (including aesthetic ones), which allow them to be proliferative and generative at the point of encounter with human subjects. Here, they might also have *another* objective value in terms of serving certain human needs – such as, say, for care, communication, nurturing and recognition – that prefigure the discourses that we use to describe and understand them[13]. Taken together, we might say that these are part of the complex reasons why art and culture might have *value* – and partly why people might choose to make or engage with them in the first place, whether in the cultural industries or beyond.

For now, it is perhaps enough to say here that the value of cultural objects is in excess of that ascribed to them either as social facts *or* as commodities.

In terms of informing a critique of creative economy discourse, this has some significant implications:

- Firstly, it retains the idea that public discussion of the objective value of cultural objects, including their aesthetic features, remains worthwhile and necessary. This is important given that, amidst a shrinking settlement and a turn away from the idea of culture as a public good, a more pragmatic, economistic approach to measuring cultural value has now become 'simply unavoidable' (O'Brien, 2010, p. 17; see also Frey, 2008; Wallis and McKinney, 2013; Yudice, 1999)[14]. Arts organisations are required to demonstrate value production in the economic and social spheres, alongside – or sometimes in advance of – the realm of cultural-aesthetic value. But while cultural objects have many potential use values and might reasonably be supported in respect of any of them, it also remains appropriate to make judgements of cultural value in aesthetic terms. This is because while the value for subjects of different cultural objects is in part socially conditioned and arbitrary, it is also tied to the different objective aesthetic qualities that an object might be said to possess, as well as the subjective experiences, and subjective and objective consequences, which encounters with such objects help afford and enact. That different objects might be valued by different people, for different reasons, and that interests and power may be implicated in judging, and that it might be impossible to identify a universally accepted standard of the 'good' or 'bad', does not disqualify that some arts and culture might simply be regarded (at a given moment) as better and more deserving of public support than others, because the community has judged them to be so, for reasons that have been arrived at (as Wolff argues) through a transparent and democratic dialogue. Of course, the history of cultural policymaking shows us that this dialogue is extraordinarily difficult to enact and achieve. Which kinds of culture get made (and get funded) remains highly controversial and often socially unjust. But judgements about the value of art and culture (whether made by academics, critics, or by bodies charged with adjudicating the levels of resource or support they might deserve to receive) cannot be sustained by the idea that the aesthetic form or content of works, and their efficacy in communicating with human subjects, has no bearing on such judgements – to argue otherwise is not simply a misrecognition of art's foundational purpose, but an act of political abandonment[15]. When it comes to cultural value, the proper aim of any informed objectivist (or 'aesthetically realist') approach must therefore be to come up with better criteria and conditions for judging, while recognising judgement's always uncertain, partial and fallible nature.
- Secondly, relatedly, in respect of commercial goods, the insistence on considering the objective properties of cultural objects is important for

helping to slow or counter those expediencies that would reduce the quality of culture to that which can be most effectively commodified or measured against standard economic criteria. As we've seen, some commentators on the creative economy have been keen to project the idea of cultural value as degraded and elitist, or else as now happily co-existent or commensurate with commercial value (Hartley, 2005; Potts et al, 2008; Nesta, 2013; UNESCO, 2013). No doubt this can often be the case. Yet, the arts and cultural industries continue to provide complex goods that can support a whole range of reactions, responses and uses   and acknowledgement of the objective qualities of such goods is part of that complex recognition. Primarily, in this respect, we still need to recognise that cultural objects have significance and value in enabling us to make hermeneutic sense of ourselves and our collective and common life. For Russell Keat (2000), cultural goods (whatever their origin or purpose) have the potential to act as 'meta-goods' – goods that significantly (if not exclusively) through their aesthetic means have the potential to provide us with the resources for helping to reflect on the value and necessity of all *other* kinds of goods:

> [Cultural goods] should be seen as *meta*-goods, as goods whose nature resides at least partly in addressing questions about the nature of (other) human goods and their potential contribution to human well-being. … Their significance resides also, and to a considerable extent, in providing a means by which those audiences can reflect on *other* goods, and hence make better judgments about their possible value for them. (Keat, 2000, p. 1567)

As Keat notes, the category of meta-goods is inclusive and might just as easily include Aristotle's *Ethics* as *Eastenders* (2000, p. 14)[16]. That we need to focus *also* on the ways in which the capacity to make reflective and evaluative choices about culture (and have them validated) is socially stratified (as Bourdieu has shown us) does not undermine that cultural goods contain 'meta' possibilities that are borne partly from their own objective qualities and partly from our subjective engagements with them. I would still propose therefore that through a more nuanced, qualified and holistic approach that considers historical context, subjective appreciation *and* objective quality, we might come to better know what the culture *is* and what it can *do* politically – and so do it justice.

In both 'public' and 'commercial' terms, therefore, the idea of objective cultural value remains a useful one for informing ongoing critique of the creative economy. Retaining a sense of this is important, not least for avoiding both referentially empty and economically reductive discussions of the value of art and culture in both public and commercial contexts. What is ultimately at stake here, of course, is how to advance discussion of what is culturally *good* (and bad) and *worthy* (and unworthy) of public and private support, in democratic societies, and while I have by no means solved that problem, a more qualified approach at least provides us with a means by which we can begin to deliberate and decide, not least by refusing to discount the objective properties – as well as the subjective judgements, experiences and effects – of cultural objects, in any given evaluation[17].

CONCLUSION: DOING JUSTICE TO CULTURE?

So, having laid some foundations, how should we aim to 'get' at this cultural value that is partly subjective and socially shaped, and partly objective? What might *this* sociology of the cultural object look like? In *Performing Rites* (1996, p. 19), Simon Frith argued persuasively for evaluating cultural objects in ways that can account for the differences in 'the objects at issue' as well as 'the discourses in which judgements are cast' and in the 'circumstances in which they are made'. A more recent version of this argument has been offered by Lee Marshall, in his efforts to call into being a newly 'materialist sociology of music' (2011, p. 154). While broadly sympathetic to a Bourdieusian approach, Marshall seeks also to find an accommodation for the 'music itself', using (as yet unspecified) methods that might take 'aesthetic specificity' as seriously as subjective apprehension and reception. He uses the example of the Sex Pistols and UK punk rock to suggest the possible contours of such an enquiry:

> It is, of course, theoretically possible that, under certain social and cultural conditions, 'Anarchy in the UK' could be a romantic song, or a mournful one, but does it really help our sociological understanding to make this point? Would it not be more effective to consider how the unrelenting loudness, the buzzsaw guitar sound, the angry conviction in Johnny Rotten's vocal, the jolt of the anti-Christ/anarchist half rhyme, and other things in 'the music itself' contribute to how the song means what it means, and how that might make some people want to violently jump up and down and bang into each other, and some other people to put their hands over their ears and turn away in disgust? (2011, pp. 171–72)

For Marshall (as for Frith), we need to look at the properties of the music itself – but less as an aesthetic unity, with an inbuilt and fixed meaning, and more as a kind of open-ended structure. Like all social structures, music both constrains and enables, and in its material and semiotic emergency – in different physical and coded sounds, temporal elements, internal structures of composition and suggestion – it encourages and prompts as well as curtails or inhibits certain kinds of response and reading. But what matters also are modes of listening and the range of sensations therein produced, despite their allegedly inherited 'social' provenance:

It's all very well stating that the claims for the emotional, non-verbal character of music are socially constructed, but that doesn't stop the hairs on my arms standing up when I hear certain songs. We need to 'buy into' this account of human experience, to believe it to be true if we are to do it justice. (ibid., 2011, p. 169)

What is the justice that we are being asked to do here? Certainly it's to take seriously and respect both the structural properties and the sensational, affective dimensions of music and its somatic and psychic effects on persons who engage in listening practices that might be in some way pre-fabricated and socially determined, but also have the potential to move them differently, and present to them with opportunities to make (at least partially) some kind of new or incremental meaning. It means to do justice to the sensational power of music objects ('the hairs on my arms standing up') by taking seriously the affirmative or otherwise transformative power that such objects afford, and it means to recognise that music matters because it can act as a meta-good that is linked so intensely to both the making of the private self and the experience of common life, in both a subjective and objective sense (Keat, 2000; see also Frith, 1996; De Nora, 2000; Hesmondhalgh, 2013). If music, and responses to it, are to be regarded as *more* than just 'norms' or 'dispositions', or mere reproductions of the habitus, then it requires some sustained effort to theorise the musical object, its conditions of listening and the patterns of mattering thereby entailed. To do otherwise, as Marshall would suggest, is to fail to fully 'do justice to the subject, and the subjects, we study' (ibid., p. 172).

As we say for music, can we not say for the products of the cultural industries more generally? Each cultural object is made from physical-material properties and contingent repertoires of signs and aesthetic codes that have objective properties and structure, as well as subjective impacts. And while their composition and presentation, and of course their enjoyment and appreciation, cannot be fully theorised and grasped outside of the social contexts which ascribe them value and meaning, neither are they reducible to mere expressions of history, power and interest. For they also have an existence that is both independent and emergent, and so partly autonomous of ideological judgements. Finally, they contain as elaborated meta-goods the potential to generate reflexive experiences and effects in excess of their conventional casting and value. What we need in cultural industries research, therefore, is a theory of creative justice that considers cultural objects in their own right – not in an idealistic sense or without reference to their social origin – but neither simply as reifications of belief or crystallisations of an external interest. Cultural objects are complex entities that have aesthetic properties and effects that might be regarded as objective

– *as well as* subjectively apprehended and socially made. To dispute this fact is not only to reinforce a kind of sociological imperialism or *hauteur*, and a theory-practice contradiction[18], but also to inflict an injustice on those objects, experiences and effects that for all kinds of reasons, and for all kinds of people, really do matter.

NOTES

1. Cultural objects I define as the variety of symbolic or expressive texts and forms produced by artists, other cultural workers, as well as by ordinary people, hobbyists and amateurs. Such objects have a cultural value that is partly – though often primarily – judged to be aesthetic in character; that is, concerned with properties of beauty, elegance, harmony (or their absence) and appreciated through sensory contemplation and judgements of taste. Andy Hamilton (2007, pp. 1–3) describes aesthetics as being concerned with 'intensified and enriched experience' which is seen to be historically 'ubiquitous' and 'democratic' in so far as it not only pre-dates modern conceptions of art, but is to be found in many different areas of social practice and across all societies – thereby existing as an 'everyday and unmysterious phenomenon' (ibid., p. 6), rather than as something rarefied and exclusive.

2. Objectivity is a term with many possible meanings, so it seems necessary to try and clarify how I'm using it here. Generally, I use 'objective' to refer to that which *pertains to objects,* as opposed to 'subjective' – that which *pertains to subjects.* Here, objective refers more specifically to the properties, powers or nature of things themselves, the very qualities they are made from, enable or contain – as opposed to what people (as conscious human subjects) might merely think about such phenomena. Objectivity in this (realist) sense therefore assumes that cultural objects have their own properties, structures and powers (including aesthetic ones) – which are not simply the *product* of human subjective perception, though they may of course be the *focus* of such perception or be influenced by it. To accept such a claim therefore involves accepting the basic realist argument that objects can exist independently of our knowledge of them – a necessary condition of any fallibilist social theory

Table 1   Objectivity and Subjectivity (after Sayer, 2000)

Objectivity (1): objectivity as in **'value-free',** 'unbiased', 'dispassionate' or 'neutral'	Objectivity (2): objectivity as in **'true'**	Objectivity (3): **'pertaining to objects'** or the character and nature of things in themselves (*e.g. the objective properties of music or the objective effects of unemployment*).
Subjectivity (1): **'value–laden',** 'partial', 'biased'	Subjectivity (2): **'untrue'** or a matter of opinion	Subjectivity (3): **'pertaining to subjects'** i.e. human beings and what they feel or think (*e.g. the subjective experience of class or the subjective enjoyment of a soap opera*).

(see endnote 7 below). So when I argue (as I do throughout this chapter) that cultural objects have 'objective' aesthetic properties, I am not making an idealist claim for the existence of some specific and trans-historical hierarchy of value, but rather suggesting that such objects contain their own characteristic qualities and capacities that are not simply the product of an ideology or discourse, even though we might well need discourses to subjectively appreciate or apprehend them. The distinctions I draw between objective and subjective, and between different kinds of objectivity and subjectivity, are based on those proposed by Andrew Sayer (2000, pp. 58–62), and summarised in the table below:

Thus, in this chapter, I mostly use objectivity (3) and subjectivity (3) to try and distinguish the nature of the objective and subjective dimensions of aesthetics – thought at times I might implicitly rely on objectivity (2), for instance in making the basic truth claim that aesthetics actually has both objective and subjective dimensions, or in offering the assertion that aesthetic experience is not simply a cultural arbitrary.

3. No doubt this is a valid concern, but it does have some epistemological – as well as practical – limits. As Russell Keat argues: '[t]he "elitism" objection, I suggest, is often based on some form of scepticism (including postmodernist versions of this) about "value-judgments": the denial that there are any objective criteria governing these, and the claim that they should instead be seen as no more than the expression of individual's preferences. Such scepticism has significant social implications: it delegitimates any form of social authority which rests on claims of "objective" knowledge or judgement, since it denies that anyone's judgement is any better or worse than anyone else's' (Keat 2000, p. 7).

4. Evidently these values are linked – cultural industry objects are simultaneously economic and cultural, and not always is this in tension or opposition; for example, it is often the most novel or challenging cultural aspect of an object that provides the main source of its economic value (Ryan, 1992; Brouillette, 2009). Yet, each value is also semi- or relatively autonomous – concerned with meaning and provisioning respectively, each suggesting different possibilities for action and change (Ryan, 1992; Sayer, 1999). The fact that these values are sometimes incommensurable should not necessarily be seen as a problem; indeed, this is part of their emergent potential, and a value in its own right (see Banks, 2015).

5. As Nick Prior aptly puts it, one of the values of Bourdieu's work is to provide 'ammunition against internalist histories' (2015, p. 352).

6. Again, this is to support the basic realist claim that 'objects can exist independently of particular knowledges or claims about them' (Sayer, 2011, p. 47). This does not mean we can *know* objects without discourse, only that the discourse and the object are *existentially* separated; even though discourse plays a role in constructing the object, and making it knowable and recognisable *as* an object, the two things – discourse and object – are not exactly the same. If they were, then it would be impossible to be wrong about anything, and unnecessary to disagree or debate, since the world would be 'simply what our concepts say it is' (Sayer, 2000, p. 34). The presumption that knowledge is fallible, and open to change, is premised on the assumption that there is a world that exists outside of our discursive constructions of it, to the extent that we can be right or wrong or have better or worse interpretations of what is going on in any situation – a point made in chapter 1 and to be revisited in chapter 7.

7. Emergence here refers to 'situations in which the conjunction of two or more features or aspects give rise to new phenomena, which have properties which are irreducible to those of their constituents, even though the latter are necessary for their existence. The standard physical example might be the emergent properties of water which are quite different from those of its constituents, hydrogen and oxygen' (Sayer, 2000, p. 12).

8. In this respect, music (and culture more widely) suggests a potential for invigorating social change by 'cultivating and enriching our inner world and by feeding processes of concern, sympathy and engagement, against helplessness and isolation' (Hesmondhalgh, 2013, p. 17). This also suggests music (and culture and arts more generally) might therefore appeal objectively to some universal qualities of our human nature – such as the need for care, and our capacities to flourish or suffer (see also Sayer, 2011, Mohanty, 2001). Others have suggested music as having other kinds of objective powers – that lie in psychology and neurology – and that can enhance our innate human powers; for example, 'What if "harmony" and "rhythm" are not merely metaphors for social cooperation but actual roadmaps laid down in ancient neural networks'? (Taylor, 2014, p. 499). I suggest this possibility – not to posit some essential causal relation between nature and culture – but to recognise the close imbrication of the two: their mutually supporting relationships and effects (see chapter 4, also).

9. As Georgina Born (2010, p. 175) notes, reflecting on Michel Foucault's discussion of painting in *The Archaeology of Knowledge* (1972), a post-structural critique identifies the components of even the most basic aesthetics (space, distance, depth, colour, light, etc.) as conceived of in, and inseparable from, the confines of a discursive practice – seemingly rendering impossible the idea of an autonomous aesthetic. A more realist or objectivist approach might counter however that 'space', 'light', etc. are actually physical, mind-independent properties that exist outside of any particular discourse about them, and therefore in some sense existing autonomously (and see Mohanty, 2001 for a useful critique of Foucault's constructionist position).

10. IRCAM; Institut de Recherche et Coordination Acoustique/Musique.

11. Referring to (Baron) John Birt, former director-general of the BBC (1992–2000) who oversaw a controversial period of organisational restructuring during his tenure – a turbulent process Born exhaustively details in *Uncertain Vision* (2005).

12. As Austin Harrington has written, 'We must reject both transcendentalism – the view that aesthetic contents in works of art hold validity *in no relation* to social facts; and we must reject relativism – the view that aesthetic contents in works of art *hold no validity other than* as social facts' (2004, p. 110).

13. The cultural and literary theorist Satya Mohanty makes a valid point in this respect: 'I would like to argue that values are not *only* socially determined, because often they refer to deeper features of human nature, our species-wide needs and capacities, which set limits on how historically "contingent" legitimate evaluations can be. Our evaluations can be objective, I suggest, because they are often about features of human nature that are independent of our own socially shaped judgments and attitudes' (2001, p. 814). Andrew Sayer (2011) has also persuasively argued against sociologically reductive accounts of cultural taste implying that the kinds of culture that people might choose to value cannot be seen as wholly free-floating or

socially arbitrary, since their choices can never be entirely divorced from consideration of the kinds of being humans *actually are* – vulnerable beings with different biological and cultural endowments capable of flourishing or suffering in various kinds of ways.

14. Increasingly, the issue of cultural value is seen to be best resolved by sovereign consumers making choices in commercial markets, or, in the public sector, by using economistic (and purportedly more 'democratic') accounting measures such as contingent valuation surveys, stated preference techniques and various 'willingness to pay' methodologies (see Frey, 2008; O'Brien, 2010). In such cases, it is the capacity to satisfy individual consumers' (or consumer-citizens') preferences that is offered as the most reliable measure of the value of a cultural object – yet this, in itself, tells us little about the source or content of those consumer preferences or their efficacy in providing the kinds of personal (or social) benefits that they allegedly provide, and nor does it allow reflection on the objective qualities of the cultural goods themselves which appear only as arbitrary or empty signifiers – as objects without objective content.

15. Or has George Yudice once put it: 'To the degree that this pragmatism reigns supreme, art and culture will be left with little legitimacy other than what is socially, politically and even economically expedient' (Yudice, 1999, p. 17).

16. A different example, but with similar meaning, Andrew Ross tells us '[l]ike all forms of popular culture, the dancehall is compromised, multivocal, and as likely to serve it's faithful with a taste of liberation as with a reminder of society's limitations' (1998, p. 67).

17. Perhaps what is needed here, then, mirroring Sayer's idea of 'qualified ethical naturalism' (2000, p. 98) is some kind of 'qualified aesthetic naturalism', that is, a theory of aesthetics that shows how the nature of the aesthetically 'good' is at least partly able to be derived from evaluations of our objective natures as human beings, and not merely through our sociologically inherited and subjectively experienced tastes and preferences – I am grateful to Jason Toynbee for this suggestion, a complex idea which (in some small measure) my own account here does gesture towards, but only in an inadequate and underdeveloped way. Something for another occasion, perhaps.

18. As Nick Zangwill has argued sociologists cannot 'live their skepticism' (2002, p. 449) since while disavowing aesthetic taste as a social construction, they also tend not to regard their own aesthetic choices as a delusion or a product of ideological false consciousness – indeed, like everyone else, sociologists are constantly making aesthetic choices that they tend to justify in terms of aesthetic, rather than sociological, criteria. To return to my earlier example, what does a Bourdieusian Bowie-lover hear when they listen to their favourite Bowie recording? Something that is meaningful, moving or magical? Or the distilled essence of their own pre-formatted taste for the necessary? What do they feel afterwards? Is it merely the bloodless affirmation of a preference that is bounded by the limits of a habitual interest – or maybe something else?

Chapter 3

Practices, Ethics and Cultural Work

As the previous chapter was concerned with doing justice to cultural objects, this chapter attempts to do the same for cultural work. In our foregoing terms, we might say that one way to do justice to cultural work would be to examine holistically all of its particular qualities – the full range of factors that pertain to its organisation, valuation and undertaking; something like the kind of comprehensive and 'enriched' criticism proposed by Born (2010, p. 199) perhaps. This would involve consideration of both the objective qualities of work, including the kind of activity that it actually is, and its social effects, as well the way it is constructed, mediated and subjectively experienced through discourse. Ideally, through such an approach, we might come to know cultural work better – and so do it justice[1].

Here, however, I want to take this general idea and apply it more specifically and substantively. I want to show that *one* particular and more restricted way in which we might do justice to cultural work is by focusing on its ethical dimensions – or its existent status within a particular kind of *moral economy*. This is useful for two reasons. Firstly, it allows us to assess what the value of cultural work might be, why people might choose to undertake (or avoid) it and what motives or interests pertain to it – which might then enable us to better understand its form and character. Secondly, it might also allow us to make a case that supports the preservation or development of 'good' or better kinds of cultural work, including work that enables people to flourish and live well in an objective sense (Hesmondhalgh and Baker, 2011; Keat, 2012; Muirhead, 2004). Such an approach therefore carries both a positive and normative value – necessary prerequisites for developing any notion of justice, we might argue (Fraser, 2013; Nussbaum, 2011).

41

WORK AND MORAL ECONOMY

Work is a moral endeavour. But that doesn't necessarily mean that it's any good. Rather it's to suggest that work's organisation and undertaking is inevitably suffused by the different moral (or ethical[2]) dimensions that shape and inform our collective and common life. Another way of saying this is that work is always subject to the norms and values of the particular society in which it is *embedded*. For moral economists, 'embedding' is the characteristic feature of all economic activity – since the economy is judged to be a constituent element of the social, and not a free-floating, autonomous entity that lies beyond it (Bolton et al, 2012; Booth, 1994). Work – whether it takes place in the home, the community or the capitalist firm – is always configured by a morality (or 'ethics') of some kind, therefore.

More broadly, the term 'moral economy' has been used to describe the ways in which ethical concerns tend to inform and shape the exercise of all kinds of economic procedures, as well as the ways in which economic interests can, in turn, disrupt or reinforce (non-economic) norms, dispositions or values (Sayer, 2003). It is the dynamic interplay between economic and non-economic values and interests that tends to feature most prominently in research on moral economy. This is not simply a descriptive exercise, but a critical and evaluative one. As Russell Keat (2004) has argued: 'Every economy is a moral economy', it's just that 'some are nicer than others' – implying the need to make normative judgements about the ethical character of economic activities, including work, usually with the intention of trying to shape or influence them for the better[3].

While moral economy approaches have variously found favour in philosophy, anthropology, political economy and sociology (e.g. see Thompson, 1971; Booth 1994; Sayer, 2003; Keat, 2004; Skeggs, 2009; Bolton et al, 2012; Arvidsson and Peitersen, 2013) they have had less influence in studies of the cultural industries, with a few exceptions (see Banks, 2006; Kennedy, 2012; Bennett, Strange and Medrado, 2015; Hesmondhalgh, 2016). However, I would maintain that, here, a moral economy approach is valuable for two reasons. Firstly, it offers a particular connection between in-depth, hermeneutic explorations of cultural work (richly descriptive, though sometimes disconnected from a wider context) and more political economy-based approaches that tend to emphasise the (somewhat 'disembedded') workings of social and economic structures. Moral economy approaches also help bring together idiographic descriptions of the conditions and experiences of work and more abstract or systemic accounts by emphasising the *normative environments* that both ground and connect different individuals, institutions and structures. This takes on a particular cast in the cultural industries where the motives to work (or to employ) are often complex and diffuse, not simply 'economic' or 'cultural' in character, but marked by diversity, and sometimes contradiction and inconsistency. Fundamentally, the moral economy of cultural work shows that it contains different and competing articulations of *value*. Firms, managers, artists and so on invest their work with varied purposes, intentions and meanings, which strongly influence the production, circulation and consumption of cultural goods – taking ethics or morality into account suggests the potential to describe and understand cultural work better than we otherwise might (Banks, 2006; Kennedy, 2012).

Secondly, moral economy approaches offer a complement to existing critiques, such as those found in critical political economy, or pragmatism[4], because they permit us to make evaluative (normative) judgements *about* the ethical qualities of work itself. This is not to supplant 'political' critique[5] but to deepen and enhance it, to bring out the substantive qualities of work and to show why it might matter to us in the first place, in terms of the specific ways it might enhance or detract from our human *well-being*[6]. Moral economy theories do tend to focus on well-being – reflecting the Aristotelian sympathies of many of their proponents – the attainment of which tends to be seen as a primary social purpose. To minimise suffering and maximise 'the good life' – however that might be identified and attained – is an idea that informs debate about what might objectively stand as the fullest realisation of both individual satisfaction and the public good[7]. In cultural work, establishing what counts as 'good' work – work that allows for the maximal well-being for the greatest number – has now become a more pressing concern (e.g. Alacovska, 2013; Hesmondhalgh and Baker, 2011; Luckman, 2012; Oakley, 2014). However, such approaches, while 'moral' and prescriptive, are not intended to be 'moralistic' in the pejorative sense of 'telling people what to do' – but rather tend to make *evaluations* and *recommendations* about situations which can be judged as more or less amenable to improving the quality of work, once they themselves have been made subject to evaluative scrutiny.

By taking the particular example of professional work in music, this chapter explores how cultural work is understandable as a socially complex 'moral' endeavour. Here, I will use a particular rendering of the concept of *practice* to inform discussion of one example of music work. However, while quite specific, the case itself is used to illuminate my wider and more significant point – that doing justice to cultural work not only involves the empirical work of describing and detailing what work *is* it also demands normative judgement *about* the qualities of work, in terms of the contribution it might make to human well- or ill-being in capitalist societies.

WHY WORK IN MUSIC?

Why do people choose to work as professional musicians? We know, for the majority, it's not for the money. Most music work is precarious, piecemeal and poorly paid. Typically then, we might assume musicians persist because they have a special talent or love for the music. Playing music helps fulfil desires for artistic expression, creation or community; it may invoke passionate or pleasurable emotion or offer the promise of some special, transformative effect. Music work, it seems, is usually undertaken – not in anticipation of material rewards – but for its own intrinsic value, for its own objective sake. But how might we begin to theorise the ethical motives for working in music, or cultural work more generally?

I want to address this question through an analysis of findings from some previous empirical research on the working lives of jazz musicians[8]. Theoretically, this analysis is informed by Alasdair MacIntyre's influential conceptualisation of *practices*. Jazz, as will be argued, might be viewed as an exemplary practice (in the MacIntyrean sense) since it is a distinctive social activity based on the ethical pursuit of various 'internal' and 'external' goods. It is argued that these two types of goods, and the relationships between them, can tell us much about the particular values attached to jazz as creative cultural activity and its role as an enduring form of cultural work. The remainder of the chapter is then concerned with outlining the usefulness and limits of MacIntyre's formulation in relation to other understandings of the ethical basis of jazz work, specifically those derived from the work of Pierre Bourdieu. Here we see a contrast – between one understanding of (cultural) work as a diverse and open-ended ethical activity and one that sees work as (more) constrained by an overriding concern with strategising and self-interest. In both, however, we begin to see how work might be objectively understood as a moral-economic endeavour – an activity intrinsically concerned with the pursuit of the different 'goods' of life.

A THEORY OF PRACTICES

In *After Virtue* (1981), Alasdair MacIntyre defines practices in the following way:

> By a 'practice' I am going to mean any coherent and complex form of socially established cooperative human activity through which goods internal to that form of activity are realised in the course of trying to achieve those standards of excellence which are appropriate to, and partially definitive of, that form of activity, with the result that the human powers achieve excellence, and human conceptions of the ends of goods involved, are systematically extended. (MacIntyre 2007, p. 187)

A most important quality of practices is that they generate what MacIntyre distinguishes as *internal and external goods*. Internal goods refer to intrinsic qualities which are practice specific – that is, rewards that can only be attained through immersion in the particular practice in question. Such 'goods internal to a practice' (2007, p. 188) can only be fully realised through a subordination to, and immersion in, the character of the practice; that is, when practitioners establish a knowledge and appreciation of a given practice's interior qualities, and an intimacy with its specific demands. MacIntyre uses the example of chess to show that only by playing chess can individuals derive its characteristic internal goods, such as an appreciation of the particular kinds of 'analytical skill, strategic imagination and competitive intensity' (2007, p. 188) that chess demands and that only chess can provide in chess-specific form. All practices, then, possess their own characteristic, internal goods, obtainable only through an application of the virtues[9] in the context of the particular demands of the practice.

These internal goods are, however, contrasted with and necessarily co-exist with external goods (such as money, prestige, esteem, praise and status), which *are* obtainable through engagement in any given practice, but exist in contingent rather than dependent relation to the practice in question – since they can be obtained elsewhere in any kind of practice, or by other means. External goods are further distinguished from internal goods in terms of exclusivity – the benefits of the former (such as profits) are objects of competition that tend to be accrued at the expense of their availability to others, while the benefits of the latter tend to be undiminished in their sharing, and beneficial to the community as a whole. Further, while the pursuit of external goods is highly likely to occur in practices, this is often detrimental to maintaining the integrity of the practice – a point to which I'll return.

As MacIntyre's definition suggests, the acquisition of internal goods and their capacity to enrich the community is strongly related to the ongoing achievement of objective *standards of excellence* – without which there can be no genuine practice:

> A practice involves standards of excellence and obedience to rules as well as the achievement of goods. To enter into a practice is to accept the authority of those standards and the inadequacy of my own performance as judged by them. It is to subject my own attitudes, choices, preferences and tastes to the standards which currently and partially define the practice. (MacIntyre 2007, p. 190)

The notion of practice therefore refers not to an unrecognised, individual ability or performance but to collective recognition and regard for the standards of worth inherent to the activity in question. What unites people in a practice is a shared commitment to the practice, which is recognised as unique and distinctive, with a set of internal standards of excellence that one must seek to uphold for the good of the practice and for the good of practitioners themselves. But it should be noted that in achieving excellence, practitioners are not simply meeting or surpassing a technical standard, but ensuring that their 'human powers' are enhanced and that individuals open themselves up to what MacIntyre identifies as 'the good of certain kind of life' (ibid., p. 190) – a sense of being part of a living tradition, immersed in a particular specificity. Thus, a practice always relates to the wider recognition of how individual skills and abilities are directed towards the 'higher' good of the community. It is partly this 'higher' communitarian dimension that distinguishes practices (as understood by MacIntyre), from ordinary non-practice-based activities[10]. The sense that the activity of the practice provides common or cooperative benefits outside of the parameters of instrumental or individual self-interest is important. In order that societies live well, then, the establishment of virtue and the continuation and elaboration of the practice itself must be judged as important as the development of any individual, 'selfish' needs.

However, while, at first glance, practices appear bound by the confines of the community and its prescribed and objective standards, it is erroneous to imagine that practices remain static and unchanging. Indeed, practitioners – through immersion in the materially specific tradition of the practice – become agents of change through the constant refinements, challenges and innovations that are introduced as the limits to the practice are explored. In this way, the history of the practice is dynamic as new standards of excellence are conceptualised and attained. Further, the notion of *competition* is central to the concept of practices. While practices are not immune from market competition – since this is often seen as the best way to accrue external rewards – MacIntyre argues that practices are more commonly associated with what he terms *emulative* competition. The difference between emulative and market competition is that emulative competitors see achieving standards of excellence and internal goods as paramount, with external goods valued primarily as resources for enabling further contributions to the practice. For the purely market-facing competitor, external goods are prioritised and production largely takes place in order for these to be most effectively obtained – and, as Russell Keat (2000) avers, there can be no ethical commitment to the standards of the practice that would not be overridden if some other, more efficient, means of obtaining these external goods presented itself. Emulative competition may well be undertaken to obtain external goods, but also, and principally, because it benefits the community as a whole – serving the practice by enhancing or transforming the standards, and so expanding the range or quality of obtainable internal goods.

Finally (and crucially), while practices might appear to be closed systems, discrete worlds populated by enthusiastic individuals or small groups of skilled practitioners, in MacIntyre's formulation the relationship between internal and external goods is made explicit by the fact that in order to flourish practices cannot stand alone, but must be contained and developed by *institutions*. Institutions (e.g. firms, clubs, societies, schools) are central to a theory of practice since it is they that provide necessary economic resources, administer the internal standards (deciding what constitutes good or bad chess, opera, painting, graphic design and so on) and cultivate the communitarian context through which the practice can be recognised, developed and refined. Practices therefore cannot survive without institutions for any great length of time. But because institutions, by necessity, must also be concerned with the cultivation of external goods – since in order to flourish they must obtain money, property and material resources, be structured according to some kind of hierarchy (in order to distinguish their expertise from that of other claimants) and be able to distribute money, power and status as discretionary rewards – they are, as MacIntyre put it, prone to exert a 'corrupting power' over practices themselves; the central paradox being, then, that practices are both supported by *and* undermined by institutions:

> Institutions and practices characteristically form a single causal order in which the ideals and creativity of the practice are always vulnerable to the acquisitiveness of the institution, in which the cooperative care for common goods of the practice is always vulnerable to the competitiveness of the institution. In this context the essential function of the virtues is clear. Without them, without justice, courage and truthfulness, practices could not resist the corrupting power of institutions. (MacIntyre 2007, p. 194)

Thus, a core contradiction is that those institutions necessary for the development and continuation of a practice are, potentially, the agents of its corruption and downfall. As the practice becomes institutionally embedded (necessary for the cultivation of standards of excellence and community that defines it as a practice), it becomes vulnerable to the demands of the institution for external goods that lie beyond the confines of the practice itself. For MacIntyre, only the virtues can serve to act as a bulwark against the pervasive corruption of the practice.

Of what relevance is this somewhat abstract theory to the work of jazz musicians? Clearly, jazz can initially be hypothesised as a practice in the terms presented by MacIntyre. It is a *coherent, rule-bound social activity* (standards and repertoires played by trios, quartets, big bands) through which application of the *virtues* (in this case, for example, perseverance, justice, courage, honesty, diligence) certain specific *internal goods* can be attained (typically creative, technical and aesthetic (co)accomplishments in the form of aesthetically valued objects, embodied skills, idioms, styles, techniques and grooves), that rely upon *education* (jazz training) and some historically developed objective *standards of excellence* (e.g. the jazz tradition or 'canon';

improvisational aptitudes), and further depend on *institutions* (record companies, labels, broadcasters, magazines, societies and clubs) in order to flourish. *External goods*, largely in the form of money, power, esteem and status, are also present and available and are pursued by practitioners and institutions, to varying extents and ends. However, I will argue that what most distinguishes jazz as a particularly acute example of a flourishing modern practice is the sharply delineated contrast and tension between the durable ethical pull of the internal goods of the practice (the virtues of community participation and engagement and the 'good of a certain kind of life' that jazz work provides) *against* the contingent external goods that musicians and institutions might seek to accumulate in jazz or by other means.

RESEARCH WITH JAZZ MUSICIANS

In this section, I illustrate the practice-like qualities of jazz and jazz employment by drawing on some previous empirical research I have undertaken (with others) on British jazz musicians[11]. As will be shown, the terms in which musicians described their working lives are strongly redolent of the qualities of a practice as described by MacIntyre. However, while I seek to develop the possibility of a practice-based inquiry into jazz work, it is clear that a MacIntyre-inspired perspective differs in some marked respects from more established social science critiques – including the Bourdieusian perspective which I outline in a subsequent section, by way of comparison, with reference to the data collected.

Internal and External Goods

The 'internal goods' of jazz evidenced in the descriptions of work offered by some of our research participants could be said to include: *making beautiful objects* (chapter 2) *and thereby attaining a sense of creative or emotional fulfilment, emulating or surpassing the established standards, the achievement of improvement in skill or technique, the feeling of community or collective unity in the group, recognition and appreciation of technical or aesthetic achievements of others, or simply experiencing the transcendental, 'in-the-zone' power of improvisation and groove.* External goods such as money, status and power were also valued (though often little accrued) and tended to be disdained or recognised as more likely obtainable in other (better-paid, higher-profile) artistic fields. Indeed, given the likelihood of immiseration and the low industry status of jazz work, our sample tended to reflect the assumption that 'producers and consumers of jazz are concerned with it for its own sake and not for some exterior reason' (Stebbins 1966, p. 198). A theory of practices (alongside a theory of objects) provides concepts to access these intrinsic motivations.

The strongest motivation for becoming a professional jazz musician was the *love of jazz*, often recollected as conceived in a moment of epiphany; since most musicians were not schooled or initially exposed to jazz, they experienced a turning point or moment of transcendence that we character-ised in analysis as the 'jazz calling' or the 'coming to jazz' :

> I don't know how to explain but the music took me – that's it, it just took me (Singer #10).
>
> So I bought this [Stan Getz] record, took it home, put it on the record player, and I just stared. ... I was totally, totally gone. ... I just went aaaah! Aaah! I've found it! (Saxophonist #1).

As in other studies of jazz musicians, many our participants came to jazz through 'love at first sound' (Berliner, 1994, p. 21). The direct, visceral and transformative exposure to jazz, and the subsequent desire to become what we might term a fully immersed jazz *practitioner* was commonly expressed. Schooling, enculturation and employment would eventually follow, inspired largely by passion and respect for the practice, and the internal goods derived from adherence and participation to its specific demands.[12]

But because professional jazz musicianship is low-paid work and largely devoid of financial security and continuity, one might expect these internal goods to be highly valued *initially,* but only able temporarily to offset the demands of economic necessity, or the lure of external rewards by other means, since it is widely known that 'earning a living from jazz is almost impossible' (Jeffri 2003, p. 40). However, as MacIntyre argues, in genuine practices, the internal goods to be obtained from attaining excellence will, far beyond that which is economically 'rational', outweigh the external goods to be obtained via other activities. So while jazz musicians must of course survive economically, either as full-time musicians or, more likely, through holding second jobs, it was common amongst our sample to find musicians choosing to endure economic hardship in order to further derive the particular internal goods that are obtainable *only* from playing and performing within the jazz community. This usually meant musicians were erratically subsisting on part-time work, occasional irregular gigs, second-jobbing here or there – all to enable dedicated and immersive commitment to jazz and the cultivation of its internal rewards:

> So I started my own band ... doing all the bookings ... writing my own music, saving money you know, I even had to get some jobs of my own to make sure I had the money to pay for the recording sessions. I was working at [an] airport, *Toys R Us*, selling ladies' perfume, all kinds of crazy jobs (Trumpeter #1).

Others saw poverty as the necessary price to pay for maintaining an immersion in the jazz practice, as this time-served professional in her mid-forties described:

> You know I just try to make ends meet ... and I'm still at home with my mother, she's oldish and we try and help each other out. I think if I was on my own it would be very different. ... I'd definitely have to go and do some full-time job and forget my music (Drummer #1).

Alternatively, external goods accrued from activities beyond the practice could be employed (reinvested) to resource the jazz practice that was viewed as a more authentic source of internal rewards. Thus, a number of jazz musicians who were given opportunities to develop parallel (better-paid) careers in pop, soul or funk reported on how the relatively lucrative rewards attained in these fields provided the means to finance jazz practice, or were themselves eventually rejected as commercial or inauthentic diversions that undermined the possibility (and avowed necessity) of playing jazz:

> I realised in the [funk] world, a lot of the sort of things that I didn't like about it, there was a lot of image. ... I used to say it was about posing not composing – and that put me off (Vibraphonist #1).

The desire to make or participate in jazz, in defiance of rational economic principles was common to the sample – for this could provide the route to the valued internal rewards that only jazz could provide.

Tradition and 'Standards of Excellence'

Amongst our sample, a lifelong (but always incomplete) education in the tradition and canon of jazz was identified as a cornerstone of the jazz practice. Acceptance of the necessity of subordinating oneself to the technical and stylistic demands and rigours of the practice was clearly a virtue characteristic of our participants – a pathway to the internal goods jazz could provide. We might go as far to venture that MacIntyre's claim that to 'enter into a practice is to accept the authority of ... standards and the inadequacy of my own performance' (2007, p. 190) could have been written specifically with the jazz player in mind. This ethical sense of discipline, sacrifice and an appreciation of tradition were strongly articulated by musicians:

> 'You know you've got to study what came before and get a really strong grasp of that, because there's a tradition there, there's a whole vocabulary of music and sound, so understanding how bebop works is crucial. You can't sidestep that music' (Singer #2).

This did not necessarily mean a slavish adherence to the established standards (though some were accused of this) but more likely a respect for historical precedent that can shape and colour new works which reinforce or transform the character of the practice. As one singer argued, attempting to move 'beyond' jazz while staying in touch with the canon, personal, creative development and commitment to improvisation was crucial:

> Why try to take a slice of time and history and preserve it, like, in aspic or something? (Singer #3).

Another musician disclaimed the sanctity of following traditions ('they're just genres') and instead emphasised the necessity of drawing on past styles and aspects of the canon in order to inform what he saw as the native improvisation and experimentalism of the jazz territory.

> If you just see jazz as spirit of exploration, or [that] you are speaking with a vocabulary in an expressive kind of way, then the vocabulary starts to develop, it's just heaven (Clarinettist #1).

One of the overriding themes of our interviews was that to learn, to be taught, and to teach others is an internal good. The intrinsic virtues of educative application, self-sacrifice, benevolence and passing on the practice (devoid of obvious egoistical concerns) were commonly expressed by our jazz musicians:

> Being an educator is an incredibly important part of my working life. ... It's the responsibility of the musicians who perform the music, to go out to school, and one-on-one, or one-on-fifteen, present the music *properly* [speaker's emphasis] to the young people (Trumpeter #1).
> Serve the music, you serve the musicians, you serve the audience, you know what I mean? And you're serving yourself, because in the long run you will have reaped the benefits (Drummer #2).

Additionally, the role of individual and inspirational teachers – who were revered and named – was a strong theme in our interviews. The role played by primary and secondary school music teachers, peripatetics, academics, band leaders and other professionals was crucial for passing on the practice, establishing the standards of excellence to be attained and providing a vital understanding of the possibilities and demands of jazz. As a key element of professional jazz practice, education (of the self and others) is presented as an intrinsic and necessary virtue – a means of 'serving the music' and 'serving yourself'.

Emulative Competition

While respecting tradition, the practice of jazz demands that musicians
dedicate themselves to emulating, and perhaps surpassing, the achievements
of the established canon. The greatest jazz player is not the one who has
made the most money but the one who has most effectively emulated and
extended the tradition. The historical accounts of jazz work are abundant
with tales that reiterate the emphasis placed on emulative, rather than
market competition, and indeed, to match or surpass the artistic or technical standards of the 'greats' has long been regarded as a primary virtue of
pioneering musicians. For the market-oriented or instrumental competitor
such striving might well be undertaken for financial or status-seeking reasons. However, for the emulative competitor in a practice, while resources
in the form of external rewards might be viewed as desirable, this is primarily because they offer a means to ensure the continued pursuit of artistic
excellence – they are not principally viewed as means to the acquisition of
economic profit. Such was the case amongst our sample, with one musician
here describing his determined efforts to emulate and surpass a cornerstone
of the British jazz canon:

> I think what I do on this is much more subtle than *Indo Jazz Fusions* [music
> made by John Mayer and Joe Harriott in the 1960s] because ultimately – I love
> that record – but ultimately John Mayer had his own kind of ideas about what
> he was composing, the instrumentation was a bit wacky, he decided to use a
> harpsichord because he thought it sounded Indian [laughs]. ... This is far deeper,
> as I've said, every single note of the harmony, the bass lines, the chords, the
> melody, the improvisations, comes from India, basically (Clarinettist #2).

A further reason why emulative competition is clearly central to jazz, much
more so than market competition, is that (at least in the United Kingdom)
the jazz economy is sufficiently small, informal and precarious to render significant efforts to establish a *market* advantage relatively futile (for example,
there is barely any 'market' to compete for in the kind of British Indo-Jazz
described above). This does not mean that musicians do not compete for
contracts, gigs or residencies through conventional means (self-promotion,
advertising, etc.). But it does mean that the rewards likely to be obtained from
doing so are sufficiently meagre to discourage a significant investment of
personal time and resources in establishing one's market advantage. Rather,
because jazz is a minority pursuit, largely uncommercial, and has a relatively
high barrier to entry in terms of skill, learning and grounding in tradition, then
the motives for entry tend *mostly* to be related to the acquisition of internal
goods. Economically acquisitive new entrants come to learn that the value of
any musician's playing is likely to be evaluated in terms that recognise *only*

the excellence in performing jazz to the highest possible aesthetic or technical standard. Put otherwise, while a musician can establish himself or herself in the market place, and glean external rewards, they will only be recognised as worthy of such rewards if they have previously demonstrated their excellence (or rather their jazz 'chops'). The few who fail to do this or achieve commercial success without having apparently 'paid their dues' (thereby disrespecting the practice) are often viewed with suspicion and contempt. The issue of conflict in the practice and the differential allocation of rewards I will return to, but it is sufficient to say here that market competition *tends,* as MacIntyre, argued, to be of less significance than emulative competition in defining the character of a practice – a condition most marked, we might aver, within the confines of professional jazz.

The Role of Institutions

In MacIntyre's analysis, the likely 'corruption' of practices is a most pronounced feature, with the acquisitiveness induced by advanced capitalist societies regarded as culpable for the unwelcome elevation of external over internal goods by institutions ostensibly charged with preservation of practice integrity. In the jazz world, the necessary institutions (clubs, labels, promotional agencies, colleges, etc.) are themselves identified as potential sources of corruption by musicians, especially when they appear to unjustly prioritise commercial over artistic decisions:

> As soon as he started trying to do something a bit different, he suddenly found himself off the label (Pianist #1).

Furthermore, the role of educational institutions such as academies, colleges and conservatories in shaping the character of the practice was frequently remarked upon. This was viewed positively when the academisation of jazz led to advancement in skills amongst younger players, and a shift in pedagogy away from informal, on the job methods to more formal styles was judged to be leading to a growth in the number of trained and technically adept players. The practice of jazz is enhanced when it is taken more seriously by the academies and when it becomes more fulsomely recognised as a legitimate art and career. However, while institutions may provide the context for the cultivation of the practice, and opportunities for full immersive engagement in the traditions and standards of excellence demanded of jazz, they also contain the possibility that the virtues of jazz might be cut or shaped in ways inimical to the good of the jazz art. Particularly, there was much discussion in interviews of how the formalisation of jazz training in higher education was leading to some rather clinical professionalisation, where graduates with a more commercially oriented attitude were colonising the practice at the expense of those who were perceived to be more 'authentic' purveyors – a sense then that those motivated by external rewards were threatening to displace those more concerned with the intrinsic and internal goods of the practice. Additionally, there were concerns that the essentially free, creative and improvisational practice of jazz can only suffer when contained within a formal, academised syllabus:

> If the kids are all being taught ... these are the chord changes and it gives you examples of what you *should* [speaker's emphasis] play, of course these kids are going to – they're not stupid. [But] where's a [Thelonius] Monk going to come from? ... Where's the next Keith Tippett going to come from? Howard Riley? (Pianist #1).

In summary, if we take the accounts of these musicians as accurate statements of their positioning in the jazz work world, we have some grounds for suggesting jazz exists as a modern form of MacIntyrean practice. This idea of practice is useful because it helps us to bring out the intrinsic rewards of jazz musicianship, the ethical interplay between internal and external goods and the role of institutions in both creating *and* undermining the practice of jazz. Above all, it reveals to us how the individual willingness to work in jazz can be understood in terms of its embedded social and ethical context (i.e. as a moral economy) – since it is the collectivised practice of jazz that unites and binds practitioners and provides the setting for the application of the virtues and the receipt of internal (and external) goods that their exercise can provide. We might even want to take jazz as an exemplary case – a model that we can try to apply to cultural work in general, an example that might help explain why any kind of cultural worker might want to commit to their art or practice – despite the evident difficulties that such a commitment might occasion.

A BOURDIEUSIAN PERSPECTIVE

While an initial reading of our participants' accounts would suggest the possibility that jazz might be understood in terms of MacIntyre's notion of practices, it is equally the case that the moral economy of jazz might be more usefully approached through alternative or contrasting theoretical schemes. One approach that has so far underpinned a number of sociological assessments of jazz work is that derived from some of the work of Bourdieu, and it is useful here to consider our data in light of some his particular theoretical propositions.

Bourdieu – Strategy and Self-Interest in Jazz?

In Bourdieu, as in MacIntyre, the idea of 'practice' is utilised, but framed within a more systemic account of how social structures beyond the practice organise the motives of individuals and their apparently freely chosen actions. As we saw in the previous chapter, for Bourdieu, the choices of individuals (in a practice, or the wider 'field') are shaped strongly by the habitus – the system of inherited and embodied dispositions that tend to frame the ways in which people act and react in different social settings. Here, while the choices and motives of individuals are not wholly predictable or pregiven, they are strongly formatted and patterned – mainly shaped by one's class background – and reproduced in the characteristic bodily practices and ways of thinking and doing, internalised by particular classed groups. Further, for Bourdieu, the habitus serves to frame the predominantly *competitive* relations he observes between the different classes and class fractions that converge to make up the variegated landscape of the social (Bourdieu, 1984).

Thus, in contrast to MacIntyre's notion of internal and external goods, in Bourdieu's world of cultural practices, the issue of motivation is more strongly linked to the 'strategic' pursuit of various kinds of 'interest' (which he claims is not necessarily 'universal' and may therefore, in a MacIntyrean sense, be 'internally' or 'externally' oriented), with a fundamentally competitive, but durably organised social world. To demonstrate this, Bourdieu famously situates artistic and cultural practices within what he terms the 'field of cultural production' (Bourdieu 1993), a structured arrangement of transactions and exchanges which is both a context and outcome of objective social forces and the strategic, habitual actions of the agents that occupy its parameters. As we saw in chapter 2, the 'field' is predicated on power relationships *between* agents who co-exist in mutable (though relatively enduring) relations of dominance, subordination or equivalence within the field, largely determined by their relative possession of, or potential access to, various kinds of 'capital'. To recap, these capitals include economic, in the form of money and financial assets, social capital in the form of personal ties and connections, and cultural capital in the form of skills, knowledge or education; artists might also accrue symbolic capital, in the form of artistic legitimacy, prestige and consecration. Thus, in the cultural field, the stakes of competition are (materially and symbolically) high, with practitioners involved in continual struggles to establish supremacy and standing through the various capital markets. The field (and its constitutive practices) is therefore premised on an *antagonistic* sociality – whereby actors are concerned primarily with striving for advantage and the enhancement of their own particular interests, linked to acquisition of the various capitals.

Charles Kirschbaum's work (2007) is exemplary in this regard in his deployment of a Bourdieusian perspective to analyse the general trajectory of the jazz career. By depicting the (bop, post-bop) jazz world as a distinctive 'field of struggles', Kirschbaum seeks to demonstrate the processes by which new, up and coming, established and consecrated musicians have variously sought to develop and protect their status through instrumental forms of alliance, protectionism, exclusion and organisation in work. The strong reliance on social ties and the patronage of established musicians, as well as the management of (frequent and myriad) conflicts and antagonisms are cited as principal features of the jazz life and indicative of the kind of 'survival of the fittest' economy that has pertained. Similarly, Diogo L. Pinheiro and Timothy J. Dowd (2009) adopt a Bourdieusian perspective to underscore their detailed account of the 'competitive struggle' (ibid., p. 491) inherent to jazz work, where success is considered only in terms of the effectiveness with which musicians are able to deploy their capitals. Combining Bourdieusian and Howard Becker's (1982) 'art-world' approaches, Paul Lopes (2002) systematically traces how an interlocking and evolutionary field of social relationships forged by musicians, bands, institutions, academics, critics, commentators and audiences has emerged as a central determining force in structuring the working lives of jazz musicians. Lopes is sympathetic to Bourdieu's notion that a 'force field' (Lopes 2002, p. 277) of social relationships defines the objective structure of the jazz world, and his own work excellently demonstrates the value of such an approach. Compared to MacIntyre, then, Bourdieu-inspired analyses have not only usefully revealed the structural context (field) that shapes the apparently self-creating and subjective practice of jazz, but have been able to highlight the centrality of power, rivalry and competition to the functioning of jazz world. The emphasis on 'interests' is central here, since this reveals something of the fundamentally self-serving ambitions of practitioners – however variably such interests might be defined.

What happens, then, if we apply a Bourdieusian scheme to our own data? Firstly, it is likely that the popular 'love of jazz' might be understood less as an ethical commitment linked to the internal goods of the practice, and more as a means of cultivating an 'interest in disinterestedness' – a particular strategy for securing a 'symbolic profit' as a dedicated and publicly avowed jazz exponent. Secondly, the MacIntyrean concept of 'internal goods' would likely be viewed by Bourdieusians as a form of misrecognition, obscuring what might better be described as the strategic accumulation of the capitals. Thus, the immersion in jazz art, attaining and surpassing its standards of excellence, achieving the 'good of a certain kind of life' and so on, might be viewed as an optimising investment in symbolic capital acquisition, and part of a negotiation for artistic supremacy, legitimation and status in the field of

struggles. Thirdly, our respondents' repeated espousal of the virtues of education in the jazz practice might well be read as a camouflaged strategy for the
accumulation of cultural capital, sufficient to set one apart from one's peers,
or (say) establish an economic advantage through promoting one's superior
teaching abilities. Fourthly, MacIntyre's notion of 'emulation' in competition
might be judged as a means of accruing economic or symbolic capital and
power, rather than a source of the non-exclusive, communitarian goods produced through the excellence of extending the standards of the jazz practice.
Fifthly, the widespread disavowal of economic capital by our respondents
(the rejection of commerciality and 'selling out') could either be seen as an
example of making a virtue out of a necessity (the disavowal is made easier
by the fact jazz is so poorly paid) or more likely an instance of 'bad faith',
since rejection of the market is often seen by Bourdieusians as a means of
investing in the potential of some anticipated future conversion of one's
symbolic profit into more conventional economic returns[13]. Indeed, this latter
point is stressed most strongly by Bourdieu when he argues that the economic
interest 'always haunts the most 'disinterested' practices' (1993, p. 75) and
when he readily accepts the view that 'painters and writers are deeply self-
interested, calculating, obsessed with money and ready to do anything to suc-
ceed' (ibid., p. 79) despite their publicly avowed disinterestedness. Finally,
even if we failed to recognise particular (either obvious or more disguised)
forms of capital acquisition amongst our respondents, we might assert with
confidence that by espousing the virtues of the internal goods of the practice,
practitioners are simply involved in reproducing the *illusio* of jazz – that is,
the collectively shared belief in the manifest and rightful necessity of a practice, which Bourdieu argues is both a 'precondition and product of the very
functioning of the game' (Bourdieu, 1996, p. 230). For Bourdieu, it is through
this uncritical and unquestioned reproduction of the *illusio* of the practice
(a.k.a the 'jazz field'), that the aforementioned struggles for supremacy and
interest are masked and allowed to develop.

Yet, before we excise all traces of the virtues from jazz, we should note
that Bourdieusian readings do contain some specific limitations. Firstly, even
though, as Bourdieu (1990b) argues, the idea of 'interest' need not necessarily
be understood in 'universal' (i.e. economic) terms, but rather as *any* kind of
specific interest (such as an interest in 'disinterestedness' or *ars gratia artis*),
the universal quality of Bourdieu's interest is its potential for 'exchangeability' *as if it were* an economic asset. Indeed, it remains difficult to disassociate
the idea of 'interest' (and, we might add, the accumulation of 'capitals') from
the world of individualism and rational economic calculation from which such
terminology is derived (Jenkins, 1992). This is especially so given Bourdieu's
consistent reiteration of a kind of 'Hobbesian interest- and power-based model
of social life' (Sayer 2010, p. 96) premised on always competitive position

taking. Further, whatever their orientation or object, the idea that (either consciously or unconsciously) people are only motivated by their 'interests' is a somewhat reductive view of human beings and tends to rule out the possibility that individuals might act, not to secure an advantage, but because of other reasons linked to their regard for others or their understanding that certain actions are right and good in *themselves* (Sayer, 2011) – such as, perhaps, upholding the values of a cultural practice like jazz. Secondly, despite Bourdieu's espoused anti-economism, it often appears in the cultural field that economic self-interest is *the* fundamental interest that tends to underpin (or override) all others – as in his sceptical view of the motives of 'painters and writers' and his repeated concerns regarding the ever-haunting 'spectre' of economy and the well-disguised fakery of economic repudiation (see Bourdieu, 1993, Chapter 2). So while there may well be a plurality of 'specific' interests, it is often *material* interests that appear to act as the foundational, generative basis of habitus, practice and field. Finally, there is the vexed issue of intentionality. While Bourdieu argues that social action is not conscious or strategic in a conventional sense, he nonetheless sometimes accepts that 'the responses of the habitus may be accompanied by a strategic calculation' (1990a, p. 53). This equivocation about the role of conscious and calculative action is problematic, for while Bourdieu wants to emphasise the habitual and largely unconscious nature of the 'strategic' pursuit of interests, (since the habitus naturally orients one to internalise pregiven and pre-established interests), others have argued that such a view of strategising is untenable:

> While accepting that interests are variable, it is very difficult to imagine how an 'interest' can be anything other than something which actors *consciously* [author's emphasis] pursue. The only alternative involves the detached social scientific observer deciding what actor's interests are – and hence what is in their interests. This is an approach which Bourdieu consistently rejects. Despite definitional protestations to the contrary, the use of the word 'interest' imports into the analysis either an unavoidable dimension of conscious, calculative decision-making or an indefensible epistemological conceit. (Jenkins, 1992, p. 87)

In spite of Bourdieu's avowed antipathy towards rational-choice theory and economistic explanations (see Bourdieu, 1990b), in his own analyses it appears that individuals in a competitive field and cultural practice are (a) primarily motivated by cultivating their exchangeable 'interests'; (b) tend to give primacy to interests that are material and economic and (c) do so at least in *some part* consciously, and must therefore be engaged in acts of calculation as to what their interests are and how best to improve their standing (and field position) in relation to them (see Jenkins, 1992; Swartz, 1997, for further discussion).

We might surmise then, in contrast to MacIntyre, that the Bourdieusian moral universe suggests that the mode of ethical orientation to a practice is not one of subordination and observance, and valuing the 'higher' good, but one of competition in the 'interest of one's interests'. This is either blatantly realised through the acquisition of the external goods of power, status and money, *or* through those internal goods which might theoretically be 'disinterested' (and thus potentially practice-focused) but are more likely (in a competitive 'field of struggles') to be used opportunistically as a mask for strategic exchangeability and the accumulation of capitals and power, linked to the established (class) interests. Put simply, any apparent investment in the internal goods of a practice would appear to act (ultimately) as a vehicle for the concealment of a strategic interest in the acquisition or accumulation of external goods.

This would be consistent with David Swartz's account who suggests that Bourdieu not only privileges economic motivations in the last instance but 'implicitly formulates an anthropology that posits a fundamental human propensity to pursue interests and accumulate power' (Swartz, 1997, p. 68). Indeed, as Andrew Sayer has similarly argued, it is Bourdieu's rather cynical view of the social that obviates the possibility that individual choices might be motivated by ethical concerns that encompass certain other kinds of reasoning, reflection and consideration:

> If we are to understand lay normativity and ethical being, we therefore need to get beyond the over-whelmingly self-interested and strategic model of action that is implicit in Bourdieu's concept of habitus and capitals. The concept of capitals reduces the use-value of things or the internal goods of practices to their exchange value or external goods. ... Practices like musicianship or medicine have their own internal goods and satisfactions, their own internal standards of what constitutes good work, and these are what many practitioners strive to achieve. (Sayer 2010, p. 97)

Thus, the main contrast between a MacIntyrean and Bourdieusian approach (to jazz or any other kind of cultural work) is the significance ascribed by the former to the 'internal goods and satisfactions' available to practitioners, who are identified as being able to exercise reflexive and ethical judgement about the intrinsic value of these goods (beyond the *illusio* as it were), based not just on their exchangeability or contribution to self-interest, but in terms of their contribution to the good of the practice as a whole, and the range of ethical and emotional rewards which pertain to its undertaking. A Bourdieusian perspective, because of its limited, 'Hobbesian' view of the social, and its preoccupation with exchangeable 'interests' and 'strategy' (and therefore its intimation of a tacitly selfish and economistic worldview, despite Bourdieu's protestations), tends to account for internal goods in terms of their role in the enhancing of the acquisition of external goods.

ACCOUNTING FOR ETHICS

Have we done justice to jazz work and its moral economy? While only a single case study, the empirical data presented here serves to suggest that jazz musicians consider the love of jazz, self-education, sacrifice and respect for tradition as vital components of a professional identity, yet also recognise the importance of the education of others, the value of collective and creative development, the infinite perfectibility of the practice and an awareness of the contribution that individual musicians can make to the practice of jazz as a whole. They endorse the view that practices of cultural work generate their own internal goods since the specific goods of jazz were deemed unobtainable elsewhere in the same form. Our interviews also showed that in jazz, while they co-exist, internal goods may be more highly prized than external goods, sufficient to render their pursuit a priority. The idea of practices as described by MacIntyre was then compared with some established Bourdieusian approaches. These were seen to offer a more systemic critique of the field of jazz work, and to highlight the important value of external goods, yet were somewhat limited and deficient in their ability to address the more embedded (non-economic) ethics and motives of jazz practitioners. Thus, while Bourdieu has very much to offer to an understanding of jazz work, particularly in terms of theorising its historically determined, structural and habitual character, as well as its (partly) competitive ontology, perspectives inspired by his theories tend only to discuss *some* of the ethical intentions that underpin jazz musicianship (largely based on the maximisation of self-interest in respect of the acquisition of external goods) and fail to fully grasp its capacity for cultivating the virtues and the specific *internal* goods that jazz generates for its practitioners. I would therefore argue that in order to extend empirically and theoretically our understanding of jazz (and by implication other forms of cultural work), we ought to recognise the role of ethical commitments that lie outside of the strategising of exchangeable interests in the field of struggles – in this way, we might do better justice to the work involved.

However, while I might want to argue that jazz is a durable practice that provides opportunities for the attainment of internal goods rewards, and fulfils many of the criteria for 'good' creative work (Hesmondhalgh and Baker, 2011), this is not to affirm any idealised, rose-tinted view of jazz, or, in fact, of cultural work in general. It does not mean that jazz (or any kind of cultural work) is devoid of exploitation, ill-being, instability and aggressive forms of competition, or that it is wholly democratic, inclusive or egalitarian (for sure, some of the bitter infighting and self-serving found in jazz *does* sometimes makes it resemble more a cut-throat field of struggles). Any focus on internal goods cannot be divorced from consideration of external goods and those wider social structures and powers that might serve to compromise, undermine or 'corrupt' the practice (as subsequent chapters will show all too clearly). However, in foregrounding MacIntyre's approach[14], I have tried to bring further to prominence the idea that the ethical principle of living 'the good of a certain kind of life' and contributing to the collective practice is at least as significant a compulsion to cultural work as any as the kinds of instrumental or less 'virtuous' motives and interests. What we say for jazz, can we not at least provisionally say for other kinds of cultural work, as well?

CONCLUSION: DOING JUSTICE TO WORK?

This chapter first argued for the need to do justice to cultural work – meaning to respect its objective properties, and give it its due. While there are many ways this might be done, one way I proposed was to consider work's foundationally ethical (or socially embedded) character. By way of example, I provided an account of the *moral economy* of professional jazz musicianship. To help do this, I compared MacIntyre's theory of practices against some previous (Bourdieu-inspired) research on the moral economies of jazz work. Here, the latter, while useful, was found to be somewhat more limited and less comprehensive than the former, which allowed for better consideration of the value and desirability of internal goods and their influence on well-being, the dynamic relation between internal *and* external goods in the undertaking of a cultural practice, and some the ways in which specific practices dialectically intersect with wider powers and social structures. But while MacIntyre's theory is – to my mind – a better theory when it comes to doing justice to the character of cultural work, no doubt we need Bourdieu's theory as well, to help us appreciate certain aspects of jazz work, such as the wider structural relations that shape the organisation of the field, as well as some of the more antagonistic and competitive relations between musicians, practices and other social actors and phenomena. Both theories have their uses in helping us to understand what jazz work is, and how it operates.

We might conclude that the first intention of a moral-economic approach – to provide better descriptions and understandings of the values and ethical character of cultural work – has therefore been demonstrated. Yet, the second purpose of such an approach – to offer normative judgements *about* this moral economy – has started to become apparent. This is because I was not only reporting on musician's own descriptions and understandings of their work, but also (at least implicitly) *evaluating* them. This was revealed in my account of the specific internal goods of jazz, and how they were effectively combined with external goods to shape the objective *well-being* of jazz practitioners – where certain goods and ways of being a jazz practitioner were tacitly identified as being better or more desirable than others. So while I tried to show how musicians described (and reproduced) the specific internal goods of jazz (e.g. the goods of groove, technique, excellence, collaboration, improvised performance and so on) the *reasons* why these were good were because they could be evaluated against external (as well as internal) referents – such as feelings of community, achievement, solidarity, self-respect or other forms of well-being that we might want to associate with good work of *any* kind. We should note here then that it was not the practices per se that were inherently good or virtuous, rather it was their aesthetic and ethical *content*, and it is this that needs to be evaluated on its own terms, but also against some kind of exterior standards that allow it to be recognised and judged. If we were to go further with this, we might also want to focus on whether the jazz practice is actually beneficial or good for *others*, who might lie beyond it (Miller, 1994). In such ways, we might begin to obtain a better understanding of what good (and bad) jazz work might actually be – and how it relates to other kinds of good and bad cultural work, or work in general.

What this all serves to demonstrate is that critical social science is inherently an *evaluative* enterprise. In attempting to describe and understand, we come across evaluations, and so begin to appraise and judge for ourselves. The purpose of critical social science, ultimately, is to use these evaluations to inform suggestions and recommendations that might translate into transformative social action – hopefully of a progressive kind:

> Critical analysis must be empirical social inquiry and be framed by normative philosophical argument – such that it can explain what is wrong with current social reality, so it can evaluate society, identify the actors to change it and provide both clear norms for criticism and achievable practical goals for social and political transformation. (Fenton, 2016, p. 348)

This is a laudable ambition – but achieving it is far from straightforward. How we might do so in relation to cultural work I will return to in the final chapter. But, for now (and to help fulfil that ambition), I want to shift the focus away from the theoretical *giving* of justice to the actual *receiving* of it – and to problems of *distributive justice* in the creative economy. In the next three chapters, we'll examine who has the opportunity to take part the practices of cultural education and work (and who doesn't) and how the positions and rewards of cultural work are socially shared. Such an inquiry will hopefully bring us closer to a position where we can offer the kind of normative critique (and plans for action) envisaged above – and so a theory of creative justice.

NOTES

1. The purpose of doing so, to reiterate, is to draw out the fullest *qualities* of cultural work; what kind of activity it objectively is, and the range of subjectively held values and meanings that pertain to it. To consider this – especially at a time when the value of such work has mainly been reduced to its economic purpose and the banalised imperatives of 'creative economy' discourse – is *not* to disregard the (many) negative features of work, or indemnify capital against its most pernicious charges, but to draw attention to complexity, value plurality and multiplicity in the structure and organisation of cultural work, and in its undertaking.

2. While some social scientists insist on the distinctive separation of these terms – ethics often being regarded as being about informal beliefs or dispositions oriented towards particular ways of living, contrasted with the more stringent associations of formal and prescriptive rule-making attached to 'morality' – I use the terms interchangeably, acknowledging their often interchangeable use more widely and presuming both to be broadly concerned with normative conceptions of the good (see Sayer, 2005, p. 8).

3. So we might say that even the most 'disembedded' (or 'free') market economies have their own morality ('self-sufficiency', 'free enterprise', 'consumer sovereignty' and so on) – the debate is whether this morality is actually beneficial or socially desirable.

4. The best example here is probably David Stark's (2009) *The Sense of Dissonance*. As a pragmatist, Stark is less concerned with playing arbiter to any *particular* values, or (as a moral economist might) establishing some rational basis for evaluating between them based on external criteria, and much more with revealing discrete empirical situations in which different values might compete and intersect, relationally, and according to their own internal logic of justification. The idea of justice is quite different to that proposed by the objectivist, therefore. Put simply, if the objectivist looks 'out' towards the possibility of shared justice principles based on objective criteria, the pragmatist looks 'in' for justice, to the particular situation or case in question. Stark's work – like pragmatism and the 'sociology of critique' more generally – rests on the assumption that justice is largely an *internal matter of dispute,* without any externally stable or accepted standard or referent, and so disavows any claims to a more general objectivity in the sense I would want to propose.

5. Some Marxist approaches have often been critical of that which foregrounds 'ethics' at the expense of 'politics'– tending to follow Marx's often-espoused view that ethics were merely an ideological expression of prevailing moralities and a poor

substitute for a communism that as a 'real positive science' could escape such illusions. Though as Sayer (and others) have pointed out, a political critique without ethical foundation is no kind of critique at all, an abstraction without content that gives us no reason to support or deny it; plus even Marx's critiques have their ethical foundations – what is the critique of capitalism but an ethical objection to the repression and indignities that prevent sentient, creative beings fulfilling their human potential? For example, the Marx of the *Economic and Philosophical Manuscripts* (1844) is a moral economist of work par excellence.

6. Well-being is defined here as objective and subjective state – a state of being that allows for human flourishing and minimal harm or suffering. Well-being can be defined through various measures such as access to health, housing or the general economic wealth (Wilkinson and Pickett, 2009), or through efforts to measure general 'happiness' (Layard, 2006). For others, such as Nussbaum, well-being lies in having access to core or basic *capabilities* – for example, the right to life, good bodily health and integrity, control over one's environment, and opportunities to connect and affiliate with others (see Nussbaum, 2011) – that are regarded as foundational prior to any *particular* choices or 'functionings'.

7. Aristotle argued that the pursuit of the good and the attainment of human well-being is the central purpose of life. The state of obtaining the good was referred to by Aristotle as *Eudaimonia,* which meant, as MacIntyre notes,

> blessedness, happiness, prosperity. It is the state of being well and doing well in being well, of a man's [*sic*] being well-favoured himself and in relation to the divine … [and] the virtues are precisely those qualities the possession of which will enable an individual to achieve *eudaimonia'* (MacIntyre, 2007, p. 148).

8. Findings are drawn from the *What is Black British Jazz?* research project funded by the United Kingdom's AHRC *Beyond Text* research programme (2009–11). The project was conducted at the Open University and led by Jason Toynbee, and featured Mark Doffman, Byron Dueck and Catherine Tackley, as well as myself, as co-researchers. One of the aims of the project was to understand the economic life of the British jazz musician, particularly for black and ethnic minority players; the aim of this chapter however is to outline some preliminary findings that reflect on the general character of the jazz practice. See Toynbee et al (2014) for an account of the wider project.

9. A virtue is defined as a quality of moral excellence, or a character trait which enables those who possess it to live well. Possessing of the virtues (e.g. courage, justice, diligence, consideration for others) allows humans to fulfil their potential as social and ethical beings; practices provide the *principal social context* for the exercise of the virtues, according to MacIntyre.

10. Some have detected an implicit elitism in MacIntyre's approach – where the kinds of activities he deems to be 'practices' appear to be valued over other kinds of (no less skilful or immersive, or internally rewarding) kinds of work (e.g. see Sayer, 2007; Toynbee, 2013).

11. Over forty musicians were interviewed during 2009–11, each interview being undertaken by a member of our project research team (see note 6 above). The sample was comprised of working UK musicians, the majority of which were of black

Afro-Caribbean origin (from a diversity of nations), mostly second or third generation offspring of families that arrived in Britain in the 1950s and 60s. The majority were men, aged between 25 and 50, and lived in London, with a smaller group of women and some occupants of regional cities (such as Manchester). None of them worked exclusively as jazz musicians, though this was often the basis of their identification and desired preference, and many were in secondary and part-time occupations (such as teaching) when not playing jazz. Most earned between £10 and 20, 000 p.a. – significantly below the United Kingdom's average annual wage.

12. In the terms of chapter 2, we might say that accounts of 'coming to jazz' are one way of doing justice to jazz, since they reveal something of the interplay between jazz's objective aesthetic properties, as well as practitioners' experiential encounters and engagements with jazz, and why it matters to them, in discrete social contexts.

13. For example, see Faulkner et al (2008) on how the public claim of independent artistry can provide a cover and means for enhancing economic self-interest.

14. Though I can claim no originality in this – this chapter owes much to Russell Keat's (2000) excellent commentary on, and critique, of MacIntyre's work.

Chapter 4

Talent, Merit and Arts Education

In the creative economy, talent is not just the source of creativity but the means to productivity – both the spark of genius and the power of innovations. Furthermore, if you possess talent then you have the means to make it personally – to rise above the crowd, to become significant and fulfilled as a creative person. Central to this belief is the idea that the creative economy is meritocratic – a place where the ladder can be climbed, or the cream can rise to the top; where individuals with natural talent and the right attitude might freely obtain their just rewards. The cultural and creative industries have long been disciples of this faith; an obsession borne from perpetual investments in 'original' talent and in the endless rotation of personalities, celebrities and stars.

However, in this chapter, I want to make two arguments. The first is precursory, outlining the position that while people are capable subjects, with their own objective capacities, the idea of creative talent is as much social as it is personal or innate. By this I mean that a 'natural aptitude' might exist, but it is extremely difficult to separate it from the social context in which it appears, to the extent that it is perhaps impossible to isolate its discrete influence in the making of creative persons. Secondly, and more substantively, even if we accept that ordinary people may possess their own creative talents (regardless of whether we believe these to be innate or socially learnt, or some combination of the two), there is no guarantee that such attributes will be recognised and rewarded because established patterns of social inequality tend not to permit it. More simply, we might say that the socially disadvantaged are less likely to be regarded as 'talent' because they lack the resources necessary to compete in markets for prestige and recognition. In respect of this argument, the main focus of this chapter is on how – even before work is obtained – issues of talent, merit and inequality are played out in *educational selection.* As we'll see, higher education in the creative arts is revealed to be much less guilty of elevating the naturally talented, than of reproducing established patterns of social advantage. Therefore, while the analysis presented here presupposes some kind of natural and objective basis for 'talent', it focuses more specifically on the currently dominant and pervasive elements of its social attribution and construction. Thus, after the critical treatment I've subjected him to in the previous chapters, this is where Bourdieu really comes into his own, as I emphasise the value of balancing notions of 'natural' talent with a more sociological analysis of the ways in which talent (and the educational opportunities that pertain to it) are socially shaped and defined. Here, also, I start to move away from the idea of doing justice to things themselves, in terms of valuing cultural objects and cultural work, and rather more to thinking about how the resources and opportunities afforded by the cultural and creative industries are socially *distributed* – a theme developed further in chapters 5 and 6.

NATURAL TALENT?

Talent is often understood as innate; a kind of 'natural aptitude' or biologically endowed capacity – or even a gift from God. In the cultural and creative industries, people are routinely described as 'naturals' or as having been 'born' to sing, dance or exhibit whatever talent they possess. It is no doubt the case that people have their own unique, personal abilities – and it would be disingenuous to claim that physical or genetically inherited factors have *no* impact on human capacities for development[1]. For example, professional musicians have been found to possess advanced cognitive processing abilities, be capable of heightened or elaborate physical co-ordination, demonstrate uncommon capacities to synchronise sound and movement, have good sense of rhythm and so on – and some of this may (in theory) derive from inborn attributes, such as (say) having more efficient synapses, long dextrous fingers or heightened pitch perception. But all these qualities are themselves as much social as biological – they are not *merely* given but also learnt and developed and only become recognised and valued as attributes, in and through socialisation (Husén, 1974; Howe et al, 1998). We might otherwise say that while people may be differently abled, at some pre-social level, the 'natural aptitude' only becomes visible in its social appearance. As Margaret Archer (2000) has argued, all human capacities (to walk, to dance, to sing soul or cantatas) only exist as talents in potentia – and are strongly contingent upon the kinds of socialisation that allow (or disallow) such capacities to be developed. Socialisation matters because while our sentient natures and biological endowments (such as, say, having a cerebral cortex or vocal chords) might be a necessary precondition for the cultural expression that is commonly recognised as an individual talent, possession of such capacities is not *sufficient* for that talent to be realised (Sayer, 2011). Yet scientific efforts to pinpoint 'natural ability' tend to be limited to identifying (often weak) correlations between some given biological inheritance and a socially expressed outcome (e.g. identifying the genetic profiles of virtuosos), or else trying to isolate those 'higher' neurocognitive abilities that might suggest some positive association to artistic or creative performance. Most of the evidence here is indirect or inferred, and usually assembled post hoc, and so lacks a convincing account of the widely assumed 'natural' (and therefore predictable) basis of talent. The innate account is further weakened precisely *because* it tends to bracket out detailed assessments of the relational interdependencies between nature, culture and the social[2].

Usually, of course, when people speak of 'natural talent' it is for reasons of good intention, as they strive to express admiration for someone's skills or qualities. A common premise is that successful artists and creative people have an inborn and exceptional talent that (through an inner compulsion) they strive continually to express – and since most of us do not possess that natural ability, artists can thereby be regarded as individual and special. Most industry observers tend to regard the uneven distribution of the 'pool' of talent as a natural fact that must be accounted for in social and economic planning. So, if some are born more talented than others, then society simply has a duty (and stands to benefit from) nurturing and supporting those innately blessed with creative gifts. In fact, some more recent liberal and market-led versions of this kind of thinking – often espoused by culture ministers, innovation theorists and creative industry educators – is that *everyone* now has some kind of creative ability, and so society must simply allow those individuals (with the volition to do so) to 'find their talent' (DCMS, 2008). At some fundamental level this is true – as has already been noted, most humans are capable of doing something. But what is significant here is that social factors are often imagined to play no significant role in the definition, cultivation or recognition of what is still presumed to be inborn or pre-existing talent. Society's role is merely to make visible that which already exists – an internal and innate capacity. But, as I hope to show, this is largely (if not entirely) a misconception.

I want to claim that such 'natural talents' do not really exist in the form they are most commonly recognised. Or rather, while there might be some objective variation in human beings' abilities and capacities, these in themselves are insufficient to explain the distribution of recognised talent. In the creative economy context I would argue that talent is not so much 'found' as serially manufactured in social inequality. If talent is a 'gift', then it is one that *tends* to be socially inherited and institutionally made. Furthermore, terms such as 'natural talent', 'aptitude', 'creativity' or 'genius' are not simply describing a self-evident reality, but performing vital discursive work that is itself constitutive of the boundaries which serve to separate the gifted from those without gifts. Thus, what we call talent, as Bourdieu and Passeron long ago revealed, should partly be understood as 'a negation of the social conditions of the production of cultivated dispositions' (1977, p. 52) – a sleight of hand obscuring the social origins of that which is commonly recognised as only essential and natural.

But before considering how talent is defined and recognised in creative arts education, it's useful to look at how talent is more generally understood within systems of educational selection. The next section examines how, in the United Kingdom, ideas of talent are strongly linked to the concept of *meritocracy* – the notion that the 'best' and most industrious will tend to be objectively (and equitably) selected for social elevation. In most of UK higher education, examination grades and formal qualifications provide the primary measure or index of merit. Yet, it is now commonly accepted by sociologists of education that these apparently objective and dispassionate criteria offer only partial and selective measures of ability, and the capacity to obtain success in them tends to be strongly shaped by social background. But as I will then discuss, while the creative arts appear to progressively disavow the necessary salience of such credentials, the issue of what *does* actually count as talent and merit is perhaps even less clear cut than in those disciplines that continue to prioritise more orthodox (largely quantitative) measures of examination and assessment – and so (in theory) selection in the arts might be regarded as being less transparently objective and meritocratic, as well as (arguably) more unfair.

TALENT, MERIT AND EDUCATION

The creative economy is widely regarded as an effective meritocracy. The foundational premise of meritocracies is that social positions are distributed according to principles of desert, rather than through inheritance, kinship or gift (e.g. see Young, 1958; Husén, 1974; Littler, 2013). Therefore, in the cultural and creative industries, it is routinely argued that individuals with creative talent *and* who work hard will get their just desserts irrespective of social background or origin – a principle espoused by everyone from government ministers, to employers, to producers of reality television:

> Talent is the life blood of the creative industries. Only an individual can decide to put in the huge effort to reach the top of these professions. ... Everyone has the chance to discover their aptitude. (DCMS, 2008, p. 19)

You can build an incredible career in media. ... All that matters is that you're truly passionate about our industry, and that you've got a bit of raw talent that sets you apart from the crowd. (Channel 4, 'TalentDays' recruitment initiative, 2014)

'Have you got an amazing talent? You could be the next winner!' (ITV, *Britain's Got Talent* recruitment initiative, 2016)

A shared assumption is that any social differences that might inhibit opportunity are less important than possessing an individual aptitude and application – one simply requires a 'raw' talent, and the 'drive' and 'passion' to pursue it. The best (most talented) will naturally thrive and the weakest (least talented) will fall by the wayside – in a sharp-elbowed (but assumedly equalitarian) competition for prestige and recognition. In this Darwinian struggle, the rewards that accrue to the successful tend not to be seen as excessive or disproportionate, but equitable and justified – since they've been 'rightfully' earned. In this way, for some, the creative economy has come to resemble 'an amateur talent show, with jackpot stakes for a few winners and hard-luck schwag for everyone else' (Ross, 2013a, p. 178); a world where few will make it to the 'top', despite the enduring promise that everyone with talent who applies themselves has the genuine opportunity do so.

However despite the rhetoric of an 'open field', and the seductive promise of instant fame offered by reality television and the like, the conventional pathways into the cultural or creative industries still tend to rely on undertaking some further (and preferably) higher education or training in arts, humanities or related creative disciplines (Ashton and Noonan, 2013). In the United Kingdom, and elsewhere, higher education (HE) colleges and universities that offer specialist creative arts and design degrees are regarded as important training grounds for future creative industry professionals – this is where 'raw' talent is recognised and cultivated. Getting into one's chosen industry therefore tends to rely on not simply having talent but possessing appropriate educational qualifications from accredited institutions that stand as evidence of that talent. For ordinary people, this is not necessarily the insuperable barrier it might once have been. As the creative economy has expanded so the breadth and range of higher education courses serving that economy has correspondingly grown – suggesting a potentially greater access and entry to the creative sector for a wider range of populations and ostensible support for the meritocracy thesis. Everyone who is talented now has a potential opportunity to develop their attributes in an education system that is both fair (most people can enter) and meritocratic (the qualified and most talented cream will rise and be rewarded with further credentials), and can then take their skills into the creative industries job market. But is this really so? And how are talent and merit actually related in education, and creative education especially?

MEASURING MERIT

Entrance to UK higher education tends to rely on meeting some prerequisite criteria or standard – such as the possession of secondary or further education qualifications. HE institutions, although meritocratic, are also often thought of as equalitarian in the sense that anyone can freely apply for entry. Talent or ability – mostly evidenced through previous educational achievement – is the most significant entry requirement, and (in theory) the opportunity to meet this requirement is available to all. In this sense – and one most enthusiastically supported by market liberals – meritocratic systems (in education or elsewhere) are regarded as inherently fair since opportunities and rewards are imagined to be distributed equitably according to individual desert and some deserving quality of the person. Under systems of competitive individualism, it is your level of 'hard work', 'application' and 'achievement' that determines your fate – and, it might seem, rightly so.

Yet, from a more egalitarian perspective, whether these judgements of 'merit' are actually 'fair' is open to question. To judge on merit is to evaluate according to the intrinsic qualities of a particular standard, regardless of any extrinsic social (or social justice) considerations. The differences (say) in the social backgrounds of university applicants are not necessarily regarded as relevant when one is judging on educative merit alone. Usually, the only pertinent question for an admissions selector is 'do they have the required grades', irrespective of the circumstances under which grades were obtained and achieved. However, to make a more socially just or egalitarian judgement is to keep in mind questions that meritocrats would likely regard as 'externalities' – issues of social context, 'distance travelled', non-credentialised qualities of the person, or perhaps even ideas of the collective rather than individual good (Roemer, 1998). The aim here would be to try and obtain an outcome that is fair in the egalitarian sense of widening the distribution of social opportunity, rather than merely upholding a standard. But while it's theoretically possible to have an education system that is both meritocratic *and* socially just – this tends not to happen. Not only are disadvantaged candidates disadvantaged in the competition for credentials, they are disadvantaged – and rarely compensated for – at the point of HE selection.

Therefore, it's reasonable to argue that just because an educative system is meritocratic, it doesn't mean to say that it's fair. An example of this is provided by Rebekah Nahai (2013) in her investigations into the admissions practices of the colleges of Oxford University. Oxford colleges are meritocratic in the sense that prospective students are judged against a set of common entry requirements which tend to prioritise academic achievements. Selection processes are therefore based on academic merit – a form of 'democratic elitism' (see Nahai, 2013, p. 686) which aims to correct for systems based on even less desirable criteria such as 'organic conservatism' (i.e. selection by blood or birth right). Here, selection is equitable in the previously mentioned narrow sense that (in theory) anyone who meets the academic standard is eligible to be selected. In this limited way, Oxford can quite reasonably be said to be 'fair' in the formal terms of uniformly applying its meritocratic standards to all who apply.

But why Oxford is substantively *unfair* from an egalitarian perspective is because the vast majority of those it selects tend to come from already privileged social groups. The reasons why proportionately few students from ethnic minorities, working-class backgrounds or state schools obtain a place at Oxford, relative to white, middle-class and privately educated peers is that they are much less likely to meet the academic standard required for admission, by virtue of their relative deprivation and social disadvantage:

> Great disparities persist in admissions outcomes between different social groups not because Oxford is 'unfair' where unfairness stands in for a breach of meritocracy, for instance through explicitly favouring socially-privileged applicants. Rather, the underlying cause of the disparity is the deep inequality that characterises British society, which leads to academic achievement – Oxford's dominant criterion of merit – correlating with social class and family income. (Nahai, 2013, p. 699)

Contrary to popular perceptions, it is therefore the persisting and prevailing inequality in society *at large* that explains the class profile of Oxford students, rather than the intrinsic 'unfairness' (or rather, lack of meritocracy) of the selection procedure itself[3]. Indeed, Nahai argues that the efforts of some Oxford colleges to make widening participation adjustments to their admissions procedures (for example, recruiting more state school pupils, and ones from poorer areas, providing they demonstrate the appropriate 'merit') shows how meritocratic systems can be more or less externally 'weighted' in terms of fairness[4]. Such adjustments, while welcome, do little to counter the fact that as long as it remains meritocratic in its current form, Oxford will also be elitist, because it continues to prioritise academic excellence over any other criteria – including those that might ensure a more equalitarian distribution for educational opportunity.

As in the case of Oxford, we would assume that selection at other higher education institutions, and across courses (including arts degrees), will be meritocratic, in so far as applicants who best meet the entry standards will be regarded as the most eligible for selection. This means that in theory the system is equitable and 'fair' (in the narrow, meritocratic sense) because the very best and most talented will enter the academy, provided their merits meet the 'disinterested' standards of the institution. But these universities and courses, while meritocratic, are also unfair – for all the same reasons that Oxford is unfair, in that their selections tend to favour pre-advantaged applicants from more privileged backgrounds. For example, while only 7% of the UK population are educated at private (i.e. fee-paying) schools, with most of the remaining 93% educated in the state sector, this minority still secures a disproportionate amount of the places available at the elite (known as 'Russell Group') universities (Boliver, 2013; SMCPC, 2014). Yet, equally, beyond the Russell Group, and in elite arts colleges specifically, more precise data on patterns of selection and enrolment are starting to materialise, albeit slowly. In 2013, the Royal Academy of Music, one of the few arts institutions to publicly publish its own data on student socio-economic profiles, revealed that only 48% of its students came from state schools in the period 2008–2012, with only 14% of those coming from the four lowest NS-SEC[5] social classes, and 7% from what are termed lowest (university) participation neighbourhoods. In more aggregate fashion, Christina Scharff (2015) estimated that around a quarter of all students (24.4%) from five of the United Kingdom's leading music colleges had been to a private school, and further found that such colleges had only around 8% black and minority ethnic (BAME) pupils, less than the 10% in HE as a whole, and much less than the 14% of the national population from BAME backgrounds. A recent investigation by *The Stage* magazine into the acting profession found a more mixed picture when it came to elite selection – with most of the leading drama schools reporting an intake of state school students that varied between 40% and 70–80% (Hemley, 2014). This still suggests, however, a significant relative disadvantage through *not* attending private school. We might add that it is also important to look at which state schools are providing the intake – since research by the Sutton Trust suggests that elite universities don't just recruit from *any* state school but from a narrow band of elites that tend to dominate in that sector (Sutton Trust, 2016).

While the data is still far from comprehensive, the general picture suggests that despite having 'fair' systems of evaluation and selection, the outcome in arts schools remains decidedly unjust from an egalitarian perspective. Poor people (and ethnic minorities) simply do not enter the very best arts and creative industry academies – and are therefore structurally denied the opportunity of high-quality education and so, in all possibility, the best kinds of future arts employment such qualifications might ideally provide[6]. As is now widely known, the social profile of employment in the creative industries tends to reflect the profile of advantage in higher education (and indeed society at large) – where the 'talent' tends to be disproportionately middle class and (especially in the very top jobs) privately educated, white and male (SMCPC, 2014; Warwick Commission, 2015; Sutton Trust 2016 and see chapter 5). In this way then, the education system reflects and maintains the broader social divisions that ensure the established class inequalities in creative economy are reproduced. If talent were simply 'inborn' and 'natural' and allowed to 'rise', this would evidently not be the case. Instead, in HE, the capacity for talent to be credentialised and rewarded appears significantly determined by the extent to which one is able to obtain the prerequisite qualifications for entry into the arena of evaluation – an advantage heavily weighted in favour of the already socially privileged. As Bourdieu and Passeron argued, material factors ensure that for the socially disadvantaged, the 'probabilities of candidature' (1977, p. 153) are likely to be much lower than for advantaged and elite groups, since they tend to lack the formal qualifications required for entry. But I now want to discuss how formal underqualification (lack of credentialised merit) might not be the only – or even the most significant – problem faced by the socially disadvantaged in attempting to access a high-quality creative arts education.

HOMOPHILY AND DISPOSITIONAL SELECTION

I want to suggest that in creative arts education there is an additional problem – one that might make creative HE both less (formally or transparently) meritocratic and perhaps even less fair than other kinds of university education – even compared with elite institutions like Oxford.

In her Oxford study, Nahai notes a potential threat to formal meritocratic procedures in that the informal attitudes and dispositions of academic selectors might (consciously or unconsciously) tend towards favouring those candidates who best reflect their own social class positions – what she identifies as a latently 'homophilic' tendency among selectors. This is more generally referred to as 'appointing in one's own image'. However, according to Nahai, this isn't a particular problem in the case of Oxford, since having the best qualifications tended to be overwhelmingly weighted as the primary criterion for selection, so reducing the possible impact of homophilic tendencies[7]. While we might agree with her assertion that Oxford selection is primarily a meritocratic process (and thereby elitist and unfair by egalitarian standards), I think we need to be more sceptical regarding her claim about the limited influence of homophilic selection – not least because claims for its insignificance derive mainly from the accounts of those academic participants in her study who were (perhaps understandably) keen to portray themselves as unimpeachably objective selectors. Consequently, I would suggest that homophilic section, or more broadly, appointing in line with established social preference and prejudice is not only likely to be more pervasive at Oxford than Nahai allows for, but is itself already a widely institutionalised problem in the education sector as a whole, as others have consistently revealed (Bourdieu and Passeron 1977; Sullivan, 2001; Zimdars et al, 2009).

In fact, as Bourdieu and Passeron have argued persuasively, selective education proceeds not simply through an objective assessment of formal criteria but a reading of the 'social marks' (1977, p. 163) exhibited by the hopeful candidate. This is not just a dispassionate reading of an (economic) class position, but an assessment of the total cultural capital exhibited by the candidate – their 'dispositions' in demonstrating a 'wide' cultural knowledge and participation, good manners, refined comportment and an ability to express themselves in an appropriately eloquent, 'academic' or 'informed' way[8]. For Bourdieu, the habitus of the applicant – visible as the expressed internalised externality of class and social position – is always 'read' by the selector and contributes, either consciously or unconsciously, to their decision to accept or reject. The tendency for homophilic selection is therefore understood as a structural process of class favouritism and reproduction – rather than simply an aberration of the biased individual – since the selector is merely a single agent in an education system that is at the very centre of the institutional reproduction of social division. We might well surmise, of course, that homophily extends well beyond the parameters of class – into ethnicity and gender, or issues of age or disability, for example. But, for now, the two specific propositions I want to make in relation to creative arts selection are:

- Firstly, that admission to elite education in the arts tends to rely on somewhat more *opaque* judgements of talent (and merit) than is the case for conventional academic subjects, in that judgements tend to be more ineffable (though based on verbal reasoning and argument) than statistically measured or based on an 'objective[9]' qualification or credential (even accepting that those schemes of credentialisation are themselves somewhat less than objective).
- Secondly, and relatedly, either implicitly or explicitly, selection in the creative arts might tend to rely on dispositional and homophilic judgements much more markedly than in traditional academic selection.

For both these reasons, I want to speculate that arts selection may not only be less (openly) meritocratic, but might also be less fair than selection in other academic subjects.

ART SCHOOL: FAIR OR FOUL?

To appreciate these issues we need to consider the following question: If demonstrating merit in the case of admission to a traditional academic course in an elite university (such as Oxford) seems at least *relatively* straightforward and standardised, how do we judge merit in a context where one of the principal criteria of evaluation is the more ineffable quality of 'artistic talent'? This is the dilemma facing those in arts education, where academic qualifications evidently matter, but are often regarded as somewhat *less* important than performative and auditioned demonstrations of 'talent', 'promise' or 'passion' (McRobbie, 2016).

The following table shows some of the standard (and typical) entry requirements for undergraduate creative arts programmes, drawn from a small sample of leading UK HE institutions; note that the grade requirement for formal academic credentials tends actually to be quite low (especially if we were to compare it with more traditional academic subjects) and that *other* criteria (one or more performance auditions, portfolios and personal interviews) are usually given equal or greater priority in the entry assessment:

On the one hand, these more 'open' standards appear advantageous from an equalitarian perspective because they seem to undermine conventional (i.e. elite-biased) credentialism by providing greater opportunities for the

Table 2 Entry Requirements for Some Leading UK HE Arts Courses in 2015

Institution	Example Programme	Standard Minimum Entry Requirements[1]
Central School of Speech and Drama	BA in Acting	2 C's at 'A' level, 3 GCSEs, assessed audition
Royal Academy of Dramatic Art (RADA)	BA in Acting	No formal academic criteria, assessed audition
London Academy of Music and Dramatic Arts (LAMDA)	BA in Professional Acting	No formal academic criteria, assessed audition and interview
Royal College of Music	BMus.	2 'A' levels (including at least a C in Music), assessed audition and interview
Royal Northern College of Music	BMus.	2 'A' levels (including Music), 3 GCSEs, audition and interview
Guildhall School of Music and Drama	BMus.	2 'A' levels (Grade E or above), auditions
Central St. Martins School of Art and Design	BA Fine Art	Foundation Diploma in Art and Design, 1 'A' level, assessed portfolio, interview
Slade School of Fine Art	BA Fine Art	3 'A' levels, assessed portfolio, interview
Trinity Laban Conservatoire of Music and Dance	BA Dance	2 'A' levels (Grade E or above), audition
London Contemporary Dance School	BA Contemporary Dance	2 'A' levels (Grade E or above), audition and interview

1. In England, Wales and Northern Ireland the GCSE (General Certificate of Secondary Education) is the standard school exam taken (in multiple subjects), usually between the ages of 14–16; 'A' (Advanced) Levels are taken at 18, prior to entry to HE. Scotland has its own equivalent qualifications ('Standard Grade' at 16, 'Highers' at 18).

academically weak (but artistically talented) to enter higher education. The arts routinely present themselves as an alternative to intellectual, more conventionally 'academic' subjects, since their principle of merit relies on the kind of talent that does not appear to necessarily correlate to a quantified intellectual ability – dancing, singing, drawing, painting, making art of all kinds are judged to be special, autonomous capacities that do not necessarily rely on a conventional and measured intelligence and might not be accounted for by established systems of credentialisation – such as mainstream schooling and exams.

There is some truth in this assumption. In fact it was this relative indifference to academic criteria that characterised much UK art and design school education of the mid-to-late twentieth century, and made 'art school' such a success in social democratic and egalitarian terms (Frith and Horne, 1987). While most local and independent art schools demanded some minimal academic qualifications, they tended to use conventional notions of artistic talent as the principal merit for selection and did so in a relatively open-ended and inclusive way, sufficient to ensure that working-class participation in arts education was hugely expanded, and not stymied by a lack of formal credentials (see Strand, 1987; Beck and Cornford, 2012; Banks and Oakley, 2016; and chapter 5). Yet in marked contrast, then, as now, the most prestigious schools of arts and culture have tended to remain much more tightly bound by commitments to both academic and artistic 'excellence' and selection of the very best from the available 'pool' of talent. As we've already seen, the chances of getting into an elite college tend to be enhanced if one is already a member of the elite – or at the very least the 'comfortable' middle class. This isn't simply down to the meritocratic likelihood that members of these social strata will obtain the very best academic or art qualifications – it is down to a particular tendency for institutions to select on a homophilic or dispositional basis.

Indeed, at the very best schools, selection is problematic both in terms of credentialised meritocracy and overall fairness. I would suggest that in selective arts academies and institutions, while academic qualifications and credentials matter, they are *much more likely* to be accompanied by, or subordinated to, judgements of creative merit which are less formally prescribed and rendered opaque through lacking a common metric or means of measure. Indeed they often derive from ineffable judgements about an individual's performed and auditioned 'talent', 'energy', 'expressiveness' 'feel', 'promise' and so on. In this way, such evaluations may be meritocratic, but in ways that are less evidently visible and verifiable than, say, selection procedures for studying mathematics at an Oxford college. Of course, a reasonable objection here might be that the creative arts have their objective standards – it's just that they are *different* to the kinds usually evidenced in

other educative or employment contexts. The qualities of a creative performance – demonstrated, say, in the dramatic intensity of a soliloquy, the grace
of a leg extension, or the musicality of an improvisation – provide some of
the objective criteria on which merit is judged. This is a plausible claim since
– as I have already argued in chapters 2 and 3 – cultural objects do possess
their own objective properties and the arts are practices that have their own
objective standards of excellence. Yet selective judgements of talent are also
less obviously standardised and 'measurable' in the arts than in conventional
academic subjects[10], and because the definition of merit in creative education
and industry is also more openly shaped by *additional* judgements about the
personal presentation and conduct of the person – including their range of
cultural and linguistic skills, their performative qualities, their manner and
appearance, whether they offer the physical embodiment (or not) of the kinds
of dispositional qualities imagined to connote artistic talent – then the idea
that talent is able to be objectively assessed independent of the social context
of evaluation becomes highly questionable.

'TALKING THE TALK ... WALKING THE WALK'

So what makes the creative student meritorious? Partly, as we've seen, it's
some conventional qualifications and credentials. But there is also little doubt
that possessing a 'natural talent' – rather than qualifications or socialisation –
is what 'really' defines a budding artist or creative and is the proper focus of
aesthetic evaluation and critical discussion in elite school selection. But the
relationship between natural talent and selective processes of arts education
are perhaps more closely entwined than is commonly recognised. Here I want
to show how attribution of talent is not a process of natural ordering but an
act of social manufacture – realised in processes of elite school selection and
training: a process of recognition that tends to value and help reproduce the
advantages of the already advantaged. Here, talent is not (just) natural capacity but material and dispositional – a quality of personhood arguably expressive of some enduring and deep-rooted social divisions.

Research by Ruben Gaztambide-Fernandez et al (2013) into the provision
of arts education in a Canadian public secondary school offer us an initial,
illustrative example of how the ideas and practices of managing 'talent' might
both reflect and manifest structured social inequality. In their study of the
School for Creative and Performing Arts (CAPA) in Toronto, the research-
ers argued that processes of selection, curriculum design and expectations
around student behaviour and conduct revealed a fundamental misrecognition of social advantage as talent. How so? Firstly, as a selective school
CAPA is entitled to choose its students, primarily on the basis of student

skill or aptitude for one of a number of performing arts. Yet this selection, apparently based on individual talent and merit alone, tended to favour more privileged social groups. This was partly because students from such groups were likely to come from social backgrounds where parents and family were able to offer the kinds of financial and emotional support liable to encourage the effective nurturing of a talent, including access to better and more extensive arts training than their less-fortunate peers. Such advantages were not invisible to school selectors but were argued to be compensated for by a rigorous and equitable selection process that allowed natural talent to 'express itself'. However, as the research showed, the apparently fair selection process demanded students demonstrated their innate and 'raw' talent only through cultivated and measured performances that required – and so strongly implied past exposure to – formal arts training and modes of bodily comportment and conduct likely to be more alien to less privileged social groups. It is worth quoting from this ethnography at length, given the richness with which it conveys the process of talent recognition and formation:

During the music audition at CAPA, the kind of musical training that is expected for admission becomes evident. Inside the band room, one of the CAPA teachers and a guest musician sit at a table covered in forms and information sheets behind the conductor's podium. Each audition follows like a well-rehearsed ritual. A tall young man arrives, hands his sheet music to the judges, and confidently strides up the risers to the music stand in the middle. As he sets up, he says the name of his music teacher and spells it for the judges. 'You pass the audition', the guest judge jokes, and asks, 'How long have you been playing tenor [saxophone]'? 'Two years', the student says, and he adds without prompting that he auditioned for the state band, where he was asked to play first tenor saxophone, and that he has traveled to the United States and played at some of Toronto's most famous concert venues. After a short silence and a chuckle, the judges ask him to start by playing 'a B-flat concert scale'. After the scale, the student prepares to play 'The Girl From Ipanema'. Before he can begin, the teacher instructs him: 'Take it with pick up to number 5.' Without hesitation, the student turns the page, and begins to play in the middle of the tune. After a minute, the teacher asks him to stop, but the student keeps going to the end of the phrase. 'Okay, that's good', the teacher insists, stands up, and gives him a sheet of music for sight-reading. 'Do you know what key signature that is'? he asks. Immediately, and with confidence, the student answers 'G major'. He plays the unfamiliar phrase without a glitch, and the teacher comments, 'Very nice, one of the best all day'. The teacher then moves on to the final step of the audition: 'Please sing or hum the first few lines of the national anthem.' The student begins to sing the familiar lyrics in a soft, clear, and well-tuned voice, with smooth intonation and gentle phrasing. 'Thank you very much', the teacher says, 'nice job'. As the student leaves the room, the teacher turns to the guest judge: 'I told you there would be no lack of "I did this" and "did that", "played here" and "played there". They talk the talk, *and* walk the walk'. Then he jokes: 'They start to question the teachers in Grade 11'! (Gaztambide-Fernandez et al, 2013, pp. 128–9)

I would venture to say that this is not an untypical scenario in contexts of music (and other kinds of art) education selection. The formalised and ritual demands of the process served to strongly define the parameters of what constitutes a demonstrably talented student. And having the dispositional confidence and ease, as well as the schooled ability, to demonstrate one's apparently innate skills, immediately puts such candidates at an advantage relative to those others (local working-class and ethnic minority students in the case of this study) who often lack such dispositions and abilities, and so tend to look more awkward, and perform less confidently at audition – and so are less likely to be selected. The research here also revealed that minoritised candidates could be rejected for an apparent lack of 'interest' in the art form they were applying to study, since when questioned on their wider appreciation of (say) music or theatre, or histories of arts participation or attendance, often struggled to demonstrate the required levels of eloquence and engagement that was deemed necessary for potential CAPA students. The fact that such 'deficiencies' were most likely due to a lack of opportunity, rather than interest, tended to be downplayed in the overall evaluation of a student's talent and ability.

Yet it was not only in the audition process where social advantage was identified as an expression of talent. Gaztambide-Fernandez and his colleagues examined how the school curriculum itself – in terms of content and underlying principles – was loaded in favour of privileged students who best embodied and performed its apparently neutral and inclusive demands. A traditional arts education, with 'classical' training, with emphasis placed on the virtues of extra homework and out-of-hours rehearsing, self-financed attendance at public auditions, underscored by an assumption of strong familial support, was taken as standard – and thereby tended to favour students from upper social strata, who duly performed at higher levels of achievement than their less socially advantaged peers. Therefore, the idea of who possessed 'talent' tended to be strongly tied to educative success and material support defined within the confines of a curriculum that advantaged the already advantaged. Black students, or working-class students – those with tastes or training in non-standard arts or approaches, who often failed to fully recognise or internalise the demands of the curriculum, or whose commitment was often compromised by economic or social circumstance – tended to struggle to obtain full recognition as a good or exceptional student. Similarly, the extent to which a student was able to routinely enact and embody an institutionally desired 'excellence' was a good indicator of them being rated as successful and talented – since turning up for every rehearsal, on time, knowing intuitively what was expected in practice and performance, and generally emulating the habits and dispositions of a trained professional – all contributed to positive evaluation of a student as a gifted performer. In all these ways, we observe how, in arts education, the capacity to express talent is not straightforwardly linked to an ability to sing, dance or play a musical instrument, but rests on routine demonstration of a preferred history of socialisation and training, an appropriate set of cultured dispositions and a resourcefulness and commitment borne largely from the possession of an established social and economic advantage.

Research in the United Kingdom reports similar problems of misrecognition and exclusion. Penny Jane Burke and Jackie McManus (2011) examined the admissions policies and procedures for arts and design courses in five HE institutions. While ostensibly offering fair evaluation in an institutional context strongly marked by discursive commitments to widening participation and inclusivity agendas, the academics interviewing and selecting students tended to betray both institutional and personal biases towards 'traditional' student applicants, at the expense of 'non-traditional' ones. As at CAPA, the range of criteria for evaluating potential students tended to be premised on established bourgeois norms and a set of classed and racialised assumptions about what constituted a promising artist. These included an expectation of a 'wide knowledge of contemporary art[11]', 'good at self-promotion', an ability to 'talk really well', and to present oneself as being 'incredibly interesting'[12] (Burke and McManus, 2011, p. 705). Other, more material factors that rated in an applicant's favour included 'willingness to budget for and cover the cost of resources', as well as showing a desire to move away from home and live in the vicinity of the college, since this was regarded as strong evidence of an 'enthusiasm' and 'motivation' that was highly prized. Students who failed to impress in these areas (usually from poorer or ethnic minority backgrounds) tended to be rejected at the application stage, even if, as happened on occasion, they possessed *stronger* academic qualifications than their white middle-class counterparts.

In similar vein, Annette Hayton et al (2014) reported on the significance of dispositional selection for the highly prestigious BA Fine Art programme at Goldsmiths College (of the University of London), where students are primarily evaluated on their portfolio of independent work and an interview process, rather than on exam scores. While, once again, this appears more 'open' to less academic applicants, the heavy reliance on a strong interview performance (with all the implications of demonstrating erudition and competence in engaging with art[13]) and all the weight of the unspoken criteria of selection, tended, in their view, to explain the low levels of recruitment of working-class and ethnic minority applicants.

Likewise, Sam Broadhead's (2014) study of 'non-traditional' (mature, ethnic minority) students negotiating their entry into UK art schools revealed much about the ways in which arts education tends implicitly to cater to the needs of (a usually unnamed) privileged majority, at the expense of social minorities whose experiences, interests and needs may differ markedly from those of 'traditional' students.

Finally, from my own collaborative research with colleagues into black British jazz musicians (see Banks, Ebrey and Toynbee, 2014; Dueck, 2014; Toynbee et al, 2014) further example is provided of how judgements of talent tend to be skewed towards standards that favour the attributes of the socially privileged. The recruitment of students to UK university jazz departments and conservatories (as for music degrees in general) has tended to favour white musicians from relatively privileged backgrounds. Despite the origins of jazz in black America and the long history of participation by indigenous and migrant black musicians in making British jazz, black students remain significantly underrepresented on UK jazz courses. Our research revealed that the academy preference for applicants with a history of formal musical training, equipped with requisite technical skills and evidence of wider knowledge and 'interest', tended to discriminate against black musicians. Such musicians had histories of training that were more often informal and inconsistently schooled, tending towards the autodidactic, and based on mimesis rather than paid-for lessons and formal instruction, as well as grounded in repertoires and styles often inimical to conservatoire jazz, developed in conjunction with others in 'community' music contexts (Banks, Ebrey and Toynbee, 2014). Thus, not only was it the case that black candidates were less likely to apply and to be accepted onto conservatoire jazz courses[14], the wider evidence suggests that in Britain, black musicians in *any* genre struggle to enter the very best music colleges, as Byron Dueck has revealed:

> English conservatoires have a much smaller percentage of black British students than most institutions of higher education in the country. According to figures published by the Higher Education Statistics Authority (HESA), in 2009–10, black British students accounted for less than 1 per cent of the total student population in at least three of England's conservatoires (HESA, 'All HE Students'); this was also the case in 2011–12 (HESA, 'Music'). Black enrolment was low enough to be recorded as 0 at two of these conservatoires in 2009–10, and at one of them in 2011–12. In contrast, black British students constitute 6.5 per cent of the English student population as a whole. (Dueck, 2014, p. 208)

In our research we found further evidence of the kinds of misrecognition reported by Burke and McManus in so far as the exclusion of black musicians from the jazz academy was often rationalised (mainly by white musicians and educators) as an expression of an innate lack of 'technical' talent, and a greater facility among blacks for styles of playing that emphasise 'feel' and 'swing' rather than scholastic technique – a resuscitation of the myth of the white 'intellectual' and the black 'primitive' (see Dueck, 2014). That black musicians *systemically* will have had less material opportunity to develop scholastic technique, or to become equipped with the 'whole capital of experience' (Bourdieu 1993, p. 21), sufficient to convince selectors of their dedication and the effortlessness of their talent, tended to go unnoticed or unacknowledged.

But jazz is not unusual – consider the absence of ethnic minorities from the most elite dance academies, and indeed the lack of black dancers in all the major UK professional ballet companies (Goldhill and Marsh, 2012). Ballet is an art form where black people have long been excluded through a combination of material disadvantage, an alleged lack of talent and a history of omission based on racial stigma and unvarnished preferences for employing only 'traditional' and 'classical' (i.e. white) bodies[15]. For example, the founder of Ballet Black[16], Cassa Pancho, has repeatedly drawn attention to how the myth that black people aren't the 'right shape', or 'technically capable' of dancing ballet, or lack the dispositions necessary to embody the required grace, has strongly discriminated against black dance talent, helping to mask the pernicious history of inequality and exclusion that has consistently prevented black dancers attaining the highest professional standards and the best positions (Pool, 2010).

CONCLUSION: ON INHERITORS AND WONDERBOYS

In chapter 1, I proposed that equality and equity must mean that people have the right to seek education and employment on an equal basis with others, and that, thereafter, any differences in the way positions and rewards are socially distributed should be the result of a fair and just process. The evidence of this chapter suggests that when it comes to elite arts education, we have some way to go before we fulfil those ideals. Current systems of meritocracy not only fail to account for the fact that people do not enter the area of competition as equals, but that in making their decisions, selectors may be reproducing some established systemic prejudices when it comes to identifying and judging talent. Indeed, if we were to believe the ideology of meritocracy, then we would conclude that working-class, black and ethnic minority people[17] must have *no* merit, because they are not capable of applying themselves to obtain a place in the best kinds of arts education and training. Yet what is more likely is that such persons lack not simply the material resources and experiences that are significant prerequisites for elevating oneself into a position of candidacy, but the social appearances and dispositions that would invite selection as talent. This is not simply a matter of class or race, but a subtle composite of a number of factors – including 'infinitesimals of style or manners, accent or elocution, posture or mimicry, even clothing and cosmetics' (Bourdieu and Passeron, 1977, p. 162); all those implicit qualities that convey the rightness of an applicant and the self-evidency of their talent. For Bourdieu and Passeron, the classification of student talent takes place on the curve of the social, the absolute ratio that determines all possibilities, from the exception to the familiar rule:

> Attitudes such as bourgeois students' dilettantism, self-assurance and irreverent ease, or working-class students' tense application and educational realism can only be understood as a function of the probability or improbability of occupying the position occupied which defines the objective structure of the subjective experience of the 'wonderboy' or the 'inheritor'. In short, what offers itself to be grasped, at every point on the curve, is the slope of the curve; in other words the whole curve. (1977, p. 161)

We might surmise that the classification of talent takes place within contexts of selectivity and discrimination that challenge the meritocratic faith that natural gifts and hard work create their own opportunity. In short, despite industry and governmental rhetorics of access and equal opportunity, there are still many more 'inheritors' than 'wonderboys' in the creative economy. To realise your 'innate' talent as musician, actor, designer or artist, it helps very much to come from the kind of prosperous and well-connected background that both values and can materially and intangibly support the realisation of your apparently natural advantages. Patterns of selection consistently reveal that, far from being open and accessible to all-comers, the cultural and creative industries, and the education systems that serve them, are becoming enclaves of privilege – that dispense favour to the favoured and give grace to the graceful.

In this respect, talent can never be reduced to an innate skill or aptitude, or a concrete capacity to *do* something (though, as I've suggested, such qualities might objectively exist) but must also be recognised as a set of social dispositions, partly defined and constructed in the performative contexts of their expression and evaluation. When, as happens in creative arts education, selectors rely less on traditional academic qualifications as evidence of merit, and more so on combinations of aesthetic judgements[18], as well as implicit (or explicit) homophilic and dispositional prejudices, then pedagogic authority becomes irresistible, and symbolic violence is enhanced. When selectors insists on the right to their own 'implicit, diffuse criteria' (Bourdieu and Passeron, 1977, p. 162) then the objective basis of selection becomes almost impossible to isolate, and so the basis of rejection becomes more difficult to oppose. Perhaps now the best guarantee of success in creative arts education (and in the creative economy beyond) is not the possession of a 'raw' talent, but the ownership of an inherited ease and the capacity to expend a dispositional currency available only to a privileged few. The role of not just selectors but institutions is most crucial here, since it is both the unspoken and more explicit criteria embedded in the processes of admissions and curriculum design – not to mention evaluation of students' work quality and performance – that reveal exclusion, discrimination and misrecognition as embedded in routine practices of 'talent' identification and development in arts and creative economy education.

NOTES

1. It's consistent with the kind of approach taken in this book to argue that people have objective qualities and capacities that are both natural *and* social; biology, the physical world and culture combining to create characteristically *human* beings, that are objectively identifiable (if not always entirely different from) other, non-human, entities. This is an attempt to avoid both natural and cultural reductionism, and instead to recognise the always imbricated and mutually supporting character of 'nature and nurture'. We have, as Sayer better describes, 'differently cultured natures', where our physical, biological capacities as humans are a precondition for our culturalisation (part of our human nature is that we are beings capable of being culturalised), but do not necessarily determine what *kinds* of culturalisation we are subjected to, or contribute to. Culture too, in turn, might well shape our human qualities and capacities, including physically and neurologically – but this doesn't mean that culture is all we are, or is the 'primary' determinant in making our objective existences (see Sayer, 2011, pp. 100–01).

2. For example, as Michael Howe et al (1998, p. 402) have noted: 'In general, the correlational evidence linking performance to brain characteristics suggests that innately determined biological differences do contribute to the variability of expertise in specific areas of competence. However, there is a large gulf between identifying neural correlates of behavioural differences and finding a neural predictor of talent. The relations between neural and performance measures are too weak to warrant conclusions about talent, and correlations diminish as tasks become more complex'. And as they further argue, the *social* account of talent, on the other hand, offers far more convincing explanations for the provenance and development of unusual or special ability – linked to histories of immersive socialisation (mainly through parenting and schooling), with all its attendant practice, discipline, repetition and lengthy and intensive training.

3. 'Oxbridge [Oxford or Cambridge] is only the final step – and a relatively tiny one at that – in an unfair, inequitable and unconscionable educational filtering system that begins at the moment of birth' (Mangan, 2012, no pagination).

4. Indeed, Boliver et al (2015) note how the more elite UK universities – stung by criticisms of elitism – have more recently made efforts to try and better account for

applicants' 'contextual data' in admissions selection processes – though not in entirely standardised or successful ways. See the Sutton Trust (2016) for how Oxbridge has attempted to meet this challenge.

5. National Statistics Socio-Economic Classification – a standard measure of class used in UK official statistics.

6. Problems extend beyond the Russell Group and their preference for private school students. For example, Annette Hayton et al (2014) found that although London's Goldsmiths College has a reputation for a 'strong tradition of widening participation', its students taking the BA Fine Art degree have tended to reflect a national picture of selection and exclusivity:

> As with similar courses nationally and other London-based courses, the majority of Goldsmiths Fine Art students are female, white and middle-class. Higher Education Information Database for Institutions data for 2008/09 reveals stark disparities in terms of gender, class and ethnicity. Nationally, 72% of undergraduates taking Fine Art are female and 28% male, with Goldsmiths students comprising 65% female and 35% male. Nationally, 63.7% of Fine Art students were in Socio-Economic Groups 1–3 and 36.3% in Socio-Economic Groups 4–7 compared with 72.7% and 27.3% respectively at Goldsmiths. The national data on ethnicity show that 91.6% of students taking Fine Art are 'white', whilst this figure is 92.3% at Goldsmiths. (Hayton et al, 2014, p. 1,259)

7. Though we should note that many Oxford colleges *also* partly base their judgements on a selection interview, as a complement to assessments of objective credentials – a point which Nahai somewhat underplays. At Cambridge, an interview is mandatory. See Sutton Trust (2016) for further detail on selection criteria at Oxbridge.

8. In fact, as Zimdars et al (2009) now argue, cultural capital, the inherited and schooled ability to convey a sense of ease and confidence with learning, might be *more* significant than both formal academic criteria and an objective or quantitative reading of class 'position' in convincing Oxford selectors of a student's 'merit'.

9. Objective in the sense of being 'unbiased', 'neutral' or 'value-free' (see Sayer, 2000, and chapter 2, endnote 2).

10. This is not to say that the acquired standard grade examinations in music, singing, dancing, etc. are not regarded as relevant objects, but to note that they tend to be *subordinated* to the quality of the in situ performance audition, the reading, the interview and so on.

11. As Burke and McManus revealed, the kinds of 'contemporary' art valued did not extend to black music or street fashion, since one of the black female applicants for a fashion degree course, possessing good academic qualifications, was rejected for being 'all hip-hop and sports tops' (2011, p. 707) in favour of less qualified middle-class contenders with more conventional or legitimate tastes.

12. To present oneself as 'incredibly interesting' is a classed quality, as Sayer intimates:

> Someone born into a high income, highly educated, high status family gains a set of dispositions that attune them to their position in the social field ... in particular an ease that derives from distance from economic necessity, and a sense entitlement and confidence that they are the most rightful inheritors of the most favoured positions, in which they will

have the power to take decisions affecting others, and be served by them, and listened to. (Sayer, 2009, pp. 11–12)

13. Similarly, in 2015, applicants for the BMus at the Royal Northern College of Music were advised that 'presentation is an important element of performance. Wear smart, comfortable clothes that you can play in with ease, jeans and trainers are not really suitable. Don't experiment with a new outfit or wear high heels if you're not used to them. On entering the room, smile at the panel. ... Demonstrate an understanding of context of your music by pronouncing the names and composers of your pieces correctly. Tune carefully, quickly and quietly, to the piano in the room. Don't be disconcerted if you don't play everything, the panel may want to talk to you for longer. They are looking for potential and temperament – not a completed artist. Engage and interest the panel, keeping your performance fresh, with a wide dynamic range and sense of changes of mood and colour. Maintain musical interest in your repertoire – it is easy to slide into staleness. Avoid this! Try to demonstrate an interest in conveying the intentions of a composer and a love for the medium in which you are working'. On the one hand, this seems like helpful advice, but on the other, it comes laden with a set of classed assumptions about the appropriate social histories, appearances and communicative competences of natural talent.

14. As Boliver (2013) notes, across *all* subjects, black students in the United Kingdom are both much less likely to *apply* to elite universities and, if they do, be accepted into them, relative to other ethnic groups. However, black students (and all ethnic minority students) are not statistically underrepresented in HE as whole – because they tend to apply to, and be accepted by, the less prestigious institutions.

15. 'Look, for example, at the costumes we mostly take for granted as standard ballet garb. Peach colored ballet slippers, nude colored tights, white powdered bodies, these innocuous seeming traditions may not be consciously hateful, but they are exclusive. White skin is not just the norm but the uniform' (*Huffington Post*, 2012).

16. The United Kingdom's first professional dance company for black and Asian dancers.

17. I have neglected to discuss gender, and there is no doubt that gender inequalities persist in the academy – but in terms of *initial* entry to HE, this is not really evident, and less so in the arts where women make up around 60% of all students (HESA, 2013). But while women might enter the arts academy in roughly equal numbers to men (though differently in different kinds of arts) – they often do less well once they have arrived and certainly go on to have less successful careers afterwards (see chapter 5).

18. These judgements, while objective and technical, also happen to be deeply subjective and impressionistic. Obtaining a better and more justified set of standards for making (either meritocratic or equalitarian) aesthetic judgements in creative arts school selection would not be an easy problem to solve, therefore. But as we saw in chapter 2, while judgements are difficult, they are also necessary – and so we shouldn't avoid trying to improve them.

Chapter 5

The Long Day Closes?

Access and Opportunity in Cultural Work

In this chapter, I want to focus on the ways in which cultural industry *jobs* are socially assigned. However, unlike in the previous chapter, the discussion is concerned less with specific processes of selection, and rather more with the general distribution of opportunities amongst different social groups. What kind of people work in culture – and what kind of work they obtain – is regarded as vitally important in terms of social justice. A job in culture is not only a significant material opportunity, it also provides the chance to secure status and recognition, as well as to participate in a practice, or more widely in the shared making of social and political life. It matters, then, from a justice perspective, that cultural industry jobs are distributed as equally and equitably as possible. Yet, as I will show, the most recent evidence suggests that we are failing to fulfil this imperative, at least in the United Kingdom. Indeed, most research now reveals that the cultural industries are becoming *more* exclusive, and public concern about inequalities is increasing. However, while the question of how opportunity is distributed in cultural work (and to whom) has recently become more pressing, this is also an issue that has been with us for some considerable time. The initial aim of this chapter, therefore, is to place current trends within their historical context – and to do that we need to return to a time when cultural work first began to be recognised as prestigious and desirable, and a new opportunity that was (theoretically) open to all. I want to argue that if we can appreciate how cultural work first came to be regarded as a meritocratic world of free opportunity, then we will better understand how it has since come to be seen as so divided and problematic.

'THE LONG BOOM' AND CULTURAL OPPORTUNITY

By the middle of the twentieth century, the United Kingdom (and other economically developed nations) had begun to experience employment increases in radio and television, newspaper and magazine journalism, publishing, advertising, the music industry and the wider creative arts. This wasn't entirely unprecedented: from the early part of the century, the more general growth of white-collar jobs and the service and entertainment industries had already shifted the emphasis towards the commercial media, arts and cultural industries as new sources of work. Employment was being rapidly fuelled by a Fordist regime that elevated wages amongst more strongly unionised labour and stimulated higher levels of consumer demand for cultural goods. People's desires for such goods had also increased partly to fill expansions in the leisure time afforded by improvements in the conditions of work. Furthermore, post–Second World War advances in welfare benefits, access to health and social care, and increased opportunities in state education helped fire the creative energies and aspirations of ordinary populations. As a consequence, commercial popular culture exploded into life, as new taste communities and consumer fractions emerged that further encouraged both specialised and diverse production niches – many of which were created by ordinary people themselves. Here, technological innovations provided faster and less-expensive printing and new art-making and design, and there were transformations in film-making, in musical instrumentation and sound recording. The rise of cheaper and more portable consumer devices such as cameras, televisions and radios, as well as new formats, such as the 'glossy' magazine or 45 rpm single, also helped fuel production and jobs. Yet, at the same time, employment in the 'high' arts was supported by the provision of public funding for 'uncommercial' activities deemed to provide society with civility and aesthetic elevation. Thus, in an unprecedented way, the mid-twentieth century saw the widest spectrum of people become involved in the cultural industries, not simply as consumers, but as workers and producers. We might conclude that in the so-called 'golden age' of capitalism (Marglin and Schor, 1992) – the 'long boom' that lasted from 1945 until the early 1970s – the cultural industries not only radically advanced the provision of public art and mass creativity but created a whole new world of cultural manufacture, employment and trade. Such is the story of the cultural industries in high modernity – and a familiar one it has now become[1].

Integral to this tale is a powerful sub-narrative of social inclusion and mobility. In this account, the cultural industries are cast as liberal institutions that have tended to be welcoming towards some of society's more economically marginal groups – such as the working classes, women or ethnic minorities. At first glance, this might seem persuasive. In the United Kingdom, in the post-war era, amidst the new 'age of affluence' and a putative social democracy, opportunities to obtain the best jobs in culture and the arts appeared to disperse, and be no longer restricted to the established social elite. The cultural industries were presented as exemplary meritocracies, where talent and hard work provided the engine of social mobility, and where a disadvantaged background offered no barrier to elevation and success. Furthermore, as the idea took hold that the material opportunities of culture were becoming more evenly spread, so the sense of a wider cultural participation and representation also increased. For example, from the late-1950s, the faces and voices of ordinary people began to appear in realist cultural texts in ways that expressed their capability and confidence, as much as their inferiority and subordination[2].

But were the new cultural industries ever *really* that inclusive to the working classes and other social minorities? And, by contrast, what are they like today? To begin to address these issues, we first need to go back to the start of the 'long boom' and ask: What exactly were the new jobs that were emerging in the cultural industries – and who was undertaking them?

CULTURAL WORK AND THE 'NEW ENTREPRENEURS'

In the United Kingdom, from about the mid-1950s, jobs in the cultural industries began to attain a greater popularity and currency. People had, of course, worked in these industries prior to this period, but the huge explosion in the number and range of jobs, the increasingly stable (and lucrative) nature of many of these industries, and their more thoroughly professionalised orientation gave rise to the idea that culture making could now be a legitimate mainstream occupation, open to the widest spectrum of society. As part of the wider growth in post-industrial, service and tertiary-sector jobs, the expanding territories of culture, arts, entertainment and 'mass communications' were assumed to be opening up to *everyone*, in an unprecedented way.

The impetus for change had already been detected elsewhere. In his book *White Collar,* published in 1951, C. Wright Mills was amongst the first to identify a new set of workplaces and occupations in the post-war United States, based on knowledge and information, services and symbol production. Mills attempted a more precise typology of the 'white collar people' inhabiting these roles, including an emergent fraction he identified as the 'new entrepreneurs'. These were young and ambitious *arrivistes*, unconventional in manner, and drawn widely from all parts of society, including the (now more) educated working and lower-middle classes. Mills noted that these 'live-wires', who 'zig-zagged' (ibid., p. 95) within and between organisations and sectors, were to be found in all white-collar environments, though, it seemed, were particularly attracted to certain *kinds* of industry:

> The new entrepreneur is very much at home in the less tangible of the 'business services' – commercial research and public relations, advertising agencies, labour relations, and the mass communication and entertainment industries. (1966, p. 94)

As Mills observed, many of these entrepreneurs (and members of the wider 'new middle class') were dealing increasingly with 'symbols and with other people, co-ordinating, recording and distributing' (ibid., p. 75) – cultural workers of an exemplary kind. The expanding worlds of marketing, advertising, PR, music, design, fashion, publishing, broadcasting and so on created opportunities that allowed ordinary people to 'get on' and so escape the shackles of their socially inherited fate. An assortment of occupations was emerging that presented opportunities for ordinary people to express their distinctive and unique talents in ways previously considered unnecessary (or even anathema) to the good ordering of work. As part of the expanding post-industrial or service economy, white-collar industries (and the more expressive and 'less tangible' ones especially) were not simply regarded as engines for the generation of mass employment, but as vehicles of personal development and mobility in an advancing meritocracy of labour.

We should note that opportunities for cultural workers were also to be found outside of the offices of the white-collar firm. At this time, a certain kind of independent cultural entrepreneur began to find favour amongst the expanding market of urban cosmopolitans and youth culture consumers. By the early 1960s, sociologists were starting to name and classify this new entrepreneurial group – including Bennett Berger who identified them as the 'bohemian businessmen':

> By bohemian businessmen, I mean the proprietors or managers of small enterprises that cater to the needs, tastes, and desires of bohemians. These enterprises range all the way from those that are central to bohemian subcultures (espresso coffee houses, small art galleries, sandal and leather shops, pottery shops, jewellery shops, and so on) to other marginal businesses serving other markets as well ('art' theaters, paperback bookstores, small nightclubs specializing in modern jazz, accessory and specialty shops for women, and so on). Often, they do not have a primarily commercial or instrumental orientation to what they sell, but rather an expressive one. (Berger, 1963, pp. 332–33)

Long before the likes of David Brooks (2000) and Richard Florida (2002) began to write about the colonisation of cities by 'bo-bos' or the 'creative class', Berger had already clocked the upsurge of a new breed of 'expressive' urban professional, riding the post-war wave of US consumerism, opportunity and aspiration. Throughout the 1960s, the rise of a commercial 'mass counterculture' (Lloyd, 2006, p. 63) offered further work opportunities for these energetic figures – drawn widely from the hierarchy of social classes.

Where the United States had led in evolving new forms of white-collar and bohemian cultural work, the United Kingdom was quick to follow. By the late-1950s, sociologists such as David Glass (1954), G.D.H. Cole (1955) and John Goldthorpe and David Lockwood (1963) had observed not only the growth of white-collar work, but the rising affluence of ordinary people who were increasingly earning and gaining ground within – and beyond – traditional manual employment. As the range of non-traditional service and office-based jobs was diversifying, so, it appeared, were the social backgrounds of those who undertook them. Now, working and lower-middle-class people were able to contemplate the prospect of a social elevation unthinkable to previous generations. By the time of *The New Classes* (1966), Robert Millar was able to confidently assert that the 'British class system is in a process of radical change', moving from one founded in heredity and ascription to one based on the 'aristocracy of achievement' (1966, pp. 18–19), where 'the old class lines are not crumbling as much as becoming irrelevant' (ibid., p. 19). Like Mills, Millar included the cultural industries in his vision, noting how the values of the establishment were being challenged by 'a new type of men' (*sic*), possessed of similar ambitions to their contemporaries across the Atlantic, and employed in ever growing numbers 'in advertising, the consumer goods industries [and] public relations' (ibid., p. 100).

Additionally, the same bohemian industries that Berger had identified in the United States had also begun to appear in the United Kingdom, in the regions[3], and most notably in London. In 1966, *Vogue* magazine invited Mary Quant, the fashion designer who had 'started the revolution in English clothes' (p. 86) to reflect on her pioneering contribution to a moment of youthful insurgency into the capital and its productive culture:

> I just happened to start when 'something in the air' was coming to the boil. The clothes I made happened to fit in exactly with the teen-age trend, with pop records and espresso bars and jazz-clubs. (Quant, 1966, 'The Youth Will Not Be Dictated To', *Vogue,* August 1st, p. 86)

The broader significance of this contribution, others later confirmed:

> When twenty-one year old Mary Quant opened her first boutique, Bazaar, in 1955, in the King's Road, London, she established something of a template for other young designers, however quixotic. ... Entire districts of London, offering an abundance of vacant premises and low rents, became magnets for young designers and retailers. (Armstrong, 2014, p. 25)

And, more widely:

> The boom businesses of fashion, design and music, together with photography,
> modelling, magazine publishing and advertising, 'created wealth for almost a
> quarter of a million Londoners, in the process giving London a new image, and
> its people a fresh sense of identity and vitality.' (Porter, 1994, cited in Gilbert,
> 2006, p. 9)

But we should also note that if the growth of cultural work in the United
States was related principally to a resurgent, consumer-driven capitalism[4],
then the United Kingdom context for growth was similar, but also quite different and specific.

THE 'SWINGING MERITOCRACY'?

In the United Kingdom, employment gains and a more diverse entry into
cultural industry occupations were not only underwritten by the start of the
long boom but also occasioned by some significant transformations in systems of education and welfare. Not least, the 1944 Butler Education Act had
led to the introduction of a new national system of free secondary education,
compulsory to the age of 15 (later 16), and by the early 1960s, a greater
number of working and lower-middle-class youth was starting to find its way
into further and higher education, supported by free tuition and government
maintenance grants (Blackburn and Jarman, 1987). This was accelerated, in
the wake of the *Report of the Committee of Higher Education* led by Lord
Robbins (1963), by further investment and expansion in a whole range of new
universities, polytechnics and colleges of higher education – including many
providing courses in both fine and commercial arts, media and design. Art
schools and polytechnics became especially significant in affording hitherto
excluded (and non-academically inclined) groups a comprehensive arts and
cultural education (Strand, 1987; Beck and Cornford, 2012). In *Art into Pop*
(1987), Simon Frith and Howard Horne reflected on the democratising energies of the art school:

> This was the period, from the mid-1950s to the mid-1960s, when art schools
> operated most liberally to provide further educational opportunities to work-
> ing- and middle-class school leavers who had neither academic nor occupational
> qualifications but whose 'awkwardness' seemed to have some sort of creative
> potential. (1987, p. 80)

Such 'awkward' (but now skilled and trained) people emerged from education keen to make their mark in what appeared a more motile and permissive

social landscape (Marwick, 1982; Hewison, 1995). Commentators and critics were quick to classify these (and many other) 'rising' people into new social types; 'the art student', the new 'bohemian' or 'beatnik', the 'scholarship boy' and 'angry young man' and so on (we should note the gendered qualification here), all of whom represented something of a challenge to the established class structure. Naturally, the strongest inclination of many such types was to try and enter (and, indeed, help create) the rapidly expanding range of arts, cultural and leisure industry jobs, occupations and labour markets. We might regard such people and the organisations they served as offering a foretaste of what would eventually become known as the 'creative industries' – the genesis of an economy yet to come.

Such a shift had been detected, however, at its earliest stage. Writing in 1959, Raphael Samuel had commented on the rise of employment in 'mass communications' running in parallel with the expansion of secondary and higher education:

> More and more, London, as the centre of economic power and the home of the spreading mass-communications industries, has become the magnet of social aspiration. Upward movement from the working class has become much more prominent, not because its proportions have changed, but because it is now organised through the Grammar School and the University, where previously it took place through the local workshop and factory. (Samuel, 1959, p. 48)

At the same time, Stuart Hall (1958) was observing the new and expanding labour force of 'the communications industry' and ruminating on the likelihood of it helping to bring about a 'classless' society of equal opportunity – which, after consideration, he concluded it wouldn't. Yet, as Robert Hewison has since observed, opportunities for ordinary people grew simply because '[the] meritocratic products of post-war higher education were needed to administer the expanding field of communications, from the BBC to the burgeoning advertising industry' (Hewison, 1995, p. 123) – a necessity that appeared to push ordinary people towards new jobs and more elevated positions in the cultural industries.

Therefore, from the early 1960s onwards, it was becoming clear that young people, many from working and lower-middle-class backgrounds, were gaining greater access to 'mass communications' and other cultural industry workplaces, and so finding ways to earn a living by expressing their creative interests. At the same time, in such positions, they were also finding opportunities to articulate their own cultural marginality or distinctiveness, as well as critically explore some of the contradictions and conditions of their own lives[5]. Their timing was perhaps impeccable. The mid-twentieth century was the moment of peak employment in the UK regional and national journalism and the newspaper industries, a huge expansion of jobs in advertising and design, in lifestyle and leisure magazine publishing, and a phenomenal rise in all kinds of music and record industry production. Similarly, an expanding and diversifying BBC, the founding of independent commercial television in the mid-1950s, and then pirate and commercial radio in the 1960s and 1970s, helped create many new roles and positions in UK broadcasting. There was also growth in the provision and consumption of public art and cultural amenities more generally, and many new jobs, as state funding increased, and slowly expanded its remit into more popular and diverse forms.

It therefore seems reasonable to claim that, during this mid-century period, there was a significant increase in the number of people from socially underprivileged backgrounds finding work as professional actors, writers, designers, dancers and musicians and so on, as well as in arts and cultural teaching, administration, technical professions and management. For such people, not only were economic opportunities more abundant than hitherto, many had clearly benefitted from the affordances of a socially democratic welfare state that made becoming an artistic worker more *possible*, both economically and socially. We might therefore feel confident in surmising that some kind of social 'uplift' occurred, whereby the sons and daughters of farm and factory workers, cooks and coal miners were brought into the cleaner and more comfortable precincts of cultural work. Certainly, this is the popular impression. For example, in this period, Janey Ironside, the first professor of fashion at the Royal College of Art, was able to reflect on the consequences of a more widespread working-class entry into the academy and professional art worlds:

> One of the best results of the social revolution in Britain since the Second World War has been the release of many young designers to the world. By a system of local and government grants, young people are enabled to go to art schools and colleges and have the freedom to experiment. Before the war most of the people who are now well known designers would probably have been maids in other people's house, miners, or working in shops. (Ironside date unknown, cited in Bracewell, 2007, p. 52)

At this time, crucially perhaps, the intensity of belief in this 'social revolution' was such that – quite quickly – cultural industry jobs came to be seen in a most favourable light, especially when it came to issues of access and opportunity. Not only were such jobs rapidly expanding in number but the kinds of meritocratic, talent-driven positions they were offering appeared to offer everyone the chance for social elevation, alongside intrinsically interesting and meaningful labour. In the spotlight of a more general uplift and progress, the cultural industries stood out as highly desirable, exemplary and *attainable*.

Such is the popular wisdom – but I think the picture is less clear-cut. For instance, can we precisely *quantify* the extent to which job opportunities in the arts and culture were opened up to ordinary people? Not really. Certainly hard data are hard to come by – neither small or large organisations or bureaucracies kept detailed records of the socio-economic profile of their employees, and union membership data, employment research and censuses of the period are only part revealing (e.g. see Ball and Bell, 2013). While academics were eagerly exploring the new environments of mass communications, arts and media, their priorities and research programmes often conspicuously overlooked routine issues of production, work and employment (e.g. see Blumler, 1964). And while a lot of popular *cultural* history has now been written about the art worlds of post-war Britain – precious little attention has been given to its employment aspects. We might be sure, in absolute terms, of some increased working-class entry into cultural work – though in the main this was most likely to have been at the bottom end, in the routine, low-paid and unglamorous jobs of the organisation. This seems a reasonable assumption. Even as Raphael Samuel was identifying the elevation of ordinary people into multiple kinds of service industry and mass communication jobs, he was also noting the unjust 'proportions' that ensured the best kinds of managerial and high-status work continued to be marked by an 'upper-class domination' (1959, p. 47). It almost all occupations, cultural or otherwise, commentators of the time remarked that the established middle classes were continuing to monopolise the better paid, higher-status, managerial and professional roles – just as they always had done (Sampson, 1962; Little and Westergaard, 1964; Westergaard, 1964[6]; Blackburn, 1967).

In UK cultural industries, most national and commercial broadcasters, record companies, museums, newspapers, publishers and advertising firms and so on remained in the charge of executives and senior managers either from the aristocracy or the solidly established upper-middle class. And so while the headlines might have made by prominent working and lower-middle-class artists like Shelagh Delaney, Alan Sillitoe, Albert Finney, Alan Bennett, The Beatles, The Rolling Stones, Stanley Baker, Michael Caine, Tom Courtenay, Cilla Black, Sandie Shaw, Bridget Riley, Peter Blake, David Hockney, Tom Jones, Glenda Jackson, Billie Whitelaw, Ossie Clark, Vidal Sassoon, David Bowie, Bryan Ferry, Marc Bolan, The Sex Pistols, Vivienne Westwood, John Thaw, Julie Walters and so on, behind the scenes, in management, in high art fields, as well in the routine structures of cultural work, many of the long-established class inequalities remained intact. Certainly, with hindsight, at a societal level, we now know that *absolute* increases in all kinds of white-collar, service (and by implication cultural) work were not necessarily matched by any significant rise in the *relative* proportion of good or high-status jobs occupied by the lowest social groups (Goldthorpe and Jackson, 2007; Kynaston, 2015). This is an important point and one to which I'll return.

We might simply surmise, for now, that while there was overall *expansion* in working-class cultural employment, there was perhaps less evidence of a significant *redistribution* of opportunities, rewards and statuses. Certainly, given the relative newness and openness of these emerging industries, and their somewhat ambivalent social status, some ordinary people were able to secure some good jobs. But no doubt also that the unprecedented visibility of successful working-class talent may have helped furnish the assumption that there was a greater parity of participation and involvement than was perhaps truly the case. Commenting on the 1960s, the cultural geographer David Gilbert has confirmed that 'despite the classless rhetoric, and the examples of new celebrities with working-class backgrounds, like [Michael] Caine, David Bailey or the model Twiggy (Lesley Hornby), many of the most prominent producers of the [London] scene were decidedly upper class' (2006, p. 7). Additionally, the historian Marcus Collins (2013) has shown how the rise of popular working-class artists of the 1960s was used by politicians of all persuasions to evidence some dubious claims regarding Britain's apparent transformation into a classless state of equal opportunity – a kind of 'swinging meritocracy' as *Time* magazine famously dubbed it in 1966 (see also Hewison, 1995; Todd, 2014). While such claims weren't entirely unfounded, and as the next decade and a half did see a wider constituency flourishing in television, commercial design, alternative theatre, film, the underground press and publishing, punk, post-punk and so on (e.g. see Hesmondhalgh, 1997; Atton, 2002; Reynolds, 2005), sectors identified as increasingly vital to the post-industrial economy and polity[7], then we can safely assume ordinary people's access to arts and cultural work continued to expand. Yet, in the absence of detailed data – and evidence to the contrary – we can only assume that the presence of such groups was never really sufficient for them to achieve equality with the established powers, in terms of the best jobs, highest earnings or an assumption of ownership and control.

OTHER STORIES? WOMEN AND ETHNIC MINORITIES

At the same time, we should note that class was not the only – or perhaps even the most significant – axis of inequality. While women were beginning to access both further and higher arts education, the gendering of professional opportunity was from time-to-time evidenced in commentary and industry reports. For example, writing in 1966, the sociologist Viola Klein examined the proportion of women enrolled in some of the United Kingdom's leading trade and professional associations. She found that while women comprised over 95% of nurses and occupational therapists, and over 55% of librarians, they were much less likely to be working as professionals in emergent

Table 3 Proportion of Women in Selected Professional Associations (c. 1966)

Professional Association	Total Membership	Total Number of Women	Women as a %
Soc. of Industrial Artists	c. 1,650	'very few'	–
Inst. of Practitioners in Advertising	1,600	20	1.2
Inc. Inst. of Brit. Decorators & Interior Designers	1,900	–	c. 2
Institute of British Photographers	2,204	145	6.6
Market Research Society	1,175	200	17
Institute of Public Relations	1,780	250–300	c. 20

Source. Adapted from Klein, 1966.

cultural industries such as PR, advertising and marketing, the kinds identified by Mills and Millar as especially emblematic of the new meritocracy:

Women were also less likely than men to find professional artistic (and managerial) work in the more established 'high' cultural industries of classical music, state broadcasting and the fine arts[8], and while they could find jobs (mainly *as* women) in theatre and television acting, or radio plays, often this was in somewhat specific, tokenistic or otherwise limited roles. As Gillian Murray (2013) has shown, in TV news and factual formats, women were often appointed to add a feminine decoration or 'glamour' to complement the more serious presentation of male presenters, broadcasters and journalists[9]. However, women more often worked behind the scenes in strongly gendered positions, such as costume, set design and make-up, and were certainly more likely to work in administration – especially in the typical PA, secretarial and support roles necessary for serving more managerial and creative forms of labour (ACTT, 1975; Ball and Bell, 2013; Murray, 2013; Tunstall 1993). More generally, by being denied the 'top jobs' – either artistic, technical or managerial – women who worked in any of the arts and cultural industries tended to be placed in subordinate roles or else diverted away from the core creative professions altogether, often ending up (ether by choice or compulsion) in training, teaching or non-arts jobs[10].

Change was painfully slow in coming. By the 1970s, in the light of more advanced equality legislation, even institutions such as the BBC – long held up as a significant and (relatively) enlightened employer – felt compelled to admit that it had failed to recruit or elevate sufficient numbers of women within its purportedly meritocratic ranks. By 1981, women still occupied only around 6% of senior positions, a figure that had actually been *decreasing* since the 1960s (Franks, 2011). Further, the Corporation's own *Limitations to the Recruitment and Advancement of Women in the BBC* (1973) and the follow-up reports *Women in the BBC* (1974, 1975 and 1981) revealed that

while women were gaining access to the education and training deemed
necessary to obtain work in the BBC, they were finding it difficult to secure
the best kinds of jobs – because of more or less blatant forms of discrimination and misogyny. Suzanne Franks has detailed how the *Women in the BBC*
reports revealed some of the more energetically expressed views of male
managers and producers about women and their alleged inability to execute
creative roles:

> [Women] are not seen by the Head and Assistant Head of [Light Entertainment]
> as natural dealers in humour. They also point out that the Producer occasionally
> has to invite Ken Dodd to lunch and believes that a female Producer would find
> this difficult. ... Producer's Assistants (P's As) are acceptable to the world of
> sport in the social sense. Admitted to the Board Room for tea or drinks they are
> often the only women present. None of them, it is said, has ever expressed any
> desire for advancement. (BBC, 1973, cited in Franks, 2011, p. 129)

Writing in 1975, in *Patterns of Discrimination against Women in the Film
and Television Industries*, the ACTT[11] union found that behind the camera,
in technical trades and production, women were being similarly marginalised and contained. Not only were women in a significant minority, their
job grades and pay tended to be lower, and they were largely excluded from
bonuses and overtime. Most technical jobs were seen as male domains, and
women regarded as physically and emotionally incapable of performing what
was seen intrinsically as 'man's work'. Male objections were often as visceral as they were lurid. One male film director imagined the consequences
of women 'tripping round the place in their mini-skirts and stiletto heels',
while an electrical engineer worried that he 'couldn't swear freely' in front
of women, who were otherwise offering him distraction by spending their
time apparently (again) 'clambering round in mini-skirts' (ACTT, 1975,
pp. 10–11). The report detailed how women were simply often blocked or
explicitly barred from skilled technical jobs; for example, the commercial
broadcaster ATV revealed in 1974 'it is not our policy to employ women
floor managers' (ibid., p. 26) while one regional television company con-
fessed that it 'had not given a woman PA the director's job she applied for
because she was a woman, even though in all other ways she would have
been suitable' (ibid., p. 26). At this time, women working in television and
radio most often found that ingrained sexism was presented to them as a 'fact
of life' – a problem that women had to learn to live with, rather than challenge, or expect managers to address on their behalf (Chambers, Steiner and
Fleming, 2004; Murray, 2013; Street-Porter, 2012[12]).

While some individual women obtained prestige positions and some sectors (such as fashion) appeared more amenable to women *auteurs* and the

very best talent, we also know from accounts of the period that women trying to break into almost *any* kind of cultural profession were quite likely to
encounter hostility and discrimination. For instance, recalling her pioneering
efforts to make a career from the music scene in the 1960s, the journalist and
photographer Val Wilmer recollected the difficulties of trying to enter the
'man's world' of British blues and jazz:

> I was seen as a sweet young thing, but once that had passed, I ran the risk of
> being treated like a groupie or a 'scrubber' – to use the terminology of the time
> – by these people. It was still not conceivable I could be there as a journalist
> once I'd passed the obvious 'fan' stage and left my autograph book at home.
> From time to time, if something went wrong backstage, there'd be a purge on
> all visitors. This never extended to the 'bona fide' journalists who were, without
> exception, male, but was basically a round-up of drug-dealers, time-wasters and
> women, myself included. (Wilmer, 1989, p. 58)

While women could at least expect some degree of employment and
accommodation in the cultural industries, the conditions of opportunity for
ethnic minorities were perhaps even less congenial. In 1976, in an important
and influential book called *The Arts Britain Ignores,* Naseem Khan was
amongst the first to identify racism as a deep-rooted malaise in the arts body
politic. By presenting evidence of the widespread neglect, underfunding and
exclusion of ethnic minority arts, and the marginal economic status of prac-
tising artists, Khan exposed the complacent and often squirming attitudes of
arts funders, organisations, and state and commercial broadcasters. A fundamental injustice was noted, rooted in material inequality, as well as lack of
recognition:

> Ethnic minority arts are an energetic but struggling sub-culture. On the whole
> they exist for the communities alone – necessarily, since little encouragement
> is given them to expand. The problems they face are those of neglect: lack of
> premises to rehearse, lack of comparable back-up that is afforded to equivalent
> native British groups, lack of acceptance within the arts infrastructure and lack
> of exposure. ... The assets of immigration – the acquisition of new cultural
> experiences, art forms and attitudes – have so far been only minimally rec-
> ognised and far less encouraged. If they were, Britain would gain a far richer
> cultural scene, and would moreover be giving minorities their due. (Khan, 1976,
> pp. 5–11)

Not only were local arts and cultural scenes woefully underresourced,
invisible or misrecognised, at the time, the number of mainstream pop stars,
actors, fine or visual artists, arts managers and executives that came from any
of Britain's diverse ethnic minority groups was insignificant. Those that did

'make it' frequently found themselves marginalised and stereotyped. Khan's book offered the BBC and IBA[13] an opportunity to justify their own practices towards ethnic minorities in this respect, which served to reveal some minimal efforts to improve participation, hitched to some clumsy and clichéd attempts at representation:

> 'Othello' is always a work that is likely to be broadcast; and so provide a leading role for a black actor. Moreover, contemporary drama is tending more and more to provide acceptable opportunities for immigrant actors. A contemporary [police drama] series like 'Z Cars' is bound to include opportunities for coloured actors to play all kinds of parts. (BBC Evidence, Appendix C in Khan, 1976, p. 154)

While more varied and leading parts for non-white actors and entertainers began to emerge, especially in the comedy and light entertainment genres, the general picture was not one of inclusion and equality, but one of black and other ethnic minority people as representing a social 'problem' that had somehow to be addressed in the confines of the text, as Sarita Malik has persuasively argued:

> Many of the comedies 'about race', were actually comedies about blacks signifying *trouble; trouble* with the neighbours, *trouble* with language, *trouble* with 'fitting in', so that if the white characters did display prejudice, this was deemed funny or understandable given 'the difficulty of the situation'. (Malik, 2002, p. 97, her emphasis)

While ethnic minorities were making their way – however slowly and problematically – into mainstream television, and more positively into commercial and BBC local radio stations (especially in London, Birmingham, Leicester and other cities with ethnically diverse populations), and by the late 1970s into pop music (especially soul, roots reggae and Lovers' Rock, 'Britfunk' and jazz[14]), more traditional industries remained closed to minority entrants. For example, Naseem Khan noted that Equity's recent report on the 'Employment of Afro-Asians in the Theatre' had revealed employment opportunities for this designated group to be 'virtually non-existent' (Khan, 1976, p. 162), and classical music, dance, opera as well as more 'serious' areas of media, broadcasting and journalism – current affairs, politics, the national press – remained enclaves populated overwhelmingly by the white majority. As it was for women, ethnic minorities were also underrepresented and disadvantaged in 'backstage', technical and craft positions, as well as mostly absent from managerial and administrative roles.

THE LONG BOOM ... BUST?

To summarise: throughout the long boom, the classism, sexism and racism that pervaded the culture industries (not to mention the training and education systems that served them[15]) are evidence that access to, and opportunity within, the arts and cultural workplace was perhaps somewhat more uneven and socially differentiated than suggested by champions of the meritocratic state. We might reasonably conclude that the cultural industries have in fact *always* been unequal – even in the alleged 'golden age'. But we need to be both general and specific in our arguments. So we might still want to claim that, overall, for the *majority* of ordinary men and women, participation in artistic and cultural production was strongly enabled by initial period of post-war economic expansion, a social democratic approach to education and planning, and a welfare system that was both relatively generous and sustaining, sufficient to grant ordinary people both the time and resources necessary to attempt to forge creative or artistic careers. In just so happens that, at the same time, some profound and pervasive inequalities were in operation. This affected both who *entered*, and who got *elevated* into the best or most valued positions. The cultural industries of the long boom were therefore both inclusive *and* exclusive, and the extent to which we can discern each condition will depend on where, and at whom, we choose to look. But we should further acknowledge that while a sense of de jure equality might have masked some de facto inequality, there was also an indelible *link* between inclusion and exclusion – a line that connected the affordances of the new 'meritocracy' with the kinds of social division that it helped both obscure and reinforce. The unprecedented expansion in total numbers of cultural industry jobs, the connotations of glamour and freedom they carried, and (in the absence of sustained evidence to the contrary) the general perception of such industries as vehicles for personal and social advancement, served to almost entirely negate serious discussion of the problems and inequalities that underpinned many forms of arts and cultural employment. As a result of such neglect, over fifty years, many such problems and inequalities got worse.

THE NEW INEQUALITY?

And what of today? Certainly, one of the main problems faced by contemporary critics is trying to shift some of the durably rose-tinted perceptions of working conditions in the cultural industries. While the last decade or so has seen many academics, workers, campaigners and activists raise questions about increasing inequality and injustice in cultural work, this hadn't necessarily had much impact on public opinion, let alone gained traction within cultural firms and organisations themselves. Yet – quite recently – something appears to have changed. The issue of who gets to work in arts and culture – and what kind of work it actually is – has become less of a 'personal trouble' and much more of a 'public issue', as Mills (1959) would have termed it. In some ways this is surprising. The official statistics continue to show expanding arts and cultural industry employment, and creative economy growth, and a buoyant entry into arts education and training. Yet there is now more than a sneaking suspicion that all is not well in cultural work, and especially when it comes to patterns of access and opportunity.

In the United Kingdom, the first indications of more recent dissent came in the form of discussion about the problems of unpaid internships. It was increasingly noticed that rather than providing the benefits of some temporary 'work experience', that might offer a route into paid employment, many employers were using interns as a core and sustained (and essentially cost-free) labour input – thereby exploiting them. Indeed, given the strong appeal attached to working in arts and culture, and the enthusiasm of wannabe entrants, some official reports began to identify the cultural sector as being particularly susceptible to this kind of unethical practice (e.g. Cabinet Office, 2009; Skillset, 2010; Low Pay Commission, 2011). Yet while the prospect of obtaining an artistic career ensured that internships remained popular, they were now also identified as being unequally distributed – strongly favouring those who could afford the luxury of working (often indefinitely) for free. Furthermore, since even *getting* an internship now seemed to be easier for those with established social contacts and good networks (especially those nepotistically blessed with family or friends already working in the industry) the chances of ordinary people obtaining that vital 'foot in the door' seemed to be diminishing. These were not new inequalities – but certainly new was the way in which the injustices they occasioned were catching the attention of journalists and commentators, as well as the public mood, as a series of articles appeared that condemned both intern exploitation and the apparent monopolisation of opportunities by offspring of the established and elite (e.g. see Gardner, 2010; Malik and Syal, 2011; Wood, 2011). The sight of various politicians, arts organisations and managers then speeding to distance themselves from the offering of unpaid arts internships (and the elite privilege with which they were becoming associated) strongly suggests how quickly the practice became stigmatised. Thus, in the United Kingdom, the public debate on internships did something important; it put issues of exploitation and class inequality back on the agenda of cultural work and helped begin the uprooting of some of those deeper-lying understandings that had been first set down in the long boom. But we can also see the internship debate as providing the initial smoke that signalled a more burning sense of concern over the fundamental inequalities that now pervade *all* aspects of access and opportunity in cultural work – and not just internships.

Recently, journalistic reporting on cultural labour inequalities has increased. Much of this discussion has happened to revolve around a number of well-known artists and celebrities whose opinions on the conditions of cultural work have somewhat unexpectedly become newsworthy. For example, the British visual artist, Gary Hume, interviewed in 2014 by *The Observer* newspaper, offered this perception of the changing profile of the art school student:

> When I was a student at art college … it was full of kids from all kinds of backgrounds, mainly misfits and outsiders. That is exactly why they were at art college. Art has become a respectable career path now, another professional option for the young and affluent. But what do all the wrong people do now? Where do they go – the misfits and the outsiders? (Hume quoted in O'Hagan, 2014, no pagination)

For Hume it was these 'wrong people' – people from the working classes or *déclassé* members of the bourgeoisie – that now seemed more absent from art schools and, by extension, art work more generally. Echoing these sentiments, a number of British actors from more modest and underprivileged backgrounds (mostly direct beneficiaries of the long boom) have recently identified the increased difficulties for working-class aspirants attempting to make passage into creative education and the wider arts workplace. For example, in the same *Observer* article as Hume, actor Julie Walters was quoted as saying:

> I look at almost all the up-and-coming names and they're from the posh schools. … Don't get me wrong … they're wonderful. It's just a shame those working-class kids aren't coming through. When I started, 30 years ago, it was the complete opposite.

Similar views have since been offered by other prominent British actors – including Brian Cox, Judi Dench, James McAvoy and David Morrissey – all arguing that working-class people face increased difficulties in obtaining access to training and acting careers. Here – continuing Hume's theme of 'mis-fitting' and the kinds of 'awkwardness' first highlighted by Frith and Horne – the actor Christopher Eccleston also articulated a growing (intersectional) unease about education and work opportunity in the acting profession:

> I was a skinny, awkward-looking bugger with an accent, as I still am. British society has always been based on inequality, particularly culturally. I've lived with it, but it's much more pronounced now, and it would be difficult for someone like me to come through. … I confess I don't watch much film or television

drama but I'm aware of the predominance of white, male roles. It's not just about the working class. There's not enough writing for women or people of colour. (Eccleston, 2015, no pagination)

In other fields, established artists have begun to express similar disquiet. For instance, in 2013, pop singer (and long boom beneficiary) Sandie Shaw informed a Culture, Media and Sport Select Committee of the UK Government that public-school educated, middle-class musicians were crowding out artists from more 'challenging backgrounds' – a theory earlier suggested by the journalist Simon Price in his conjectures on the 'poshification of pop' (see Price, 2010; 2014). Writing in *The Guardian* on the occasion of the death of Cilla Black, the 'archetypal British working class pop star', the journalist and musician Bob Stanley lamented that 'Cilla's passing reminds us that we are finally leaving the twentieth century. Or, at least, losing the twentieth century – losing the certainties of a particularly British kind of pop culture, a working-class culture, that have slowly been erased since the 1980s' (Stanley, 2015, no pagination).

Much of the recent 'celebrity' commentary on cultural work has also focused on women and ethnic minority discrimination – including controversy over the alleged BBC bias against older women broadcasters such as Miriam O'Reilly and Judy Spiers (O'Reilly, 2015), the 'invisibility' and lack of roles for older women actors identified by Meera Syal (Syal, 2015), and the 'calling out' of film industry sexism by such high-profile stars as Cate Blanchett, Emma Watson, Eva Mendes and Geena Davis (Day, 2015; Ledbetter, 2015). Previously, the actors Paterson Joseph, Sophie Okonedo, David Harewood and Parminder Nagra, and the comedian Gina Yashere have all commented publicly on the significant lack of work opportunities for non-white artists in their professions in the United Kingdom, compared with more favourable conditions across the Atlantic (e.g. see Joseph, 2013; Wyatt, 2014)[16].

These higher-profile interventions should not lead us to underestimate how public discussion has been both mirrored and fuelled by an enormous amount of activity on the part of ordinary artists, academics, campaigning groups and unions who have worked to counter the inequalities of the cultural workplace and to expose the difficulties face by ordinary people trying to break into its precincts. But by drawing attention to some of the recent interventions by journalists, artists and celebrities I am highlighting the growth of a *popular* discourse of opposition to some of the injustices and inequalities of cultural work – a critical public sensibility that seemed almost entirely absent during the years of the long boom. But why has this hitherto negligible concern now emerged as a major issue of interest, for journalists, critics and public alike? I think there are a number of reasons.

Firstly, we might argue that the shared freedoms afforded by the long boom have come under more sustained (and possibly now terminal) attack – and this has not gone unnoticed. At the heart of this has been the slow dismantling of a welfare system that (as we've seen) once offered state-funded cultural opportunities for the significant majority of ordinary people. Certainly, the continued divide between high-status (and arts-rich) private (fee-charging) schools and their state-funded counterparts, the end of free HE for lower-income groups, and the more recently accelerated shift towards a system of high student fees and loans, means that many of the kinds of 'wrong' or 'awkward' people who were able to more easily enter cultural education and work during the long boom are now more likely to be priced out of pursuing an artistic education or career. Additionally, as cuts are made to out-of-work benefits, and the opportunity to incubate and practice one's talent while subsisting on other forms of welfare or public subsidy have declined, then the chances of ordinary people making it in arts and culture are further diminished. Most such people are unlikely to be able to rely on their families (the so-called 'Bank of Mum and Dad') to subsidise the now obligatory internship, or low or unpaid work, while they strive to 'make it'. Broader cuts to arts and local authority budgets are further reducing opportunities and access to scarce public resources, disadvantaging the very poorest candidates striving to make a living from art. Writing in the *New Statesman*, the music journalist and critic Stuart Maconie summarised quite well the productive affordances of the long boom and the more recent closing down of career opportunity for the aspiring working-class artist:

> The great cultural tide that surged through Harold Wilson's 1960s and beyond, the sea change that swept the McCartneys, Finneys, Bakewells, Courtenays, Baileys, Bennetts et al to positions of influence and eminence, if not actual power, has ebbed and turned. The children of the middle and upper classes are beginning to reassert a much older order. In the arts generally – music, theatre, literature for sure – it is clear that cuts to benefits, the disappearance of the art school (where many a luminous layabout found room to bloom) and the harsh cost of further and higher education are pricing the working class out of careers in the arts and making it increasingly a playground for the comfortably off. The grants are gone and the relatively benign benefits system that sustained the pre-fame Jarvis Cocker and Morrissey is being dismantled daily. (Maconie, 2015, no pagination)

Secondly, there is perhaps now more acute public awareness of the fine-grained inequalities embedded in higher education. During the long boom, working-class entry into HE was expanding, but not quite as rapidly as arts and cultural employment was growing, meaning that graduate jobs in the arts were more readily available and there was less onus placed on which kinds of degree one possessed and where one had obtained it – since having any kind of arts degree or HE qualification was regarded as an advantage. Today, even if more people might be *entering* arts and creative industry HE than ever before, it is the *kinds* of HE they enter – and the enhanced competition and discrimination between the elite and non-elite courses and institutions – that tends to more strongly affect the type of employment opportunities people will subsequently have access to. Roberta Comunian et al (2010) have found that the majority of jobs (and the best jobs) in the UK creative sector tend to be taken by graduates who attended Russell Group (i.e. elite) universities, regardless of whether they have an arts-based degree or not. A more vocational or industry-facing qualification from a non-elite institution is less likely to translate into a good job or steady work. Further (and as Comunian and colleagues also noted) for ordinary people, having an arts degree is now no guarantee of even *entering* the cultural industries, let alone obtaining a good job or salary. This is not just an issue of there now being a crude 'oversupply' of arts (and other) graduates – but the consequence of a much finer process whereby the 'very best' tend to be recruited through the kinds of informal, homophilic and discriminatory systems of selection that were discussed in chapter 4. I would suggest there is now more awareness of this (first evidenced by the internship and free labour debates) and this has provoked something of a critical backlash.

Thirdly, and relatedly, and as Hume intimated, cultural work is now more fully established as a 'respectable' professional career for the social elite – and so no longer carries with it the taint of illegitimacy or transience that marked its emergence at the start of the long boom[17]. So while the children of the privileged might always have aimed at becoming doctors, barristers, politicians, bankers and accountants, they now strive equally to become actors, comedians, pop stars and artists – attracted by the cachet of a creative career and supported by the inherited advantages that afford them the luxury of its pursuit. Accordingly, as some journalists have noted, it is no longer the art schools, but the private schools – and the most prestigious of them – that seem increasingly to be regarded as richest sources of our future artistic talent:

> From Wellington to Gladstone, and Macmillan to Cameron, Eton College has long been a seedbed for British politics and for the diplomatic service. ... Now though, that famously establishment school near Windsor is increasingly being hailed as a first-rate launch pad for a theatrical career. Leading Old Etonian actors such as Tom Hiddleston, Harry Lloyd, Eddie Redmayne, Henry Faber and Harry Hadden-Paton are suddenly at the top of the list for casting directors on the most prestigious film and television projects. (Thorpe, 2012, no pagination)

It appears that acting, pop music, television, publishing, radio and so on, those (relatively) open fields that once attracted Mills's 'new entrepreneurs' or Millar's meritocratically selected mass, are becoming monopolised by more socially privileged groups who now regard such endeavours as eminently respectable – and therefore worth colonising and protecting. In contrast, ordinary people working in arts and culture must contend with a 'class ceiling' (Friedman et al, 2015) that might always have existed but seems now more firmly secured.

Fourthly, the recognition of continued inequalities for women and ethnic minorities (as well as disadvantaged others, such as those with disabilities) and a greater sense of the ways in which disadvantages are often multipart and intersectional has awakened concern that despite legislation designed to effect equality of access and opportunity to all, the cultural workplace is foundationally unequal – and the burdens of inequality are disproportionately carried by those with multiple disadvantages (Acker, 2006; Tatli and Ozbilgin, 2012). Put more bluntly, black women, for example, do not get jobs as CEOs, Directors or Senior Executives in major UK media, advertising or broadcasting organisations – with the absolute rarest of exceptions.[18] Only a handful of working-class women have ever edited a UK national daily newspaper – and only one (Janet Street-Porter) edited a 'quality' broadsheet. This is not because people from such backgrounds lack 'talent' – as chapter 4 revealed – but because, for many, social inequalities tend to be cumulative and cross-compounding, a fact now accepted in even the most mainstream discussions of the arts and cultural work (e.g. Achola, 2015; Stern, 2015).

Fifthly, at the wider scale, the GFC and ensuing slump has sharpened sensitivities to *all* kinds of inequality, especially as many of the corporate architects of the recession appear to have evaded its destructive backwash, with states and ordinary citizens left to pick up the tab for bank bailouts and other forms of capitalist subsidy. The hollowing out of 'good jobs', to be replaced by low-paid and precarious work, barely supported by corroding systems of social security, has heightened awareness of the division between the secure lives of the more socially privileged and the debt-laden subsistence endured by the remaining majority. In arts and cultural work specifically, while the GFC heralded some initial haemorrhaging of UK creative industry jobs, swingeing cuts to state arts and culture budgets, and the accelerated advance of free or unpaid work into industries already divesting themselves of commitments to fair remuneration, the 'rebalancing' of the economy has both exposed (but perhaps further institutionalised) the 'economy of superstars' (see chapter 6), as well as reinforced those social divisions that tend to leave social minorities outside of regular employment, or serially disadvantaged within it. One of the consequences of systemic crisis has therefore been to publicly expose some of those pat assumptions about working in arts and culture that have endured since the beginning of the long boom – not least that everyone is treated equally and equitably in the workplace, and that the negative consequences of a downturn are always evenly distributed.

Finally, and most crucially perhaps, what we also have now and didn't have before – *because the questions that would have been necessary to occasion the data were not deemed necessary to ask* – is a more robust body of empirical evidence that has revealed inequity and inequality as foundational in cultural work. Let us move towards a conclusion by looking at some of this more recent research.

THE EMERGING DATA

While research on class participation in cultural work remains far from comprehensive, more substantial evidence is emerging to support the idea that the most elevated and well-paid positions routinely cleave to the elite or established middle class. For instance, using educational background as a proxy indicator for class, the Social Mobility and Child Poverty Commission's report *Elitist Britain?* (SMCPC, 2014) found that 33% of BBC Executives have been to Oxford or Cambridge universities, and that 26% of them had attended a private school, compared with the overall population figure of 7%. The same report found that 43% of national newspaper journalists and 44% of people working in executive roles in TV, film and music has also been privately educated, as had – more surprisingly perhaps – 22% of pop stars[19]. Similarly, and focusing on class inequality for the first time, Creative Skillset's most recent *Workforce Survey* (2014) identified that 14% of all creative media workers had attended private school, a figure that reached as high as 19% in independent television production, and 18% in digital media – again, somewhat high when compared with the 7% national average. More recent survey research by a team led by arts organisation Create (2015) found that over three quarters (76%) of respondents working in the arts had at least one parent working in a managerial or professional job, suggesting that for art workers, having a middle-class background is pretty much a standard prerequisite for entry.

Further sector-specific research in 2006 by the Sutton Trust looked at the educational backgrounds of 100 leading journalists, and discovered that over half (54%) of the country's foremost news and current affairs journalists were educated in private school, and that 45% of these attended the universities of Oxford or Cambridge. This was not identified as a problem of legacy – but an advancing trend[20]. The research also reported that the latest new recruits to the national news media were even more likely to come from privileged backgrounds than those from previous generations, since traditional routes of entry for working and lower-middle-class journalists – through serving apprenticeships and gaining experience in the local and regional press – were becoming increasingly difficult to obtain as those branches of the industry fall into decline. The Sutton Trust also found that the standard entry point for journalism was a London-based internship, often organised through existing personal connections, and indirectly supported by family wealth. The Social Mobility and Childhood Poverty Commission more recently confirmed this by reporting that '83% of new entrants [now] do internships, which are on average for seven weeks and 92% of these are unpaid', speculating that 'this might be freezing out those from less advantaged backgrounds' (SMCPC, 2014, p. 83). In other sectoral studies, work by Sam Friedman and Dave O'Brien has found that less than 10% of actors came from working-class backgrounds (defined as having had parents with manual jobs) and that this minority could also expect to earn, on average, around £11,000 per year less than their middle-class colleagues (see Snow, 2015). Others such as Keith Randle et al (2014) have also drawn attention to patterns of class inequality in screenwriting and film industry employment – but we should further note, as Randle has more widely acknowledged, 'class, in the context of creative industries employment, [still] remains relatively understudied' (2015, p. 337).

More widespread and established evidence can be found for gender inequality (Creative Skillset, 2014; DCMS, 2015). Research has shown consistently that women continue to be underemployed at upper levels in almost every arts, cultural or creative economy sector, and tend to occupy lower status, lower-paid roles across all industries, as suggested here in relation to the creative media sector, for example[21]:

> In the UK, the Fawcett Society's annual *Sex and Power* ... audit report indicates that there is not a single female Chair or Chief Executive of a Television company; men outnumber women by more than 10 to 1 in decision-making roles in media companies; and women constitute only 5 per cent of editors of national newspapers. The only senior roles where women outnumber men are in women's and lifestyle magazines. Similarly, the British Film Industry's *Statistical Yearbook* (2013) records that only 7.8 per cent of films were directed by a woman and 13.4 per cent written by a woman. (Conor, Gill and Taylor, 2015, p. 7)

As I write, women are estimated to comprise only around 36% of the creative media workforce, even though they continue to consistently make up around 60% of those undertaking HE education and training in the arts, media and creative disciplines (Ratcliffe, 2013; Creative Skillset, 2014; DCMS, 2015). Making the transition into creative media work – and into the best kinds of work[22] – may be becoming more difficult for women, rather than easier. Wider research has revealed that women make up 61.3% of the museums and galleries workforce, and 54.5% in publishing, but only comprise 19.7% in IT, software and computer services, 26.6% in architecture, and 35.1% in film, TV, radio and photography combined (DCMS, 2015). This confirms the idea that, generally, women are much more likely to work in lower-paying and less prestigious industries, rather than those industries more lucrative and esteemed. The more prestigious and dynamic industries tend also to display some of the starkest employment inequalities. For example, the UK Commission for Employment and Skills (2015) found that women now make up only 26% of the digital media workforce, down from 33% in 2002, suggesting that women are also leaving this industry – not joining it. Research has shown that while women are now the majority consumers of digital games, they still only make up around 12% of the gaming workforce (Jayanth, 2014). More traditional industries also retain their own particular patterns of division. Research on the classical music profession found that while women have tended to make up a majority of conservatoire students and the wider pool of prospective labour, they are much less likely to get jobs as professional musicians, especially in orchestras – which tend to be majority male (as well as white and middle class), and certainly so in the leading positions (Osborne and Conant, 2010, Scharff, 2015). Commenting on the music industry more widely, Christina Scharff (2015) noted that the gender profile of music organisations funded under the Arts Council England's scheme of National Portfolio Organisations was 38.5% women and 61.5% men – compared with an average of 46.9% and 53.1% for all art forms combined. Further, the Sutton Trust's (2006) journalism research found that only 18% of the top journalists were women, further suggesting that it's not only class that puts a brake on meritocracy, but gender as well.

Finally, as well as being less well paid, and working more precariously, we know women are serially disadvantaged when it comes to securing promotional opportunity or attaining executive positions. Gendered assumptions about the leadership and management capacities of men and women tend to suppress elevation for women while over-rewarding men, as well as containing women in prescribed and subordinate roles that best accommodate their 'natural' feminine attributes of support and nurture (see Adkins, 1999; Banks and Milestone, 2011, Reimer, 2015). It's well-established also that women are disadvantaged by the undue emphasis placed on youth, out-of-hours networking, sacrificial labour, unfettered creativity and performative excess – all features that discriminate against those who (still) carry the principal burdens of domestic labour and external responsibilities of care. Whether in film and television production (Leung et al, 2015), screenwriting (Conor, 2014; Wreyford, 2015), journalism (Sheth, 2015), design (Reimer, 2015) or games (Harvey and Fisher, 2013) many of the enduring problems of exclusion or disadvantage continue to recur, and, in some areas, now appear to be deepening and intensifying.

Most UK cultural industries continue to underemploy BAME workers, further belying claims that the arts and culture are vehicles for ethnic inclusivity – in fact much of the evidence suggests precisely the opposite. The official statistics reveal that while BAME workers now comprise around 12% of the total UK workforce, they make up less than 10% of the workforce in most cultural industries, including the music industry (6.7%), film and television (8.2%), advertising (8.2%), graphic design (6.2%) and crafts (4.2%), with only the somewhat capacious (and not necessarily entirely 'creative') category of IT and software (15.1%) appearing to offer greater than average opportunities (DCMS, 2014). The Warwick Commission (2015), while reporting similar figures, also pointed out that ethnic minorities now make up around 40% of the population of London, which is where the majority of UK cultural and creative industries are actually located – so making exclusion all the more evident and pernicious. Where they are employed, ethnic minorities tend to occupy lower-status or entry-level jobs and more often find it difficult to secure stable, consistent work or elevation into the most senior or secure positions. Evidence presented by Creative Skillset (2012) has also shown how the proportion of ethnic minorities employed declined sharply in the wake of the GFC, as industries laid off workers, especially those on temporary contracts, or in part-time or lower-status jobs, suggesting that these more precarious positions were where ethnic minority workers were principally located. This lack of general participation, as well as *containment* for those ethnic minority workers who do make an entrance, has an obvious impact on BAME incomes and career opportunity.

There are clearly other difficulties for BAME cultural workers, ones not experienced by the white majority. For instance, Anamik Saha has written of the 'arts funding governmentalities' (2013, p. 831) often produced through the public funding and employment of ethnic minority artists; so while ethnic minority arts are no longer necessarily as 'ignored' as Naseem Khan once described, they are often supported through ring-fenced diversity programmes or funding streams that – while welcome – do tend to create certain kinds of expectations that the work produced will, or should, self-consciously be about the 'difference' of minority experience. The implicit or explicit obligation to 'represent' the community or the everyday culture of being other, in various kinds of ways, ought not necessarily be used to underpin minority arts funding, given that white artists are not routinely expected to serve such expectations. Even if artists *do* want to explore such concerns, that the kinds of difference that are recognised and valued by funding agencies tend to be somewhat limited in scope and drawn from an already established (and largely pre-commodified) symbolic repertoire of ethnic otherness is a further problem that BAME artists often encounter. For example, Saha reported on a British-Asian led theatre company being criticised for its lack of attention to Bollywood genres and for being 'not Asian enough' (2013, p. 832) – and no doubt commercial cultural industries display the same prejudices. A different kind of problem comes in the form of racialised assumptions about the *absence* of difference. Our own work into black British jazz musicians revealed the experiences of BAME artists who were refused spots at music festivals on the grounds that the organisers already had an 'ethnic act' on the bill, suggesting the operation of a kind of unofficial and regressive quota system that denied access on the grounds of a presumed lack of difference amongst the homogenous body of non-white talent (Banks, Ebrey and Toynbee, 2014).

We might also point to emerging evidence of other kinds of exclusion in cultural work, such as that based on disability or age for example (Randle and Hardy, 2016; Warwick Commission, 2015) – though even then we would not be complete. What should by now be clear, however, is that the evidence for injustice and inequality is widening and deepening, and criticism of cultural work becoming more vocal and sustained.

CONCLUSION: THE LONG DAY CLOSES?

Have the cultural industries ever been genuinely meritocratic? Perhaps, to some degree. On the one hand, the absolute mobility occasioned by the long boom propelled large numbers of working-class people into new white-collar industries and occupations – of which the cultural industries were amongst the most valued and desired. No doubt the relative newness of much of the cultural sector, its illegitimate and unformed character, and the manner in which many industries were being invented in the moment of their undertaking, allowed many of the more adept and ambitious of working-class entrants to elevate themselves into positions of prestige and success. Especially in 'mass communications', in youth and popular culture-oriented industries, in the 'expressive' and 'intangible' occupations of the consumer society, the sheer demand for labour enabled ordinary people to enter into new kinds of jobs and careers that seemed unavailable or unimaginable to previous generations. In doing so, ordinary people appeared to gain a greater cultural recognition and political participation, as well as an economic opportunity. That we actually know very little about the *precise* numbers and levels of entry of such people, and their specific movement within the occupational structures of cultural work, should not lead us to disclaim the idea that the long boom helped create opportunity, and that this opportunity has now been quite significantly damaged or made to disappear. Not least this has occurred because of the current crisis, but is also underpinned by the migration from a socially democratic and welfare-conscious state capitalism to a more aggressive variant that tends to favour competitive individualism, toxic forms of self-sufficiency, and the creative exploitation of one's socially inherited advantages and assets. Yet neither should we overexaggerate the extent to which ordinary people were able to break the established patterns of privilege that marked out the cultural industries then, as they continue to mark them now. The long boom may have given working-class people some unprecedented degree of cultural recognition and visibility, but rarely was this provided at the expense of the elite and the established, which tended to retain the best jobs, most of the profits and all the benefits and advantages of management of control. We should also acknowledge that throughout the long boom, as is the case today, women, ethnic minorities and others not blessed with the advantages of white, male privilege, were never able to enjoy the fruits of the 'golden age' in quite the same way. Indeed, most of the evidence suggests that such people spent most of the long boom seriously disadvantaged, and strongly discriminated against.

But if the picture was once mixed, then what might we say of today? Certainly, the official statistics now show more people are employed in the arts and culture than ever before, though this brute data hides a multitude of differences – especially when it comes to inequalities. The opportunity for ordinary people to secure good creative jobs, and obtain the kinds of social elevation that the arts once routinely promised, now appears to be fading fast – if indeed it ever fully existed in the ways that have so often been claimed. Except for a few cultural occupations and jobs, women continue to be significantly disadvantaged and discriminated against – despite generations of legislation, intervention and campaigning. The prospects for ethnic minorities – which once appeared to have improved – now seem diminished as BAME workers struggle to secure and hold onto creative and arts employment in the post-GFC context. Only purveyors of the most blinkered industry and government rhetoric can now seriously believe the cultural industries are foundationally meritocratic. It has been repeatedly shown that cultural work, and the creative economy that contains it, is not a meritocracy, or an open field, but a fixed and unfair game; one marked by serial inequalities and minority disadvantage, and where the socially privileged are always better equipped to force the hand of chance. While it's perhaps no longer surprising to learn of the inequalities that occur in artistic and cultural work – so familiar and compelling has the evidence now become – what *does* remain shocking is the blind faith placed by governments, industry and employers in the cultural sector as a solution to problems of social and economic disadvantage amongst social minorities, since it's becoming abundantly clear, at least for the most part, that the arts and cultural industries don't just fail to alleviate inequalities, they actively exacerbate them.

NOTES

1. For example, see the accounts variously offered in Garnham (1990); O'Connor (2007) Hesmondhalgh (2012); Hewison (1995); Kynaston (2015); Marwick (1982).

2. For example, see Higson (1984) and Lovell (1990) on the rise of aesthetic realism and working-class representations in popular media and the arts.

3. For example: 'Bristolians are well provided with social and cultural activities. Excellent bookshops abound in and about the city centre. Black, blue and red stockings, "beatniks", dimly lit coffee bars and a chicken barbecue that remains open for the later diner' (*The Times,* 'Prosperous City under the Eye of an Ample Neptune', March 14, 1960, p. 8) and 'Mr Leslie Blond ... Merseyside impresario and promoter of specialized film productions, gave an "at home" party tonight to 200 guests to mark the opening tomorrow night of his newest venture – a specialized cinema, art centre, licensed club, and later, a venue of experimental plays' (*The Times,* 'Cinema to be Art Centre and Club' May 8th, 1961, p. 7). More recently Mick Brown reports that 'in 1959 [Jim] Haynes opened The Paperback in Edinburgh, the first bookshop in Britain to stock the writings of the American "Beat" authors and Henry Miller at a time when his books were banned under the obscenity laws. Moving to London, he was one of the founders in 1966 of IT, Britain's first underground newspaper, and in the same year he established the Arts Lab in Drury Lane – London's first space for the artistic "happenings" which so characterised the period' (Brown, 2012, no pagination).

4. Though as George Yudice has noted, the growth of the post-war US cultural economy was also significantly enhanced by the 'burgeoning infrastructure' (1999, p. 28) of government funding, foundation money and the expansion of HE in the 1950s and 60s, and not simply by a revivified capitalism.

5. Such opportunities allowed working-class cultural workers to reflect on their own newly acquired cultural status – which many found to be deeply ambivalent. For example, in the *New Left Review* in 1960, working-class writer and journalist Ray Gosling found himself feeling uneasy with the kinds of class opportunity being offered in the new consumer society:

> The boy does not understand his new power. All he knows is that they are wooing him. It is the feeding of the line that he is most afraid of. For centuries his people have slaved for them, but he is the boss now. The Labour Exchange wants his labour. He does not have to plead for a job. He has the money. He has the power. He is the one with something to sell. He reads it in the papers. He sees it on the television. He is constantly being told of the dreamland that now lies within his own reach, just around the block, just across the green. (1960, no pagination)

The ways in which the working classes were both culturally enabled and contained by the new consumer society would go on to become the staple concern on the new discipline of cultural studies (e.g. Hall and Jefferson, 1976) – but from the earliest stages of the long boom, ordinary working-class artists and cultural workers were alert to the contradictions and tensions of their own changing social and cultural conditions, precipitating anxiety as well as much creative endeavour.

6. As John Westergaard, writing in the *New Left Review,* suggested:

> For in fact the evidence flatly contradicts some of the formulations of this [equality of opportunity] thesis; and it leaves others open to serious doubt. First, so far as can be seen, overall inequalities of opportunity for social ascent and descent have not been reduced in either Britain or the United States during this century – or, for that matter, in most other western countries for which information is available. In comparison, for instance, with the son of a professional or a business executive, the odds against a manual worker's son achieving professional status, or just a middle class job in general, have remained very much as they were at the turn of the century. (Westergaard, 1964, no pagination)

7. Nicholas Garnham (1987) had first noted the rising value and significance of commercial popular cultural industries in London in the 1980s, backed by market expansion and the so-called GLC (Greater London Council) model of increasing state investment in popular arts and cultural activity. Though never really a formal policy as such, in London, or elsewhere, the principle of using culture to both engage and employ ordinary populations underpinned much of the shift towards cultural industry-led social renewal and economic regeneration in a number of post-industrial UK cities at this time – with aims of increasing democratic participation as well as employment. How this promise then became absorbed and transformed into the 'creative industries' discourse is by now well known (e.g. see Garnham, 2005).

8. Though, again we should note the general paucity of the record, compounded by the particular invisibility of women's labour in the cultural industries:

> Historically women have worked in pre-production as casting directors, on the studio floor as continuity 'girls' and in postproduction as editors, assistant editors and vision mixers. They have been employed in the Art Department as costume designers, have worked in wardrobe and makeup, in processing laboratories as negative cutters and assemblers, and as publicists, film librarians and researchers, as well as in the ubiquitous secretarial role. Many of the roles in which women have been employed leave little or no archival trace. (Ball and Bell, 2013, p. 551)

9. Often the clerical and the decorative roles were combined into idealised visions of the woman cultural worker – as Gillian Murray notes,

> The glamorous representation of the 'telly-bird' was promoted outwardly as a form of female aspiration to provoke the audience's interest in the television industry. It was also used inwardly to promote clerical jobs at ATV as the first step towards a big break. In doing so, women were also framed as glamorous focal points of heterosexual desire. (2013, p. 641)

A point made more prosaically by the ACTT forty years earlier as they lamented the prevalence of 'dolly bird' roles for women behind the scenes as well as front of stage and screen (ACTT 1975, p. 11).

10. The point about teaching as a woman's destination was more generally made by Viola Klein:

According to the Robbins Report, 7.3 per cent of the women … entered full-time higher education in 1962; of these, 52 per cent are students in Colleges of Education; and of the women qualifying from universities over 30 per cent become teachers in maintained schools. That is to say, about two-thirds of all women with higher qualifications – excluding re-entrants -head for the teaching profession. (Klein, 1966, p. 184)

11. Association of Cinematograph and Television Technicians absorbed in 1991 into BECTU (Broadcasting, Entertainment, Cinematograph and Theatre Union).

12. What has more recently come to light, in the wake of a series of sexual abuse charges and claims made against television personalities and broadcasters, initially prompted by the Jimmy Savile case, is evidence of a deeply ingrained culture of sexism and misogyny in the media industries of the 'long boom', one that was taken for granted and rarely able to be challenged. Writing in *The Independent* in 2012, television presenter, broadcaster and journalist Janet Street-Porter offered a frank account of the mood of the times:

In 1975, I started work as a presenter for London Weekend Television in my late twenties. I was amazed at what went on behind the scenes. I have no doubt that sexual favours were offered (by record companies and the like) to get acts on certain music shows at the BBC and ITV. On one series, a young female secretary would service an elderly male presenter in his dressing room in the tea break. Other men drilled a hole in a dressing-room wall to spy on a glamour star as she undressed. When a celebrated singer appeared on one show, he demanded two girls be sent to his dressing room to help him 'freshen up', i.e. give him oral sex. Another household name, still alive, was famous for dropping his trousers and waving his bits at the make-up ladies. They never complained, the assumption being that the ratings-hungry executives wanted their expensive stars to be happy at all costs, and sod the women in the workforce. (Street-Porter, 2012, no pagination)

13. Independent Broadcasting Authority – then the regulator of UK commercial television.

14. Black British musicians and groups that had emerged by the mid-late 1970s included the soul-funk group Cymande, reggae acts Aswad, Janet Kay and Steel Pulse, the 'Britfunk' bands Light of the World and Hi-Tension, as well as successful mainstream pop-soul acts such as Hot Chocolate and The Real Thing; later, black British jazz artists such as Cleveland Watkiss, Courtney Pine, Julian Joseph (and many others) emerged, in parallel with popular early 1980s jazz-funk and soul artists like Linx, Junior, Freez, Imagination and Phil Fearon (see Toynbee et al, 2014; Stratton and Zuberi, 2014). Again, however, while black Britons may have had some emerging *presence* in the music industry, they usually had little power, and less sustained success than white acts.

15. As McRobbie and Forkert (2013) have warned, there is a danger of 'romanticising' art schools, and certainly there were many inequalities within them – felt especially by women and ethnic minorities. The kinds of 'awkward' people they encouraged and nurtured best, tended to be young white men, who were more likely to then go on to establish themselves in cultural industry careers (see the many examples cited by Frith and Horne, 1987).

16. Not that the United States is necessarily seen as a bastion of opportunity in the screen industries; as I wrote this chapter, a public row broke out about the lack of

black talent in the nominations for the 2016 Oscars, with Hollywood becoming more widely exposed and condemned for its inability to recruit and reward black talent (see Gray, 2016).

17. In the early years of the long boom, cultural work was not necessarily viewed as an entirely serious and respectable career for bourgeois youth:

> The 1960s have perhaps been under-recognised in terms of the development of creative industries because it was hard for contemporaries, particularly within the government, media, and academia to take this new urban milieu seriously. The most visible aspects of the transformation of 1960s London – youthful fashion and popular music – also seemed the most transient and frivolous. A view was shared by many on both right and left that the development of fashion, music and other parts of the creative economy were essentially trivial, a sideshow in a longer story of metropolitan decline. (Breward and Gilbert, 2008, p. 167)

18. For example, see Anderson (2014) on MediaCom CEO Karen Blackett.

19. So corroborating Simon Price's original article on pop's 'poshification' written in *The Word* in 2010, which – by his own admission – may have been based on some dubious statistical reasoning, but does appear to have been broadly accurate in argument.

20. Indeed, follow-up research by the Sutton Trust (2016) revealed that the percentage of Oxbridge-educated journalists in the 'top 100' had risen from 45% in 2006 to 54% by 2016; though the percentage educated at private school had fallen from 54% to 51% – hardly a seismic shift, however.

21. This is a subsection of the wider cultural workforce identified as comprising broadcasting, film, games, digital, animation and SFX.

22. Women are also disproportionately employed in lower-status roles in creative media – often in the same kinds of positions that ACTT and the BBC found them routinely occupying in the 1970s.

Chapter 6

The Wages of Art

'Basic Economics' or Basic Inequality?

Preceding chapters have revealed how elite education and the best jobs tend to accrue to the more socially privileged – and increasingly so. Yet, perhaps unsurprisingly, the inequalities do not end there. Foundational to arts and cultural work is the unequal distribution of earnings, in terms of *incomes and pay*. In justice terms, one of established concerns of critical social science has been to challenge material inequalities in the workplace and their associated social divisions. The case for this has become more pressing in the cultural sector, especially as the idea that incomes are fairly and evenly distributed (according to either 'merit' or the 'market') seems increasingly taken for granted by those charged with promoting and providing creative jobs and employment. That the established powers have had no particular interest in exposing material inequality should not surprise us, of course. The success of the creative economy – at least for its principal beneficiaries – has been very much founded on denying the existence of any kind of economic injustice, rather than drawing our attention to it.

In this chapter, I want to consider in particular how cultural workers – and mostly *artists*[1] – are variously discriminated against in terms of pay and income. While most occupations tend to be poorly paid in arts and culture, the focus on artists – as a particular kind of cultural worker – is meant to draw attention to their role at the centre of the cultural industries labour process, and their elevated standing in the hierarchy of prestige attached to the creative economy. The artist is often held up as the *exemplary* cultural worker[2] – and, as we'll see, it is this that is both their blessing and burden when it comes to pay and rewards. First, I'll argue that beyond a few singular 'stars', and outside of the most socially privileged, the majority of artists are obliged to eke out a living on levels of pay that are low (in both absolute and relative terms), working in economies where the prestige of participation is imagined to compensate for a lack of security and a liveable income. Yet a focus on artists is to draw attention also to the ways in which the existing opportunities to earn a living in culture – to be rewarded for producing the objects and partaking in the practices I outlined in the opening chapters – are becoming unfairly distributed, and denied to an increasing majority of ordinary people, as prevailing patterns of pay and remuneration permit only a privileged *minority* to sustain artistic careers.

EARNING A LIVING?

Currently, in the United Kingdom, the *Creative Industries Economic Estimates* produced by the Government's Department of Culture Media and Sport (DCMS) are the official measures that account for the economic contribution and patterns of employment in the arts, cultural and creative industries – though (somewhat unhelpfully) they contain no information about workers' earnings or incomes. However, other authorised sources have suggested that artists might actually have little to worry about when it comes to securing fair pay and steady income. In 2012, the UK Government's Annual Survey of Hours and Earnings (ASHE) suggested that professional artists received an average income of £26,398 per year[3], almost identical to the national average wage across all occupations. The Arts Council of England (2015) used more recent ASHE data to estimate that the average gross (rather than net) income for full-time workers in the Creative, Arts and Entertainment activities (the SIC R90 industrial category defined by the Office of National Statistics) was £33,784 in 2013, and that over the period 2008–13, full-time earnings had increased by 6%, with part-time earnings increasing by 17% (Arts Council England, 2015). Yet the ASHE estimates are deceptive; they focus only on pay-rolled employees, and so don't reflect the earnings of the self-employed, which make up a significant proportion of the artistic labour force, and tend to have lower incomes. Other measures, such as the United Kingdom's annual Labour Force Survey similarly omits the self-employed from its estimates. Indeed, one of the more generic failings of official statistics in this field is their inability to adequately account for the majority of work that occurs in the sector – most of which is undertaken by individual freelancers and small or micro-enterprises. Arts Council England's own research estimated in 2009 that 41% of people working in the creative sector were self-employed and more than 70% of those working in its regularly funded organisations were employed on a freelance basis (Arts Council England, 2009). The DCMS also estimated that around seven in ten of all jobs in the sub-sectors of music, performing and visual arts were undertaken by the self-employed (DCMS,

2014). Other research has accordingly suggested that arts and culture professionals are doing less well than is proposed by ASHE-based estimates. The UK Arts Salary Survey 2013–14[4], conducted by the industry organisation ArtsHub UK, revealed that artistic workers[5] typically take home a salary of just under £20,000 per annum – around 75% of the national average wage and around two-thirds of the average professional wage.

How does the United Kingdom compare with others? In the Australian context, research by David Throsby and Anita Zednik (2010) found that in 2007–8 over half of all artists[6] earned less than A$10,000 per annum, with the mean creative income (income from purely artistic work) being around A$18,900 p.a. (around £10,000 at time of writing) Even when additional income streams from non-art work were included, Throsby and Zednik still found that artists' total incomes on average were 'lower than those of all occupational groups, including non-professional and blue-collar occupations' (2010, p. 9). Most artists were unable to obtain anything like a professional (or average) wage, or sustain themselves as artists, only. In 2014, the Australian Bureau of Statistics was continuing to report 'Arts and Recreation' as one of the lowest paid industrial sectors, with a worker's weekly earnings appearing to be around 25% less than the national average[7].

Somewhat more positively, in the United States, the Bureau of Labor Statistics (2014) offered that the mean annual wage was $51,120 for fine artists[8], $69,410 for multimedia artists and designers and $73,690 for fashion designers, compared with an national average wage of $47,230 (around £30,000) – suggesting that some artistic and creative occupations are as well-paid as other professional careers. However, the Bureau of Labor Statistics (BLS) survey (like the ASHE) focuses on established businesses with a full-time workforce, employed on a permanent (or at least a rolling) basis, rather than the individual self-employed, freelance or portfolio workers, who make up a significant proportion of artistic labour (conservatively, around 35–40% of all workers). One of the other problems with the BLS, as Andrew Ross (2000, p. 10) has previously identified, is that it only requires workers to specify the job in which they worked the most number of hours in the week of the survey. This means artists who just happen that week to be working their 'second' jobs will be counted as members of those occupations – even if they identify (and work) primarily as an artist. Other US evidence has also suggested that workers in the creative industries and arts are far more likely to be self-employed than in other sectors, less likely to be in permanent full-time work and, on average, will earn less than comparably qualified professionals (NEA, 2011; Woronkowicz, 2015). Further, the most recent National Endowment for the Arts data for occupations such as actor, musician, dancer, photographer and choreographer reveal levels of pay significantly below the kinds of pro rata estimates typically suggested by the BLS (NEA, 2011).

A 2006 report funded by the Canadian Council for the Arts found that artists earned a mean income of around C$22,700 (around £11,000) a year, compared with the national average income of C$36,300 – an earnings gap of around 37% (Hill and Capriotti, 2009). This research also identified that the median[9] income of artists stood at around C$12,900, compared with a national average of C$26,900. As in the United Kingdom and Australia, Canadian artists' earnings were not only found to be low but also *declining* – a trend further compounded by the GFC. The *Waging Culture*[10] survey of Canadian visual artists also identified median earnings of C$21,788 in 2007, which, by a 2012 follow-up to the survey, had fallen to C$21,603.

The picture is perhaps more positive in mainland Europe. Many Western and Northern European countries continue to offer equivalent (or relatively higher) wages than those available to artists in the United Kingdom, though admittedly, as yet, there are few robust data to show this. However, there remain some clearly established *dirigiste* commitments to providing social subsidies for artists, either through core funding provided through state arts organisations, individual grant-aid, more generous unemployment or in-work benefit, or contributions to (often free) training and education. In France, artists receive relatively generous out-of-work benefits from the state, through the well-known *régime d'intermittence,* which provides a form of income subsidy (the *intermittents du spectacle*) to support artistic workers between jobs[11], and artistic workers enjoy a wider variety of funding options from national and regional arts organisations, compared to their UK counterparts. Artists in Holland enjoy a similar guaranteed income benefit (the *Wet Werk en Inkomen Kunstenaars* [WWIK] scheme), and those in Germany (a country that actually increased its culture budget at the height of the GFC) are offered a low-contribution social insurance programme that guarantees pension and healthcare rights (the *Künstlersozialkasse* [KSK] scheme). Barnett comments parenthetically on some of the range of other benefits, currently unavailable to the UK artist:

> In Denmark, for instance, 275 artists are granted an annual stipend of between 15,000 and 149,000 Danish krone (£1,750 to £17,000) every year for the rest of their lives. In France, public funds are awarded through regional bodies not unlike our arts councils, except that the range of awards is much greater: artists in the Ile-de-France region, which includes Paris, can, for instance, claim up to 7,500 (£6,545) specifically to equip their studios. (Barnett, 2010, no pagination)

Here then, the picture of low income and precariousness appears less stark than in Anglophone contexts, with their more unbridled laissez-faire economic approaches, though it's noted that some commentators have drawn attention to worsening conditions for artists in some of the wealthier European democracies, especially under prevailing conditions of post-GFC austerity (e.g. Krikortz et al, 2015; Osborn, 2014, Umney, 2015).

Returning to the United Kingdom, it is at sub-sector level where we can see some further (more fine-grained) variations in incomes and stronger evidence of low pay. For example, in a 2013 survey[12], the actors' and performers' union Equity found that 67% of its professional members had earned less than £10,000 in the previous calendar year. At the same time, the Musicians' Union was identifying that over half of all UK professional musicians earned less than £20,000 per annum, with one in five earning less than £10,000 (Musicians' Union, 2012). Research in 2014 by the industry group Stage Directors UK found the average salary for directors working in publicly subsidised theatres was £10,759, less than half the average national wage of £26,500. Over half of directors were actually earning less than £5,000 a year, and some were being paid the equivalent of less than £1 an hour (Ellis-Petersen, 2015; SDUK, 2015). Writers are faring no better, as research from the Author's Licensing and Collecting Society (ALCS) recently revealed:

> According to a survey of almost 2,500 working writers – the first comprehensive study of author earnings in the UK since 2005 – the median income of the professional author in 2013 was just £11,000, a drop of 29% since 2005 when the figure was £12,330 (£15,450 if adjusted for inflation), and well below the £16,850 figure the Joseph Rowntree Foundation says is needed to achieve a minimum standard of living. The typical median income of all writers was even less: £4,000 in 2013, compared to £5,012 in real terms in 2005, and £8,810 in 2000. (Flood, 2014, no pagination)

Some sectors appear to offer better prospects. Most optimistically, the UK digital games industry reports average earnings at around £34,000 per annum, more than double the norm in fine art, craft or music industry occupations (Creative Skillset, 2014) – though others have identified more modest incomes in this sector (e.g. Weber, 2012; Chapple, 2015).

As in the United Kingdom, sub-sector variation has been observed in the United States, Canada and Australia (e.g. see Caves, 2000; Throsby, 2010, NEA, 2011), however since the data are often fragmented and difficult to benchmark or compare, we should be cautious of making too many claims and generalisations, both within and across sub-sectors and territories. Nonetheless, while the figures and estimates do vary, as does the category definition of 'artist' or 'creative' used in different national censuses and surveys, some *general* patterns are remarkably consistent. Regardless of territory, the mean and median incomes of professional artists do tend to be lower (and often significantly so) than counterpart earnings in other professional occupations. Patterns at sub-sector level might reveal some specific internal and comparative variations (e.g. classical musicians are paid more than folk musicians, as well as photographers and poets), but little to contradict the overall picture of low pay, both relative to other (non-arts) professions and in absolute terms. Previous estimates have suggested between one-third and one-half of artists in advanced economies are receiving incomes that place them at, or below, their nationally defined poverty line (Abbing, 2002). Since the general tendency is for low-paid employment within the cultural industries, it's evidently the case that a significant majority of artists subsist on income generated from other sources, including their partners or families. Further, as has long been known, having a second job is usually a professional necessity for any working artist (Filer, 1986; Wassall and Alper, 1992; Throsby, 2010). Indeed, it's been claimed that, depending on the territory and the specific artistic field, somewhere up to 90% of all artists have some kind of supplementary or second job (Abbing, 2002). That the official statistics tend to ignore or obscure these issues remains a problem for establishing any accurate calculation of earnings in the cultural sector.

'NATURAL LAWS' AND OTHER REWARDS

For those working within a cultural economics perspective, the fact that ordinary[13] professional artists are paid so poorly, and work so precariously, might simply reflect their true economic worth (e.g. see Adler, 1985; Filer, 1986; Towse and Khakee, 1992; Caves, 2000). The argument goes something like this: firstly, there is always going to be a limited pot of money available to pay artists, partly because subsidies are restricted, but mainly because royalties, wages and salaries only derive from what people are prepared to pay for artistic works. This tends to be as little as possible, and, for some art forms – in an age of downloading, 'open' and 'free' digital distribution and the promotion of the so-called 'sharing economy[14]'– fast reducing to zero. Secondly, the sheer number (or 'oversupply') of those both training and identifying as professional artists helps force down the price of artistic labour; there are many more people who want to be artists than positions available or attainable in the market – and as artists tend to be younger than other workers, this will also keep pay low. Thirdly, relatedly, the prevalence of non-professional enthusiasts[15], hobbyists and amateur artists, and their tendency or potential for substituting the work of professionals, suppresses wages by offering a significant 'reserve army' that can be drawn on if the cost of labour is deemed too high[16]. Fourthly, the 'low barriers of entry' to the art world, at least in terms of specific and formal credentials (compared with, say, entrance to a career as an aircraft engineer or paediatrician), ensure that wages are more dispersed among a larger body of workers, who might be 'trained' but not as exclusively (or as necessarily) qualified as those working in the rarest and most specialist professions that can command the highest salaries. Finally, the financially marginal status of 'the professional artist' reflects an ethical incommensurability with other professions: compared with medical doctors, lawyers or bankers, the artist is widely perceived to produce only 'ephemeral' or 'luxury' goods of a peripheral social value. In the United Kingdom specifically, the low (economic) status of art and artistic careers is also institutionalised in an education system that has consistently subordinated arts and creative disciplines beneath what are now called STEM subjects (Science, Technology, Engineering and Mathematics) which are regarded as more vital and important, and worthy of investment. For all these reasons therefore, it's simply not realistic for a common-or-garden painter, dancer or cellist to expect an income comparable to that of an engineer, scientist or accountant. Artists are simply paid what 'the market can bear', and that artists' pay is significantly lower than that of other professions merely reflects the general value of art to society.

This kind of reasoning is not just an academic or governmental perspective, but a lay truth. Many artists take for granted these brute facts of economic life, as this jazz musician eloquently testifies:

> [Basic] economics dictates that when demand is high, prices are high; when demand is low, then so are prices. At the moment you may be getting paid peanuts for playing 'Misty' in restaurants but that's because there's no real demand and there are forty other musicians in town who could do the same for each available gig of that kind. This is why the money is so dreadful – because the supply is greater than the demand. Demand is low and so is the price. (Dallman 2011, no pagination)

Certainly, 'basic economics' does play a role in keeping the price of creative labour low – yet too often perhaps, the reified agency of the market is allowed to provide a convenient alibi for the intentional suppression of the artistic wage. The artist feels resigned to a condition that appears natural and irresistible – but is in fact imposed, and potentially contestable.

Yet, according to cultural economists, another reason ordinary artists might be low paid is simply because they themselves *choose* to be so. In classical market terms, this might be regarded as an optimal rationalisation of an economically precarious position ('if I don't take it, someone else will'), or else motivated by the 'non-pecuniary' rewards of the art itself – the kinds of 'psychic incomes' (Throsby, 2010, p. 81) that art is judged typically to provide. Robert Caves assesses the consequences of these economic motivations for artists' wages:

> The artist's willingness to sacrifice in order to devote herself to creative work (*art for art's sake*) implies several properties of artists' incomes and activity patterns. Given the elastic supply of would-be artists, their competition will depress the average wage earned from creative work below the wage of humdrum labor,

by an amount reflecting the strength of their preferences for creative labor. Artists engaged full-time in creative work should then earn lower incomes than
persons in humdrum occupations but equipped with the same basic ability and
stock of human capital (education, training and experience). (Caves, 2000, p. 78)

Additionally, even if the pay is low, then *other* forms of 'external' good –
such as the prestige and social status of being recognised as an artist – may
also provide the motivation to labour for low pay. Indeed, while professional
artists may not so readily accrue the wealth of other professionals, they do
occupy class positions that – as Bourdieu has shown – come with cachet
and prestige. As we saw in chapter 2, the artist occupies a field where status
is measured less in terms of money and income and rather more in a self-
elaborated distance from necessity, where value is realised in the extent to
which one is able to demonstrate an expressive temperament and the restless
and inventive spirit of the aesthetic disposition. Touched by genius, the work
of the 'true' artist is untainted by mundane concerns of the material world –
such as rates of pay or levels of economic profit. Yet while this might serve
to secure kudos for the artist, it has also proved congenial to the capitalist,
who is able to more effectively exploit those who self-consciously disdain
the need for earnings and who seek to obtain a 'cultural credit' through
their wilful 'pecuniary neglect' (Ross, 2000, p. 15). Andrew Ross has drawn
further attention to the impacts of what he termed the 'cultural discount',
the principle 'by which artists and other art workers accept non-monetary
rewards – the gratification of producing art – as compensation for their
work, thereby discounting the cash price of their labour' (Ross, 2000, p. 6).
Beyond an economistic register, numerous writers have referred to the innate
'passions' and more affective benefits realised in the undertaking of creative
work (e.g. Gregg, 2009; Arvidsson et al, 2010; Duffy, 2015; McRobbie 2002,
2016) – those emotional gains and intensities which serve as compensation
for a lack of money incomes, or obviate the desire to pursue such rewards.
Of course, a further way of parsing this choice (as was discussed in chapter
3) is to say that art and culture are MacIntyrean *practices*: activities strongly
driven by communitarian goals, and the 'internal goods' that practices provide, in their own specific form. Practices, as we saw, are often undertaken
for their own sake – and not just for any particular kind of external reward
they might contingently provide.
    Regardless of motivation, and whether we understand this more from the
cultural economist's or sociologist's perspective, we know that, routinely,
artists will form an attachment to their work that is often sufficient to override
the sense of being poorly (or un-) paid or unfairly treated – with two corollary
effects perhaps being to diminish the will to challenge or organise for higher
incomes, *and* to push 'self-exploitation' to excess. Most recently, Angela

McRobbie has noted how the 'joyful-excitement factor' (2016, p. 104) of cultural work not only indemnifies against low pay but strongly lends itself to a more individualised politics and lack of self-care. Thus, taken together, the laws of the market and the variously motivated choices of individual artists might seem to explain quite well the poverty of the artistic wage. Yet there are other explanations for the relative modesty of most artistic pay – and for its distinctive distribution.

INEQUALITY AND UNEQUAL PAY

[Art] income is more unequally distributed than humdrum income, and it is more unequally distributed among artists holding humdrum jobs than among artists able to devote their efforts only to art. Some evidence also suggests that the upper tail of the distribution of artists' incomes is elongated, as the superstar effect implies. (Caves, 2000, p. 82)

The idea that artists' pay is determined by a combination of market logic and the various 'personal choices' made by individuals tends to obscure that within the art world itself there are *systemic inequalities* that shape patterns of earnings and income. In this context, the paying of the given 'market rate' by organisations and employers is perhaps less of a neutral response to price signals and more a reflection of a system that seeks to supress equality and guarantee continued privilege for an elevated few. Such inequalities derive not from a natural shakeout of talent but from the most basic principle of capitalism – the drive to secure unfettered accumulation and a monopoly of profit. From the largest, most profitable organisations, down to the smallest venues, galleries, publishers or record companies, the surplus value derived from artists is the primary means to subsistence or growth. Notwithstanding the now evident plurality of counter-capitalist and cooperative institutional models and cultures, this imperative continues as the most common impulse driving artistic economies and exchanges.

How is inequality visible? Firstly, it's notable that the rates of pay and rewards for executive and managerial employees have rapidly increased in recent years, just as ordinary artists' pay has been diminished – a problem identifiable in both private and public sectors. In 2013, research by Reuters revealed that the total earnings of CEOs in the FTSE top 100 listed firms was highest in the Media, Marketing and Telecommunications sector, outstripping even that of Financial Services (IDS, 2013). In 2015, the UK's independent television company ITV announced a 23% rise in its annual profits to a staggering £712 million – while simultaneously refusing to offer anything above a 2% rise to its rank-and-file journalists and production talent – so prompting strike action. BECTU (2015) criticised ITV for its refusal to offer a 'decent' pay rise to television workers, while managerial and executive salaries continued to rise in disproportion. While UK commercial theatre profits have risen steadily, reaching a record £530 million in 2013, dancers in the West End might now earn as little as around £500-£600 per week – reportedly the same amount they earned in the early 1990s (SOLT, 2016). To give even further example, Jones (2013) notes how in UK public sector arts, in the past decade, rates of pay for administrators and managers have increased far in excess of those for ordinary artists, whose incomes have remained static or been diminished.

That it is corporations, organisations and their owners, managers and executives that are the principal financial beneficiaries of artistic labour is perhaps not in doubt. But this doesn't mean that (some) artists are not well-paid. What is notable, however, is that the pattern of artists' remuneration tends to skew towards rewarding small groups of elites at the top of the pay pyramid, over a majority of others, and at the expense of a potentially more equal distribution of financial rewards among the wider workforce. Partly, income differentials in the arts are testament to the system of over-rewarding the 'superstars', the most successful artist-workers, at the expense of ordinary artist and performers, as well as the 'below-the-line', craft or detail labour. This is often justified in terms of satisfying the 'talent' – or rather those whose works command the highest premium (see Sherwin Rosen, 1981 on the 'economics of superstars'[17]). It's argued that such workers rightly accrue their financial advantages, since their unique 'talents' are singular and inimitable. However, even if this were the case, which is of course debatable, the income differentials between ordinary artists and their extraordinary peers are often quite staggering, and much more marked in the arts than the majority of other professions (Caves, 2000). In the arts, we can witness both extreme inequality, and inequity in disproportion.

As we've seen, a typical UK professional musician might struggle to earn the average wage – even when employed regularly as, say, a pop session musician, or a member of the pit in a West End production. Yet a list of the world's highest-earning musicians produced by the US *Forbes Magazine* in 2014 revealed UK artists such as Calvin Harris, One Direction and Paul McCartney each earning in excess of $70 million a year. The *Sunday Times Rich List* (an annual parade of the ultra-rich, much anticipated by UK elites) calculated that even the relative newcomer Ed Sheeran had already accrued a personal fortune of £20 million by 2015. Pop isn't the only site of income inequality in the music industry. Despite much industry secrecy, reports on the rewards garnered by the 'millionaire maestros' playing or conducting alongside the rank-and-file orchestra musician do periodically emerge

(Ibbotson, 2009; Service, 2009), and it's known generally that while conductors of the most prestigious UK orchestras can earn six or seven figure salaries, their ordinary musicians may struggle to earn the average wage. For composers of original works, there are also significant variances in income; research by Sound and Music (2014), a UK agency promoting new classical music, found the best paid 1% of composers received over 25% of all new commission income. For the remaining 99%, total annual earnings from commissioned compositional work averaged under £5,000 per year. Similarly, while the majority of ordinary Equity actors and performers struggle to get by on an annual income of less than £10,000, the James Bond star Daniel Craig is the United Kingdom's highest-paid actor, earning over £17 million pounds in 2015 (Furness, 2015).

Such comparisons might seem somewhat crude and reductive and fail to account for the objective talents of the talented, as well as the commercial complexities of specific cultural labour markets. But even if we were to accept this, we might still feel morally justified in questioning the *scale* of the disproportion between the very highest and the lowest paid. And if there still might seem to be no *direct* connection between the astronomical incomes of the superstar and the labours of the ordinary artist – we would have to say this is not the case. The rewards for 'superstars' come at the expense of a more equalitarian dispersal, since companies can only afford to offer 'top' artists their exceptional financial rewards by controlling costs in other areas of the production process – including the work undertaken by other rank-and-file workers, as well as other artists. The rumbling disquiet caused by recent multimillion pound salaries paid by ITV to their own 'superstars' (on screen, as well as some excessive bonus packages for management executives) clearly foreshadowed the 2015 pay dispute I earlier referred to (BECTU, 2015). To give a more specific example, in 2008, the British visual and conceptual artist Damien Hirst sold a collection of his work for £111 million at Sotheby's in London. Less than two months later, Hirst made redundant around half of the workforce at Science Ltd, the company that employed the workers that physically produced most of his art. It was estimated by *The Guardian* newspaper that these operatives – professional artists who assembled materials for his pill cabinet series and produced his butterfly paintings – were on average paid around £19,000 per annum, significantly less than the average UK wage. In June 2007, Hirst's *Lullaby Spring*, a cabinet filled with hand-painted pills, sold for £9.65m (Jones et al, 2008). Even if we were inclined to admit (like Rosen) that Hirst's gifts and talents were sufficient to justify his 'superstar' income, it is hard to accept the gross differentials between the labours of concept and execution, as well as the disregard for upholding decent standards of pay (and continuity of employment) for what is presumably highly skilled and precise work undertaken in the service of an artist whose status

and commercial value are second to none. Once again, we note the inequality
and the scale of the inequity.

But even if 'talent' and 'the market' appear to determine artists' incomes
in the commercial sector, one might reasonably expect to find decent pay
and a greater sense of distributional equality in the context of the public arts.
This isn't necessarily so. Income differentials in even the most high-profile,
state-funded arts and culture organisations increasingly mirror those of their
commercial counterparts. For example the BBC, through a combination of
compulsion and choice, has increasingly come to adopt more market principles in its operations, including paying 'competitive' salaries that differ-
entiate strongly between categories of employee. While most ordinary BBC
employees are on a single transparent scale, and each job awarded a grade
on that scale[18], a select cadre of 'talent' – the most highly rated on-screen or
on-air employees – are paid significantly higher salaries than their peers and
often employed on freelance basis to allow them to receive incomes that are
literally off the scale. In response to criticisms that public money was being
inappropriately deployed to fund the excessive salaries of a privileged elite,
a recent independent review found the BBC had taken significant steps to
reduce 'top-end talent costs' by 29% since 2009, partly by easing reliance
on this category of employee, and by diverting production into more cost-
controlled or low-cost genres and productions (Oliver and Ohlbaum, 2015).
Nonetheless, the same report identified that the BBC was committed to competing in an inflationary market for 'top talent' that was likely to intensify,
and drew attention to the corollary effects on the ordinary, grade-scale BBC
employee whose salaries had been effectively frozen for the previous five
years.

WORKING FOR FREE

While low and unequal pay remains a problem, one of the more controversial
issues in the recent politics of cultural work has been the amount of unpaid or
free labour that supports the creative economy[19]. Partly, of course, it is artists
themselves who might offer to work for free, to gain experience or a 'foot
in the door', to obtain the various kinds of rewards or incomes I've already
discussed. No doubt the youngest or most inexperienced entrants are more
susceptible to this, since, as Caves has it, 'fledgling artists trying to catch the
gatekeeper's eye' are more willing to 'accept near-zero artistic wages as an
investment in creative success' (Caves, 2000, p. 78). Yet, by doing so, such
workers leave themselves (and potentially others) open to exploitation.

It should first be noted, however, that not all unpaid work is exploitative,
in the conventional (Marxian) sense of failing to provide fair reward for

expended effort. For example, it's not uncommon for labour to be freely gifted to an amateur, experimental or 'artistic' production that is evidently non-commercial or operating without public subsidy, as a means of supporting a fellow artist or project. Artists may otherwise choose to forego earnings to work in a low-budget or unfunded project that suggests aesthetic quality or adventure – a commitment commonly found in all art forms. Working for free can also be undertaken to cement intimacies and friendships or to support some charitable or convivial social initiative; not all freely given labour should be condemned, therefore. More broadly, it would be hard to imagine *any* economy or society functioning without some kind of gifted or voluntary work. As writers such as Ross (2000) and Hesmondhalgh (2010) have argued, for artists to give the gift of one's time and labour to social events, community clubs, charities or other non-commercial activities and enterprises is very different to working for free in the context of a profit-making firm in the creative economy.

However, there are occasions when working for free presents more of a problem – especially in commercial contexts. For example, in 2013, Equity research revealed over 45% of its members had worked unpaid in the previous 12 months – a situation now becoming accepted as routine[20]. Yet, while average film and theatre jobs (in acting, dancing, singing) might not ordinarily be expected to pay hugely significant salaries or expenses, the assumption that people *should* be paid – rather than working for 'exposure[21]' or the 'experience' – was once a commonplace. Now, while London theatres and the more significant provincial venues and productions are still likely to provide at least an Equity minimum to the majority of affiliated actors and dancers, and significantly more to the 'stars', the spread of free labour in routine commercial theatre work has served to significantly undermine the idea that theatre is produced by working professionals whose labour should warrant an income.

Similarly, the UK Musicians' Union (MU) 'Work not Play' campaign is designed to address explicitly the issue of union members being routinely asked to work for free in evidently commercial (rather than social or community) contexts. In its campaign, the MU has drawn attention to a number of commercial ventures that were seeking to exploit musicians. This included, in 2012, LOCOG (the London Organising Committee of the Olympic Games) and their efforts to recruit musicians either as volunteers or as unpaid or low-paid contractors at cultural events (events where other contractors were fully paid), the restaurant chain Café Rouge which recruited unpaid musicians for a charity event that also generated commercial income, and various other profit-making organisations from television companies to theme parks, all of whom offered unpaid work as 'exposure' and a 'showcasing' opportunity for professional musicians – but rarely any pay.

Writing and authorship is another creative profession where the obligation to work for free – or at least for significantly less than preestablished rates – has now become a standard. Indeed, in areas such as journalism and magazine publishing, a generation of erstwhile media professionals (reporters, writers, graphic designers, photographers and so on) have largely been separated from secure and regularly paid positions, as intense competition and revenue depletion has led to unprecedented cost-cutting, as well as significant job losses. Writers (mostly freelance) must now compete to have their work recognised and valued in an industry increasingly divesting itself of commitments to paying for (what is now predominantly online) news, factual and feature content. In the United Kingdom, freelance writers for such established and prestigious newspapers as *The Guardian, The Independent* and *The Daily Telegraph* might still expect to receive a two or three hundred pounds for a 1,000 word article, whether online or offline (Turvill, 2013), but many providers of content, such as bloggers, reviewers, writers of comment pieces, photographers and so on, go largely unpaid. New titles that have emerged in the era of online journalism, such as *The Huffington Post*, tend not to pay for the majority of contributions.

Relatedly, more widely, the explosion of social media (and the content that drives them) has led to convincing claims the productive labour of ordinary people (rather than paid professionals) has become the foundational source of value for many content and platform-owning corporations, who either monetise people's willing and gifted media contributions, or else make money through the harvesting and selling of personal and shared online activity and data. The extent to which people are 'gifting' and 'sharing' both their creative and ordinary online labour (or simply having it unwittingly appropriated and commodified) cannot be underestimated given the heavy reliance of new social media giants such as Google, Facebook and Amazon (and others) on monetising user-generated content, and the more general dependence of news outlets, entertainment sites, games makers, music providers and so on, on the products of the freely given labour of ordinary people – who effectively operate as digital workers without pay. This is not only a substitution for artistic or creative labour but a profoundly unequal relation – as Andrew Ross describes:

> By far the most substantial rewards are allocated, on an industrial basis, to those who build and maintain the technologies of extraction, who hold the system's intellectual property, and who can trade the aggregate output of personal expression as if it were some bulk commodity like grain or beets. The real spoils, in other words, do not go to the aspiring stars, ranked and rated by the battery of metrics that measure Internet sentiment and opinion, but to behind the scenes content hosts and data miners, who utilise these and other metrics to guarantee their profits. The outcome, for this latter group, is a virtually wage-free proposition. (Ross, in Scholtz, 2013a, p. 19)

Yet, while private and commercial media and arts organisations are often identified as principal exploiters of free labour, they're far from the only culprits. Indeed, the UK public sector is increasingly cultivating its own indelible sense that paying the artist is not a necessary feature of any state-funded artistic project. For example, Susan Jones, writing as co-ordinator of the national campaigning group *Paying Artists,* recently highlighted how UK state-funded art galleries have steadily retreated from a sense of an obligation to pay, a situation that compares unfavourably with counterpart countries:

> In many other countries it's taken as read that artists get a fee when showing work in publicly funded exhibitions. In Poland, for example, artists are paid a fee linked directly to the average working wage and can negotiate from there. In Norway, they are paid according to number of works and duration of the exhibition; in Canada, artists' rights for payment when their work is used in exhibitions are legally enshrined. The UK is a different kettle of fish. Contrary to public expectation, but not the experience of many in the sector, most UK galleries do not pay exhibiting artists. In the past three years, 71% of artists didn't get a fee for contributions to publicly funded exhibitions. And this culture of nonpayment is actually stopping artists from accepting offers from galleries, with 63% forced to reject gallery offers because they can't afford to work for nothing. (Jones, 2014, no pagination)

Arguably this has occurred – according to galleries themselves – because of stringent public funding cuts, and the more intense commercial pressures now faced. No doubt there is some truth in this, yet, still, the principle of drawing down or generating funds to support artistic activity – but neglecting to use any of that funding to pay the artist involved – smacks strongly of an avoidable injustice.

FAIRNESS WITHIN PRODUCTIONS

Given these difficulties, how are we to determine who should be paid, and when? And what (if any) kinds of unpaid work might artists reasonably accept? Such questions are difficult to answer – not least for artists themselves, whose desire to work is often powerful enough to convince them that any kind of job be accepted, whether it pays or pays only in kind. However, there is perhaps a general distinction to be drawn between offering oneself for unpaid work in some obviously non-commercial 'community' context and working for free in the commercial sphere, or on a project known to be (significantly) publicly funded. Under such circumstances, it seems reasonable for working contributors to expect – and receive – some wage or share of income or subsidy. Producers and employers have a moral (and legal) obligation to pay their workers where they have opportunities to do so. Whether this happens or not is of course hugely contingent – every artist has a tale of some unpaid commission, salary or debt. But while it's the case that any expectation of rewards might depend on the status, finances and working arrangements of the project in question, this is also shaped by the particular characteristics of the art form itself.

For example, in their survey of UK independent television and film sectors, Neil Percival and David Hesmondhalgh (2014) identified some strong resentment among workers towards unpaid work in the television industry, but much less concern about equivalent work in the film industry. This was because television tended to be regarded by workers as a more formal and commercially structured activity, operating according to an established (and largely financially driven) model of practice; one that had historically taken into account the real costs of (well-organised and unionised) labour and the necessity of managing it in the context of established funding formulas. Accordingly, the workers surveyed felt that if one was working in television, then it wasn't unreasonable to expect to get fairly paid. In contrast, film tended to be regarded as more diverse both in respect of its finance, the relative weight afforded to aesthetic over commercial priority, and in terms of its relationship towards remunerated labour. It was noted that outside of the mainstream commercial blockbuster, film tends to be speculative, often made on a small or uncertain budget, and frequently lacking in terms of marketing investment or distributional opportunities – it may even be produced on a cooperative or non-profit basis, or even as an 'artistic' project made by an underresourced auteur or an impoverished aesthetic collective. The labour of film is therefore of a more mixed constituency – and for various reasons is not necessarily organised or unionised, and often informal, volunteered or paid in kind. In many such cases, where there is no obvious wage or income, to *not* work for free might mean that the film doesn't get made at all. Thus, among Percival and Hesmondhalgh's survey sample, while exploitation in both television and film was condemned, in film there was also a greater tolerance towards non-standard employment and informal working, including unpaid working. Similarly, we might note that in other art forms where capital investment or subsidy is lacking, and making money not a principle criterion or expectation – let's say for example in the practices of poetry, contemporary dance or folk music – attitudes tend also to be more pragmatic and sanguine about (if not always tolerant of) the need to work for free.

So when it comes to unpaid work, the context clearly matters – both in terms of project and art form. However, Percival and Hesmondhalgh do suggest a good rule of thumb for helping to affect a greater justice – one which they term *fairness within productions*. That is, if *someone* is being paid (or where there is evident subsidy or where a commercial return or profit is anticipated) then *everyone* should have some entitlement to pay, or a reasonable share of the available resources or rewards. This reflects a more general sentiment conveyed by the ordinary television workers they surveyed:

> The strongest condemnation of unpaid work was reserved for scenarios where inexperienced workers were expected to work for free while others were profiting from the same production, and a sense of injustice or inequality was expressed. (Percival and Hesmondhalgh, 2014, p. 200)

This sense of 'fairness within productions' offers a useful departure point for developing more equitable remuneration policies for artists. It's also an idea others are starting to propose. Recently, following its critique of unpaid work, the Paying Artists campaign recommended that all UK arts funding organisations (such as Arts Councils) adopt a policy of insisting that any organisations in receipt of their direct support must guarantee a commitment to paying the artists involved in funded projects. Currently, any such arrangements are at the discretion of the funded organisation – with too many of them choosing not to honour the commitment. In 2015, the online campaigning group 'Stop Working for Free' was consistently advising its community of members not to 'write, act, photograph or design for free (unless it's for someone or a company that is demonstrably not profiting from your work)'[22].

Yet 'fairness within productions' is not mere idealism – for some, it already operates as a working principle. The Paying Artists campaign has recently cited several examples of good practice in the United Kingdom, including here, at the Fabrica Gallery in Brighton:

> The value of its commissioning programme is circa £30,000 each commission. Fees to the artist are between £2000–£6000 plus expenses, with full technical support, installation, promotion, marketing and accompanying education programme provided. The residency programme is intended to relate to and accompany the main exhibition, and often employs a regionally-based artist. It pays £150 a day and has a total budget of £1500–£4000. There are no requirements to produce a piece of work and an open line of enquiry is encouraged. (Paying Artists, 2014, no pagination)

This is not yet a policy widely adopted by others – though doubtless it is spreading given the awareness raised by artists and campaigning groups. Nonetheless, such practices *do* offer a blueprint for a more equitable approach, firstly in recognising the ethical necessity of providing full costs and support, and secondly in attempting to offer artists more than the barest minimum of payment, where there is the capacity to do so[23]. This is important in terms of giving artists their *due*.

Yet, even if we accept that artists and cultural workers should be better paid and that 'fairness within productions' might provide a useful and basic principle, problems of 'how much', 'what proportion' or 'what precisely *is* fair', remain difficult to resolve. For the relatively powerless individual or freelance artist, it might not even be possible to identify a 'fair' reward, let alone demand one. While those affiliated to trade unions can seek guidance on union-recommended pay rates, obtaining any fair rate is also difficult if (as is increasingly the case) freelance workers are negotiating as relatively powerless individuals, on their own behalf, and may well find themselves pressured into accepting low rates and longer hours in return for the guarantee of work. In such a context, identifying consistent and common standards of pay, as well having them applied and upheld, becomes extraordinarily difficult to achieve without collective effort, more prescriptive state and legal intervention, and the consent and co-operation of those who stand to lose most from equalitarian gains. Additionally, of course, it is not just freelancers who are struggling to secure fair pay and good conditions. More broadly, the pervasive undermining of full-time (and mostly unionised) jobs, challenges to collective bargaining agreements, and increased flexibility over conditions of contract, not to mention standard rates of pay – even for the minority still employed as full-time labour – have given employers the whip-hand in determining pay structures across all arts and cultural industry labour markets.

SELF-SUBSIDY AND NEGATIVE PAY

While UK wages have declined or stagnated, opportunities for commercial or state subsidy been eroded, and working for free or 'below the minimum' made more widespread, a further difficulty is that many more artists are now being asked to actively fund their own careers – either directly or indirectly. The direct subsidy is realised in the rise of various kinds of 'pay to' arrangements, whereby artists are charged financially in order to participate in a show, production or event. Informal or indirect subsidy is evident when, say, a promoter, exhibitor or curator offers zero or a limited fee for performance or participation – thereby shifting the cost of any preparatory labour or expense to artists themselves.

A good example of a direct self-subsidy comes in the form of 'vanity galleries' (akin to 'vanity publishers') – now one of the marked features of the contemporary art scene (Phillips, 2014). Such establishments make most of their money from charging artists to exhibit, rather than selling art, and correspondingly have little commercial incentive to promote sales or nurture artistic careers. In fact, the business model relies on a particular kind of exploitation of the ambitions and desires of (mainly) new and inexperienced artists keen to get some 'exposure' and 'become known' in the art world. Reviews and encounters with such galleries tend to focus on the expensive cost of participation, the lack of promotion and support and a general sense of being 'ripped off' – with unapologetic proprietors insisting, in return, that their business model proffers significant 'showcasing' and 'profile-raising' opportunities for nascent artists at a 'reasonable' price[24].

The rise of 'pay to play' in the live music industry is similarly pervasive, and here there are various models or schemes (e.g. see Bentley, 2011; Dodgson, 2013). At the top end, a prestigious slot supporting a major artist might be offered to the highest bidder. A more common arrangement is the ticket deal, whereby venues or promoters require musicians to pre-purchase a significant bloc of tickets for their own gig, which they must then themselves sell in order to recoup their outlay – thereby shouldering the burden of the principal financial risk. Another kind of arrangement involves venues or promoters simply charging working musicians for a one-off or regular gig or residency. Promoters will claim the 'exposure' helps smooth the artist's path to some future commercial opportunity – one that tends to be somewhat vaguely defined, and usually elsewhere located. As illustration, the following invitation was received by a musician from a commercially successful company that provides UK urban street festivals and was posted on a Facebook page dedicated to exposing worker exploitation in the music industry[25]:

> Hi, your music sounds great. Are you able to come this Saturday night?
> There is no electrics on site, please bring your own battery powered equipment. There is no fee but good exposure. The music needs to be upbeat / rocky. We love covers of well-known songs, but mix in a few of your own too if you like. You will have a few slots throughout the night. Musicians play from 5 p.m. to midnight.
> Let me know.
> SO ... should anyone fancy this really attractive offer, do send Jessica@urbanfoodfest.com a note.

Evidently, there is little sense of equity or 'fairness within productions' here. Yet, as Leslie Meier (2015) has reported, even the more corporate elements of the music industry now offer opportunities to work for free, as well as self-subsidise one's career by committing oneself to forms of labour historically undertaken by others (such as promotions, marketing and managing, as well as recording and distributing) that the industry has now significantly outsourced to its artists.

CONCLUSION: THE DISAPPEARING WAGE?

Pay and incomes for ordinary artistic work have been in sharp decline, or disappearing, not merely because of the GFC, and the stringency of public sector cuts, but because of the acquisitiveness of commercially minded managers and organisations, who strive to extract maximum value from artists at minimal cost. While this has always been the case, the more recent, arresting rise of a minority of 'superstars' (to use Sherwin Rosen's term) and well-remunerated capitalist, managerial and artistic elites, at the expense of a more precarious majority, indicates both a hardening (and widening) of established structures of material inequality in artistic work. This has had objective consequences, not just in terms of materially disadvantaging the majority of artists but in diminishing the range of the population who are able to enter and sustain a living in culture. These are real social costs as judged from any egalitarian perspective.

We might surmise that the observations of Pierre-Michel Menger, made over fifteen years ago, in an influential article examining art workers in France, still seem to summarise quite well the general condition of artistic labour in *all* advanced capitalist societies, including the United Kingdom:

> Artists as an occupational group are on average younger than the general work force, are better educated, tend to be more concentrated in a few metropolitan areas, show higher rates of self-employment, higher rates of unemployment and of several forms of constrained underemployment (non-voluntary, part-time work, intermittent work, fewer hours of work) and are often multiple job holders. They earn less than [other] professional, technical and kindred workers ... [and] they experience larger income inequality and variability. (Menger, 1999, p. 545)

In fact, in light of the emerging evidence, we might suggest things have got markedly worse, both in terms of precariousness and in terms of income inequalities. Of course, this state of affairs has not gone unopposed – as I've tried to describe. The question of what might be done to further address these issues, I will return to in the final chapter. For now, we should simply note that, for the ordinary artist, securing the means of life requires a particular relation to necessity – not least an acceptance that if one wants to work in arts and culture then one might have to be materially disadvantaged (in the short term at least), and simply take that which is offered. But, for the ordinary artist, work now seems to involve a more *prolonged* financial struggle. The reality now is that most ordinary artists will never secure regular work or a liveable income, let alone attain the consecration, prestige and riches so volubly promised by proselytisers of the creative economy. We might also note that artists' own internalised commitments to their practices, and to the 'sacrificial labor' (Ross, 2000, p. 28) they often demand, may have helped secure the dominance of precarious jobs and dwindling pay, with investments in practices of culture-making and the 'internal goods' they occasion serving to shore up (as much as offset) tendencies towards greater exploitation. In the terms of chapter 3, whether the necessary balance between external and internal goods can be maintained – sufficient to ensure the integrity and continuation of practices of cultural work – might now appear to be in considerable doubt.

Yet, finally, we should also recognise that prevailing conditions rely on artists having not just the willingness but also the *capacity* to tolerate them. It should by now be evident that the ability to sustain in this kind of low-paid but highly prestigious work is unequally distributed, socially. Those who have access to stable secondary incomes or independent wealth are much more likely to be able to afford to work discontinuously, 'below the minimum' or for free. Likely also, is that a significant proportion of professional artists are in some way subsidised by others – usually their spouses, partners or families; indeed, this might be the only reason they are able to work in art at all. Such people are also better able to invest in the 'opportunities' offered by vanity galleries, pay-to-play deals and the like, or subsidise their own labour in other kinds of ways, over time. Thus, for the privileged, middle-class artist, set free by independent wealth, spousal incomes or inheritance, a passionate, aesthetic lifestyle is comfortably tolerable and affordable – for others, much less so. Finally, we should also note (as we saw in chapter 5) that the class and gender pay gap and wage inequality for black and other minority groups remain highly significant in arts and culture – strongly influencing the social distribution of incomes and rewards. The creative economy is therefore *divided* between those with advantages and those without them – and, as we saw, this has ramifications that go way beyond the wage relation.

NOTES

1. A.k.a. the 'creative', the 'talent', the 'author/auteur' – those seen as primarily responsible for the imaginative production of symbolic goods and commodities, as opposed to those engaged in other kinds of labour in the cultural sector.

2. See Stahl (2013) and Toynbee (2013) for more (critical) discussion of the idea of the artist as being an exemplary, 'limit' or 'special' case.

3. http://www.thisismoney.co.uk/money/article-2269520/Best-paid-jobs-2012-Official-figures-national-average-UK-salaries-400-occupations.html

4. http://www.artshub.co.uk/news-article/feature/all-arts/uk-arts-salary-survey-2013-14-197894

5. ArtsHub UK defined these as visual and performing artists, plus managerial and administrative workers, working freelance or in arts organisations.

6. In this case, defined as writers, fine and visual artists, performers, musicians and artistic community workers.

7. http://www.abs.gov.au/ausstats/abs@.nsf/Latestproducts/6302.0Main%20Features5Nov%202014?opendocument&tabname=Summary&prodno=6302.0&issue=Nov%202014&num=&view=

8. http://www.bls.gov/oes/current/oes_nat.htm#00-0000

9. As Hill and Capriotti (2009, p. 6) neatly summarise:

> The median is a measure of the earnings of a 'typical' worker in various occupations. Half of individuals have earnings that are less than the median value, while the other half has earnings greater than the median. The median is less influenced than the average (more appropriately known as the 'mean') by extreme observations, such as a few individuals reporting very large incomes. As a consequence, median earnings are typically lower than average earnings.

Given, as we'll see, the distorting influence of 'superstars' on the mean, the median is perhaps a better estimate of where the majority of workers sit on the spectrum of earnings.

10. http://theagyuisoutthere.org/everywhere/?p=4414

11. The *Intermittents du Spectacle* (IdS) is a social insurance scheme available to artistic workers engaged in the (inevitably) discontinuous world of cultural work – here, Charles Umney summarises the benefits:

> It was created in the 1930s for cinema production workers, and extended to include musicians in 1969. When creative workers are engaged for work, they and their employers (should) pay social contributions. Workers can then claim a basic minimum income compensating for periods between jobs. ... To qualify, workers must undertake 507 hours of work over 10 months; 'declarations' from employers for one performance normally count as 12 hours' work. (Umney, 2015, p. 712)

However, plans to curtail the benefit were tabled by the French government in 2012, leading to strikes and public protests (Osborn, 2014).

12. http://www.equity.org.uk/documents/2013-equity-membership-survey-summary/

13. We come back to *extraordinary* artists – aka 'superstars' – later in the chapter.

14. A term generally, often liberally, used to describe companies that find ways to extract value from pooled or peer-to-peer sharing of resources, without actually owning those resources (or even very much in the way of employees or capital infrastructure) such as AirBnB, Uber, Taskrabbit and others; social media companies such as Facebook and Twitter are also often included as examples of network or informational capitalists that exploit the sociability and sharing capacities of others for a commercial return.

15. Randall Filer (1986, p. 58) puts it bluntly enough: 'The community theater is a well-accepted part of [American] life while the amateur insurance salesman is not'.

16. Yet, as Jason Toynbee (2000) has noted, many of these people are not simply awaiting their call to market, but already operating in quasi- or proto-markets for cultural labour; occupying a shifting and sometimes indeterminate space between making culture for their own amusement as hobbyists or amateurs, but also occasionally making efforts to make money or obtain some kind of professional status as artists. This is a zone of partial commodification, and indeterminate employment

status – where 'selling out' is often disdained, and 'making it' eschewed in favour of something more 'authentic', or simply more rewarding and manageable. This might include (say) local orchestras, bands, record labels, etc., or artists collectives, (semi) amateur production of various kinds. Proto-markets of cultural production tend to be marked by mixtures of 'experiment, hybridity and parochialism' (Toynbee, 2003, p. 52) as much as they provide substitutes for market failure. This clearly raises further difficulties also in terms of measuring and calculating, and clearly defining, what counts as employment in cultural work.

17. In 'The Economics of Superstars' (1981), Sherwin Rosen identifies twin processes at work that, for him, explain the rise of unusually high wages differentials between ordinary and extraordinary artists. Firstly, he argues that there is an 'imperfect substitution' between artists, meaning that (say) the work of two bad painters will never achieve the same value as the work of one good one, and so we will pay significantly (and disproportionately) higher premiums for the work of the perceptibly talented (talent being a given in Rosen's formula). Secondly, Rosen argues the low costs of reproduction of the art commodity and the rapid expansion of 'joint consumption technologies' (technologies that allow us to more easily distribute and consume a talented artists' work – basically, different kinds of media hardware and software) allow the talented to rapidly accrue disproportionate incomes and profits as their work is now made so easily accessible to larger audience. When these factors combine, 'the possibility for talented persons to command both very large markets and very large incomes is apparent' (Rosen, 1981, p. 847).

18. For BBC pay scales in 2014, see http://downloads.bbc.co.uk/foi/classes/disclosure_logs/employment/RFI2014-0491-most-recent-salary-grades.pdf

19. In an important and influential essay, Tiziana Terranova (2000) was among the first to draw attention to how the emergent new economy rested significantly on the freely given labour of unsalaried individuals external to organisations. The gifted or solicited inputs of a literate and self-resourcing (but largely unpaid) class of creative and intellectual workers were becoming more central to innovation and change in the new economies of symbol and knowledge production. While Terranova wished to highlight conditions of emergent forms of computerised knowledge work especially, the social relations underpinning free digital labour now seem more generically embedded in the creative economy as a whole.

20. http://www.equity.org.uk/documents/2013-equity-membership-survey-summary/

21. Wages for art (in all sectors) are increasingly paid in 'exposure' – a currency that, while potentially valuable, often fails to materially sustain. We might think of exposure is a kind psychic *honorarium*, as Martha Woodmansee (1994) describes it in relation to emergent literary markets of the eighteenth century. Here, publishers tended to pay out only token sums to poets and writers, as bare acknowledgement of their authorial contribution, a prestige which writers were encouraged to receive with unflinching gratitude. As Woodmansee notes, these modest compensations 'bore no relationship to the exchange value of that work' (1994, p. 42) and 'resembled the gifts made to poets by aristocratic patrons' (ibid., p. 43).

22. https://www.facebook.com/groups/263804607094399/

23. Though it's also perhaps worth noting that even a reasonably generous policy such as this one only offers artists up to £6,000 for a commission, and given that most professional artists may only be capable of fulfilling one or two such commitments a year, it is easy to see why even successful artists, backed by enlightened employers, might struggle to earn anything approaching a living annual wage.

24. One of the most well known of these 'vanity' galleries in the United Kingdom being the Brick Lane Gallery in East London; the merits and demerits of which are debated in *Arteological* (2015)

25. *Stop Working for Free* https://www.facebook.com/groups/263804607094399/ (accessed June 2014)

Chapter 7

Concepts for Creative Justice

In this book I've proposed the need to think more urgently about justice in relation to cultural industries, given the growing importance of such activities to the social and economic organisation of contemporary societies. This first involved giving culture its *due* – trying to better understand what the cultural industries produce (cultural objects) and how they're produced and why (in cultural work). It then entailed examining how the opportunities and rewards that might be occasioned by such work are socially *distributed*. It was shown that the cultural industries are far from ideal in the ways they allocate and dispense their opportunities and rewards, and that creative *in*justice – evidenced in patterns of discrimination, misrecognition and inequality – is now an endemic feature. The creative economy is not only failing to provide the conditions that would allow ordinary people to enter the labour market and participate in the production of culture but also actively exacerbating social inequalities *in* work through its own structures and patterns of organisation.

Yet, in the spirit of practical and normative critique, I want to use this final chapter to suggest three concepts (and some associated principles) that might help advance the cause of 'creative justice' in cultural education and work. These concepts are intended to be heuristic, propositional and non-comprehensive – and open to refinement or challenge. Yet they also play a quite specific role. Firstly, they allow me to bring together some of the key arguments and understandings of this book. Secondly, they're offered to help illuminate the efforts of practitioners who might already be using the same (or similar) ideas to inform their own struggles for progressive workplace change. Thirdly, they're used to signal the need for discussions about the kinds of wider and more systemic changes that might be required to help occasion a genuinely transformative creative justice. In this way, the concepts are designed to provoke further discussions that go beyond the limits of the immediate context in which I invoke them.

OBJECTIVE RESPECT

In *Spheres of Justice* (1983), Michael Walzer proposed that since humans are 'culture-producing creatures', it's vital 'we do justice to [them] by respecting their particular creations' (1983, p. 314). The initial chapters of this book were very much concerned with respecting human creations – trying to do justice to cultural objects and cultural work, in and of themselves. Indeed, we might refer to this as an attempt to offer *objective respect* – that is, to understand the objective properties or qualities of phenomena, as much as the subjective experiences that pertain to them.

Chapter 2 considered the problem of cultural objects and criticised the conventional sociological approach to aesthetics which has tended to relativize cultural value and disclaim the notion of objective quality. It was argued that informed decisions about the value of art and culture (whether made by academics or by providers of various kinds of resources and support) should continue to recognise that cultural goods have aesthetic qualities that not only objectively exist but also have some significant bearing on how they are judged, and why they matter. I proposed that by thinking through holistic forms of valuation that consider historical context, subjective apprehension and objective quality, we might come to better know what the culture *is*, and what it can *do* – and so do it justice. This was judged to be important, not only in terms of understanding culture in an ontological sense but also in retaining some sense of its potentiality as a source of creative economy critique – since culture remains recognised as having its own objective value, beyond that which is deemed to be commercially expedient or purely 'subjective' (and by implication socially arbitrary).

Chapter 3 noted that one of the objective features of work is that it is a socially embedded practice (a kind of 'moral economy') that contains a variety of both 'internal' and 'external' goods, which are mutually constituting and best understood together, rather than separately or in isolation. I therefore proposed one way we do justice to cultural work is by appreciating it as a complex activity, subject to a plurality of ethical procedures, processes and claims.

There are of course many *other* things we might say about the qualities of objects and work, but, for now, we might simply state that offering 'objective respect' suggests the need for something like the following principle or course of action:

- *To respect cultural objects and practices, by evaluating them in terms of their own objective qualities, as well their subjective apprehension and value.*

Evidently, as we've seen, when it comes to *objects*, one issue for academic and critics (and of course for consumers, public funders, sponsors and practitioners of culture) is coming up with evaluative criteria that allow for the paying of objective respect, while not reproducing unwarranted cultural hierarchies and established inequalities. Another important challenge is how to take into account (inevitably different) aesthetic evaluations, and how these evaluations might themselves be made subject to a more objective evaluation or critique. This is not an easy job, to say the least. Yet, political complexity and the diversity of cultural forms (and their interpretations) should not lead us to disqualify or relativize judgements of cultural value, but simply means that we now have the task of making more difficult appraisals – ones that have ideally to be conducted in a dialogue (as Wolff describes) that must strive to be sensitive to history, social context and the objective (aesthetic) qualities of the objects in question. We need to embrace this complexity simply because, overall, questions of cultural value remain 'unanswerable without some prior analysis of why culture *matters*' (Crossick and Kaszynska, 2014; O'Connor, 2016) – as both an objective entity and to its comprehending human subjects. While (quite rightly) critics and commentators continue to emphasise the difficulties of choice and the injustices of current methods of appraisal[1], we should still continue to recognise the importance (not least for producers and consumers) of valuing culture in ways that lie beyond that which is merely 'pragmatic' or socially and economically expedient (Yudice, 1999) – otherwise we will fail to fully do justice to culture and to all that it can be or do.

Similarly, in the case of cultural *work*, objective respect means not simply describing but also critically appraising the fullest qualities that work can offer. One thing this suggests is the need to appreciate that while cultural work is often exploitative and damaging, it can also be positive and fulfilling, and provide various rewards and compensations, both personally and socially. In chapter 3, I argued that one of the characteristics of cultural work is that it is comprised of 'practices' that provide socially embedded, ethical work and that offer the chance to obtain 'the goods of a certain kind of life', as well as various kinds of contingent external rewards. In 1969, when Carl Andre of the New York-based Art Workers' Coalition, one of the first organised art activist groups, made the following demands:

1. ART, OUR WORK, BE WIDELY AND HONORABLY EMPLOYED
2. ART, OUR WORK, BE JUSTLY COMPENSATED
3. ART, OUR WORK, BE ALL THE BEST THAT WE CAN LIVE OR DO[2]

Here, a claim was being made to have work recognised and respected in practice-like terms, and appropriately valued, both ethically and aesthetically.

Similarly, the example we saw in chapter 6 of the Fabrica Gallery respecting the work of the artists (in line with the kinds of recommendations made by the Paying Artists campaign) suggested an organisation giving due and balanced consideration to the internal and external goods of cultural work. But while the overall understanding of cultural work (and work in general) is enhanced when we 'take the promise of fulfilling work seriously' and examine what it entails 'with rigour and sympathy' (Muirhead, 2004, p. 8), this certainly doesn't mean we accept *any* kind of cultural work as being good. We must not lose sight of the fact that cultural work is often far from pleasant or beneficial, and that to respect something is not necessarily to leave it unchallenged or unchanged. Indeed, much of the motivation for this book is dismay at the profoundly unequal and unjust way in which cultural work is currently organised. But I would argue that only though understanding how and why such work has become so vital and meaningful to so many – why it matters to people – will we come to better appreciate what is at stake when cultural work's structures and organisations appear so damaging, unfair and unjust, and what might then be done to remedy or repair them[3].

Thus, as this suggests, by paying objective respect, and in doing justice, we not only need to describe cultural objects and work but try to *evaluate* them – since the purpose of critical social science is not merely to provide a positive account but a normative one, also. Our research needs to contain evaluation and judgement in order to be effective *as* critique; that is, to be able to say why some things are better or worse than others, or indeed to argue for any kind of value position[4]. This does not mean of course that the judgements of social scientists (or other kinds of critic) should always be regarded as right – quite often they can be wrong – but it *is* a requirement of critique that it seeks to posit a fallible alternative to the actual, otherwise it can only ever merely describe what already exists, and by doing so exclude the possibility of theorising any kind of social progress or change. As Bulent Diken (2015, p. 6) has rightly noted, 'the promise of emancipation' is quite central to any properly critical social science – a necessary vision of alterity beyond the same. This must apply to how we engage with both cultural objects and work, alike.

Finally, one vital question raised by the idea of 'objective respect' is how it might help us theorise and account for the specific *relationship* between objects and work. We know that there is no necessary connection between beautiful objects and good work; one might create the best art through the worst kinds of labour conditions, be these self-inflicted or imposed by others. Similarly, virtuous practices and ethically minded production are no guarantee of a great art. But if cultural objects are the *product* of cultural work, then we need to consider carefully where the focus of our justice concerns needs to be, in the context of the connections and relationships occasioned and necessitated by the industrial production of aesthetic objects. For example, while I've argued that cultural work matters because it offers the prospect of labour that is especially creative, meaningful and rewarding, and therefore, in the interests of justice, ought to be made more widely available, then what happens if this labour leads to the 'aesthetic injustice' of the production of what is judged to be objectively bad art? Similarly, is it 'just' to allow the production of aesthetically rich and generative work, that qualitatively advances an art form, and perhaps even occasions other kinds of positive social and cultural benefits, but that is produced under oppressive conditions of work or by elites whose social elevation has come at the expense of a subordinated minority? Any theory of creative justice must inevitably grapple with the questions raised by what is – by its very nature – a combined set of aesthetic and ethical concerns that contain a number of these internal dilemmas and contradictions.

PARITY OF PARTICIPATION

In the middle part of the book, attention shifted to the idea of distributive justice – or who gets to receive a good education, the best jobs and the highest earnings and rewards. Generally it was shown that, far from being open and meritocratic, the cultural industries are a relatively closed and homogenous social field where career success relies less on talent and hard work and rather more on the gains occasioned by inherited social advantage. As a consequence, socially *dis*advantaged and minoritised groups were revealed to be much less likely to secure an elite arts education, to enter and become elevated in the cultural industries job market, and to enjoy the material benefits of a secure, steady work with a liveable income. Chapter 5 revealed the latest research which shows that even *partaking* in cultural work is becoming more of an elite or middle-class privilege. However, a particular concept that might help us to anchor a more egalitarian challenge to this injustice is one borrowed from the political philosopher Nancy Fraser – *parity of participation*.

Fraser defines parity of participation as 'social arrangements that permit all (adult) members of society to interact with one another as peers' (Fraser, 2013, p. 184) and is intended as way of bringing different kinds of justice under a common measure, namely the degree to which people are able to engage and interact in different spheres of activity as moral and juridical *equals*. Parity of participation therefore offers a point of commensurability between different types of justice claim. It first supports claims for economic justice (e.g. through redistribution of wealth in the form of fairer pay, taxation and social support), as well as cultural justice (e.g. through equal recognition of the legitimate cultural rights and statuses of persons). Fraser (2008, 2013) has also more recently identified a third kind of justice claim (one she terms 'representational' or political justice) which also demands parity of participation in the political systems and architectures of (national and transnational) organisations and states. When it comes to parity of participation in our more specific case of the cultural industries, we might adapt this concept and seek to substantiate it through supporting the following principles:

- *Advancing social arrangements that allow for the maximum range of people to enter and participate in cultural work, in which they will be fairly treated and justly paid and rewarded for their efforts, relative to their peers;*
- *Ensuring that people are not prevented from entering cultural work on the grounds of any unfair cultural discrimination or prejudice, and that they have equal opportunities to participate and develop once they become engaged or employed;*
- *Developing the cultural industries as democratic arenas where minority and marginal groups can advance their own fair representation and secure a more equal share of the public communicative space.*

Fulfilling these ambitions would increase levels of participatory parity (in the terms understood by Fraser) since they would provide the necessary improvements in patterns of *distribution, recognition* and *representation*. This is consistent with the definition of equality I outlined in chapter 1 and, it must be said, throughout this book, the need for a fuller participatory parity has been implicitly assumed as a prerequisite for creative justice. For instance, the analyses of chapters 4–6 were premised on the presumed need to tackle an interlocking set of *dis*parities in relation to cultural education and work. These included the ways in which coming from an economic (and culturally) disadvantaged background tended to preclude acceptance onto programmes of elite arts education, as well as the propensity for employers to discriminate against women and ethnic minorities in employment recruitment and selection (while also paying them less). It also included the ways in which the sexism and racism that prevents women and ethnic minorities securing the most elevated and executive positions in cultural work also undermines the political power of such groups, mainly because they lack access to the environments and platforms which might allow them to challenge the kinds of inequalities that are invisible to the majority of their more privileged co-working elites.

Parity of participation is therefore a concept and principle that allows us to recognise and connect different dimensions of injustice under a single justice claim – the right to interact with fellow workers as *equals and peers.* It is worth highlighting of course that it is a general and specific lack of participatory parity that has often exercised *other* critical approaches to cultural work, whether their authors have stated it in such terms or not. Writers such as Rosalind Gill, David Hesmondhalgh, Angela McRobbie, Toby Miller, Kate Oakley, Jack Linchuan Qiu, Andrew Ross and so on have tended to work from egalitarian premises that take for granted the need for marginal or minoritised groups to achieve moral and juridical equality in the workplace and to be treated with an equal respect – in terms not dissimilar to those that Fraser has more formally proposed. I want to take their approaches as offering further assent for suggesting 'parity of participation' as a normative principle for underpinning what I'm presuming to term 'creative justice'.

Parity of participation is of course extraordinarily difficult to achieve. As long as the social backgrounds of people wishing to enter cultural work so markedly differ, then the provision of equality of opportunity *only* within work is unlikely to lead to equal outcomes[5]. This is because some people are already disadvantaged when they come to enter the competition for positions – and equality of opportunity only works if the starting conditions are the same for all candidates. Thus, in order to obtain anything like parity in cultural work, the more fundamental issue we will need to address is the prevailing inequalities in society *at large* – not easy in contexts where inequality seems to be becoming more socially ingrained and difficult to oppose. Nancy Fraser has herself argued that 'transformative' justice requires the deepest restructuring of social relations 'in multiple dimensions and on multiple levels' (2013, p. 204) – a claim which is difficult to refute (and one to which I will return).

Yet, here, I just want to pause and draw attention to some of the benefits of more modest and specific ('affirmative') measures that seek to compensate for pre-existing social disadvantage and increase participatory parity in cultural education and work – since these offer us more immediate prospects for change and might well propel our thinking into the kinds of spaces that suggest more transformative options. Instilling principles of equity and equality can begin from the ground up, and in the smallest measure – in ways that might support or encourage more ambitious or systemic initiatives, both in and out of cultural work. Three (indicative) examples I'd cite in passing are *blind auditions, industry quotas* and *fair pay*.

Blind auditions – where candidates initially perform behind a physical or virtual screen, out of sight of selectors – are an intervention designed to raise levels of participation in the arts by social minorities and have been most widely used in the context of trials for professional orchestras in the United States (see Goldin and Rouse 2000). It's notable also that some technology and games companies have started introducing 'blind coding' exercises into recruitment, as a particular effort to tackle gender imbalances in employment. A US company called GapJumpers has had some success with software that allows companies to screen their prospective tech employees through blind competency and skills tests. Here it's been found that women tend to perform very well on such tests[6] – and better than men – and where they're used in recruitment decisions, proportionately more women get hired. We should acknowledge that blind auditions may be of little use in other art forms – acting or dance for example. Yet we might propose that a more *general* principle of seeking to standardise tests of entry as 'blind' at some initial stage would go some way towards challenging ingrained perceptions of talent in a whole range of cultural education and work contexts – if not, of course, entirely solving the enduring problems of homophilic and discriminatory selection we looked at in chapter 4[7]. Nonetheless, blindness – in principle – might make for a fairer and more just assessment, we could argue.

Being unseen is one possibility, being made visible is another. In the United Kingdom, arguments for introducing specific employment *quotas* or forms of positive discrimination that favour social minorities are gaining ground, prompted, perhaps, by the kinds of concerns and anxieties that were discussed in chapter 5. Recently, the black British actor and comedian, Sir Lenny Henry, has called for the introduction of 'ring-fenced' budgets in the BBC to support a dedicated BAME commissioning and production unit, which would work with production companies that could guarantee at least 30% of its ownership was BAME controlled, or at least half the cast of its productions, in terms of cost, came from BAME backgrounds (Jackson, 2015). The journalist Lyn Gardner has called for quotas in UK theatre to ensure that women and ethnic minorities are adequately represented in the industry, citing the example of the theatre company Headlong which recently introduced a policy of having a 50:50 gender balance for commissioned writers of new plays (Gardner, 2015). BECTU representatives have similarly called for 'enforceable targets' (if not 'quotas' per se) for BAME employment, backed by financial penalties for non-compliance (Bell, 2014). Directors UK have also argued for 'specific diversity targets' (2015, p. 17) to tackle BAME underemployment. Even mainstream broadcasters such as BBC and Sky have slowly started to recognise the value and necessity of moving towards more binding targets, not least Channel 4 which under the terms of its own '360 Degree Diversity Charter' has set itself (the difficult) target of having 20% BAME employment by 2020, and LGBT employees of 6% – with bonus and salary deductions for those executives whose departments fail to make the grade. Yet these efforts remain voluntary (and can often seem tokenistic) and lack the backing of legal instruments that could impose punitive and binding penalties for non-compliance – though we should also acknowledge that support for quotas (or 'targets') remains far from universal even amongst broadcasting professionals, or in other cultural industries more generally (Elan, 2015; Fritz, 2016).

One of the most common objections to quotas is that they promote individuals on the basis of social characteristics rather than on 'merit'. This is deemed to be unfair and counterproductive, in so far as the best talents are denied their due, and those unfairly advantaged are more likely to produce suboptimal work than those promoted on 'ability'. There is also the sense that it might be patronising to elevate individuals on the basis of their social characteristics, and such individuals themselves might suffer further discrimination or stigmatisation at the hands of colleagues if they appear to be appointed only *as* minorities, rather than as capable workers. These objections might appear reasonable – but none seems sufficient to outweigh the fundamental purpose of quotas generally, *which is not to distinguish individuals but to challenge structural inequalities.* The overriding problem here is not so much that a selected person might not have talent, but that the criteria for judging capability are themselves deeply problematic. As we saw in chapter 4, while creative talent may have some objective basis, there is really no such thing as talent divorced from socialised judgement; such judgements are – amongst other biases – already classed, raced and gendered. So, while talent may have a value in itself, to object that the 'best' people might be disqualified through a quota system is to assume that the best exist outside of the socialised arenas of judgement that substantially determine quality – which is simply not the case. In some small measure, therefore, we might suggest quotas and 'targets', if sensitively developed, and made concrete and binding, might well offer ways to counter structural biases and improve parity of participation. But we should acknowledge that though quotas may have benefits, the most important need is not simply to 'increase the numbers', but to challenge the preconceptions that have led to the initial discrimination[8]. So while quotas offer a kind of crude (but potentially effective) way of tackling a problem in empirical terms, they don't necessarily meet the more fundamental priority of tackling underlying ideas, both about what talent *is*, and who might have it.

Finally, as we saw in chapter 6, the chance to participate in the creative economy depends significantly on the possession and securing of material resources that furnish the capacity to study and work. To participate as an equal, in the way Fraser describes, one must have access to incomes or earnings that support livelihoods and sustain engagement over the course of a job or career. *Fair pay* is proposed as a prerequisite for parity of participation and a more egalitarian justice, therefore, and the current effort of many workers' organisations is testament to the struggle to secure it. As I write, most of the major UK culture, arts and entertainment unions have recently launched fair pay campaigns, as well as initiatives against unpaid work. As well as the Musicians' Union's 'Work not Play', this includes campaigns by Equity ('Professionally Made, Professionally Paid'), BECTU ('Say No to Exploitation in TV') and the National Union of Journalists ('Fair Pay Fortnight'). Smaller no-nunion organisations have entered the fray such as the Paying Artists campaign, as well as more grassroots and activist groups such as the Ragpickers, Precarious Workers Brigade, Interns Anonymous and the Carrotworkers Collective, who have condemned free labour and internships in unequivocal terms:

> [the] internship is functioning as an access filter to professions perceived as desirable, a regulatory valve that replicates the most classic lines of class division. In order to be able to work for three or six months for free, the intern/volunteer needs to have the economic possibility of doing so. Internships finally are not so 'free' after all, as the cost of the unpaid labour is absorbed by the families or by the self-exploitation of the worker who then seeks complementary jobs. (Carrotworkers Collective, 2009, no pagination)

Such sentiments are shared with counterparts in other countries, such as the Working Artists and the Greater Economy (W.A.G.E) group based in New York, USA:

> 'W.A.G.E. BELIEVES THAT THE PROMISE OF EXPOSURE IS A LIABILITY IN A SYSTEM THAT DENIES THE VALUE OF OUR LABOR.
>   AS AN UNPAID LABOR FORCE WITHIN A ROBUST ART MARKET FROM WHICH OTHERS PROFIT GREATLY, W.A.G.E. RECOGNIZES AN INHERENT EXPLOITATION AND DEMANDS COMPENSATION' (W.A.G.E, wo/manifesto 2016, no pagination).

Such campaigning has met with mixed success – but some real gains have been made. The broader international perspective reveals that art and cultural workers' organisations can have significant influence over pay and labour conditions, as in the example of the Canadian artists union CARFAC (Sibley, 2015). Such organisations continue to offer a valuable source of 'counter-power' in the terms of Enda Brophy, Nicole Cohen and Greig de Peuter whose own 'Cultural Workers Organize[9]' project has done valuable work in bringing to light many new arrangements of solidarity focused on pay (and other) issues of workers' justice, both nationally and internationally (see de Peuter and Cohen, 2015; Brophy, Cohen and de Peuter, 2016). We might say that such campaigns and the organisations behind them already recognise parity of participation as a normative principle, *since the provision of a fair and guaranteed pay or income for cultural workers* (or at least 'fairness within productions' as we discussed it in chapter 6), is seen as necessary to support the life chances and career capacities of the greatest proportion of the existing or aspirant cultural workforce.

If blind selection, quotas, fair pay (and other 'affirmative' initiatives) fall some way short of offering full parity of participation, we should still acknowledge their value in their own context, as Andrew Ross has argued in relation to the United States:

[It] is important to remember that affirmative action policies were conceived as a first step, not the last, towards solving the problems of cultural and social injustice. As such, they established and important break with the occupational caste system, breaching the walls of socio-economic segregation. With the liberal retreat from race-conscious legislation in full swing, it is important to stand firm in support of these policies and their achievements, while searching for ways to plant the seeds of what Fraser calls transformative justice. (Ross, 1998, p. 193)

I would want to support this view but (as Ross himself recognises) stress that we also need to think about the more sustained oppositions and compensations that might be necessary to bring into effect a truly egalitarian creative justice – the kinds of structural transformations that would ensure a fuller participatory parity in culture[10]. In a post-GFC context, and amidst the kinds of setbacks and defeats currently being inflicted on social democracy in the arts (and everywhere) – this has become all the more pressing.

REDUCTION OF HARMS

Reducing the physical and psychological harms and injuries inflicted by cultural work, based on assessments of objective conditions and their human effects.

The third concept I want to propose is *reduction of harms*. This is closely related to the other two. Firstly, as we saw, the principle of paying 'objective respect' to cultural work is one that is designed to elicit both positive and normative accounts, as work is subject to both empirical description of a kind that might reveal its objective properties and qualities, as well as its subjective experiences, all within a broader context that seeks to evaluate these qualities against a set of external normative standards. Establishing what those standards are, and what forms of benefit or harm they might occasion, is clearly an important priority for effecting any greater justice at work. Secondly, even if we have greater 'parity of participation' in the form of improved redistribution (of funding and pay), recognition (a more diverse and integrated workforce) and representation (polyvocal cultural democracy), we might still need to intervene to ensure explicitly that *in* work people are treated fairly and justly, and with appropriate consideration and respect, sufficient to ensure that principles of participatory parity are upheld.

We might think of harm as a condition of physical or psychological hurt or ill-being induced (in this case) by the self- or other-imposed practices of cultural work. These might include exploitation (or self-exploitation), overworking, stress, bullying, intimidation, domination, aggression or violence, for example. Some of these harms we can locate in the forms of class, gender and race-based discrimination and misrecognition already discussed; others might be more personal or indiscriminate, or derive from some kind of institutional carelessness or indifference. Regardless of source, 'reduction of harms' is an important principle, not least because its activation suggests the possibility of a positive and complementary effect coming into force – an increase in human well-being through *flourishing*. Flourishing consists in being able to expand or develop one's human faculties and capacities – which derive from being able to live well and work in environments that are safe, supportive and sustaining (as we saw in chapter 3). The reduction of harms – and an increase in flourishing – therefore seems to be a principle worth pursuing in a post-GFC context where firms and employers seem increasingly divested of strong commitments to treat their workers either very fairly or very well.

One objection to the idea of a reduction of harms, however, might be the relativist one that would suggest harms (like 'goods') are actually quite difficult to define, especially given that people's experiences and understandings of what constitutes harm can differ quite markedly. One person's bullying can be another's 'strong leadership', for example. 'Overworking' can be a difficult condition to specify or identify, especially in the kinds of cultural work we're concerned with here. Certainly, these are tricky issues to deal with – and matters of dispute in most cultural (and other) workplaces. Yet, consistent with the approach of this book, I would also argue that it's quite possible to argue for a reduction of harms using objectivist grounds that can accommodate a diversity of understandings of well-being, without adopting a purely relativist position. This 'plural objective' approach to well-being is one previously proposed by Andrew Sayer (2011) and summarised thus:

> [The] objectivist conception of well-being does not assume that there is only one good way of living – [so] it is compatible with pluralism, but not with relativism. Pluralism in this context is the view that there are many kinds of well-being, but that not just any way of life constitutes well-being. ... Relativism (is) the idea that what is good is simply relative to one's point of view. (Sayer, 2011, p. 135)

Sayer therefore rejects relativist understandings of well-being and focuses instead on the rational possibility of specifying the conditions under which people might be seen to objectively *better or worse off*. His work here is strongly influenced by writers such as Martha Nussbaum who, through the development of the well-known 'capabilities' approach, has offered an account of human well-being that emphasises the necessary conditions under which humans might be judged to flourish or suffer[11].

This is relevant here since my view of much of the critical cultural work literature is that it *already* adopts a plural-objectivist (rather than relativist)

position, in that it tends to assume foundationally – though usually implicitly, by inference or in sotto voce – a set of objective and external criteria by
which any current or better or worse reality might be assessed[12]. Generally,
such research tries to do this by describing and understanding the consequences for human beings that might arise through their good- or ill-treatment
in the cultural industry workplace. In such approaches, 'exploitation', 'sexism' and 'stress' (say) might conceivably be understood as both social and
linguistic constructs, discursively made and subjectively experienced, and
as real forms of harm with objective consequences. So, for example, a
writer such as Jack Linchuan Qiu (2016) tends to assume the humiliations
and degradations suffered by workers on the iPhone production line are
objective and real, rather than socially constructed, and it would be better
if they didn't happen and workers were treated more fairly and humanely.
This isn't just Jack's unfounded 'opinion' but a reasonable assessment of
people's needs based on an objective sense of what makes humans suffer
or flourish. In Angela McRobbie's (1998) work, the ill-treatment of women
fashion workers isn't presented as a discursive construct, or simply a bloodless transgression of social norms by some firm or manager, but a genuine
form of suffering imposed upon vulnerable and disadvantaged persons[13]. In
such contexts, the views and voices of workers, and their accounts of their
own lives, are taken seriously as expressing something of the reality of their
condition and situation. This is not to say that these views (or the views of
social scientists) are infallible and incontestable – indeed, as I've stressed,
they might well be mistaken or wrong[14] – but neither are they *merely* a
'subjective[15]' opinion or merely a product of discourse. To regard them as
such would not only be reductive and patronising, but potentially dangerous,
since it might lead us to misrecognise or misunderstand the genuine harms
or suffering felt by others – and prevent us from doing something about them
(Sayer, 2011).

  If the most effective critical approaches to cultural work already proceed
from a plural-objectivist principle – that humans are vulnerable beings,
capable of flourishing or suffering in some objectively definable (as well
as subjectively experienced) ways – then this is entirely consistent with the
assumptions that inform the range of organisations now emerging to challenge the forms of harm and injury occasioned by the organisation of cultural
work. For example, in the United Kingdom, BECTU's *Respect and Dignity at
Work* survey, conducted in 2012, found that 79% of respondents had experienced bullying at work and identified that BBC (the major employer of media
industry freelancers) had strongly contributed to an 'undercurrent of fear' that
prevented freelance workers challenging an ingrained culture of bullying and
harassment. Partly in response, the Federation of Entertainment Unions[16] created its own survey and report (*Creating without Conflict*), designed to draw

attention to bullying and intimidation in the cultural workplace, and it too found the following:

> The worlds of the media, arts and entertainment are often seen as glamorous, however a survey of 4,000 workers has revealed these industries are 'hotspots' of bullying. More than half of those questioned (56 per cent) said they had been bullied, harassed or discriminated against at work. The results showed shocking levels of ill-treatment, inappropriate behaviour and a culture of silence, with only one-third of those suffering bullying and harassment reporting the incidents. The survey showed there was almost an acceptance of the prevailing culture of bullying; an attitude of 'if you can't stand the heat, then get out of the kitchen'. Although managers were the main perpetrators, half the respondents identified co-workers and colleagues as offenders. (Federation of Entertainment Unions, 2014, p. 1)

Creating without Conflict was an attempt to force employers to take bullying more seriously and has met with some initial success, as Anne-Marie Quigg reveals:

> Leading from the findings of the *Creating without Conflict* report and the BBC's *Respect at Work Review*, the unions were able to agree a Grievance Policy and Bullying and Harassment Guide at the BBC, which came into effect in February 2015. ... Significantly, for the first time the policies covered freelance workers as well as employed staff. ... In March 2015 the high-profile [freelance] television presenter Jeremy Clarkson was suspended from the BBC pending an investigation into an alleged altercation between himself and a producer. ... The Clarkson incident was widely regarded as the first 'test case' for the new [policy]. On 25 March [the BBC] announced that Clarkson's contract was not to be renewed at the end of the month. (Quigg, 2015, pp. 95–6)

While bullying is one kind of problem, other forms of harm can derive from a more fundamental disdain for the most basic standards of human health or safety. For instance, testimonials reveal that, in the United States, the Dancers' Alliance has campaigned successfully for minimum industry standards for dance workers, including the provision of 'hazard pay' for dangerous work where dancers are required to undertake complex or physically risky performances under difficult conditions, and a right to refuse where the dancer perceives a 'threat to [their] physical well-being'[17]. The principle of harm reduction and objective respect for the person is built into the recent code of conduct developed by Equity for the employment of professional models in the United Kingdom. Here, employers are urged to 'ensure that the safety, health, well-being and dignity of the Model is protected and maintained at all times'[18], an approach mirrored in the efforts of the US-based Models Alliance, whose 'bill of rights' quite reasonably demands that models be treated with professionalism and respect, as well as being afforded the contractual facility to exit from jobs that are considered unsafe or degrading, and to be able to confidentially report mistreatments in an industry where the physical and psychological abuse of young women is especially rife. Meanwhile, in 2015, the Canadian Media Guild's *Fairness for Factual TV Workers* campaign was launched in response to concerns about poor working conditions, including the harms associated with industry shifts towards making higher-risk or 'extreme' reality TV formats that have led to an escalation of injury and death for crew and production staff, a trend not helped by the fact that 'most of reality television is non-union, and there are no rules' (CMG, 2015).

CONCLUSION: TOWARDS CREATIVE JUSTICE

Throughout this book the idea of 'creative justice' has been suggested as a provocation; a way of focusing attention on some of the prevailing *in*justices within work and education in the cultural industries. This has involved thinking about both the 'giving' and 'receiving' of justice – giving respect to cultural objects and the practices of cultural work (and acknowledging their complex value), but then exposing some of problems of distribution and sharing that have arisen as cultural work has become more capitalised and commodified – or 'corrupted by institutions and external goods', as MacIntyre would no doubt put it. Overall, the cultural industries have been shown to be profoundly unfair and unequal when it comes to dispensing opportunities, positions and rewards. I've argued that this is to the detriment of society from an egalitarian perspective – and diminishes the quality of society in economic, cultural and political terms.

The concepts and principles I've outlined in this final chapter simply suggest one way of thinking through what a better creative justice might actually *consist* of – but in terms that are perhaps less abstract and scholastic than we might imagine. We can see that ideas akin to 'objective respect', 'parity of participation' and 'reduction of harms' are already informing the specific efforts of many of those engaged professionally in cultural work – and so are helping to shape the standards of justice therein. The key issue here of course is whether these current standards are actually *sufficient* or being properly and justly applied. Much of the evidence would suggest not – as the previous chapters have shown. Therefore the challenge now, for critics and practitioners alike, might be to try and harness these concepts, and the principles that underpin them, to try and inform more sustained and systemic successes in the fight for creative justice – a campaign that may need to take us into higher order theorising, more concerted action, and way beyond the confines of the cultural industries themselves. So, as to whether these concepts are adequate for this challenge or have a genuine currency and meaning others are now free to decide – but what they *do* draw attention to is the need to raise consciousness of injustice and inequality, and to help advance the conversation about fairness and parity in cultural work; a discussion in which I hope the voices of workers and campaigning organisations (as well as academics) will continue to be voluble and resonant. Such conversations can only aid in the ongoing struggle for creative justice.

NOTES

1. For example see Stark, Gordon and Powell (2013); Arts Council England (2014); O'Brien (2015) and Crossick and Kaszynska (2016) for some flavour of current debates.

2. http://artsandlabor.org/wp-content/uploads/2011/12/Lippard_AWC.pdf

3. This reformist or reparative line is of course contested by writers who see no good work under capitalism and argue that what is required is the end of work *tout court* – amidst the revolutionary dismantling of capitalism itself – and much of anarchist and autonomist Marxist literature adopts such a position of course. For Franco Berardi ('Bifo') the GFC is merely an indicator of capitalism in terminal crisis, hastening and necessitating the need to establish new kinds of autonomous social organisation that allow humans to work together beyond the confines of employment and the wage relation. Here, human beings might 'rediscover their intellectual and psychological integrity' and begin to create a better community that is 'aware and free, cohesive and erotic' (Berardi, 2009, p. 115). The idea of post-work societies is now being more widely discussed (e.g. Srnicek and Williams, 2016), and some compelling and well-argued positions staked out, including the idea of societies where work is both limited and decentred (and organised around various basic income systems, forms of work sharing, shorter hours), such as that eloquently proposed by Kathi Weeks in *The Problem of Work* (2011). With specific respect to cultural work, Stevphen Shukaitis (2016) has recently explored some emerging practices in avant-garde artistic labour, including various 'compositional' strategies of work refusal and disruption, sabotage and obfuscation that seek to dethrone the kinds of organised cultural industry work I'm predominantly concerned with here.

4. It's worth reiterating that even a negative evaluation of evaluation is itself an evaluation, even if it claims to offer no alternative value (Connor, 1993). Or rather, rejection of value already *implies* a future better state where value has been surpassed – which is itself a value judgement; albeit an implicit (or 'crypto-normative') one. To underscore the point made in chapter 1, all social science (like all social life) is normative – and inevitably so.

5. Yet, we should also note that, for others, such as Paul Gomberg, a more fundamental problem is that 'competitive equal opportunity is impossible', simply because jobs and positions are in *limited supply*, so that even where social background is

accounted and compensated for, there will still be 'winners' and 'losers' – some who have desired jobs and some who don't – simply because there aren't enough good jobs to satisfy all demand, and many bad jobs still remain in need of performing. Compensating for social disadvantage might help in terms of the social distribution of positions, but leaves intact what Gomberg regards as a more fundamental injustice – the fact that 'opportunity is a scarce good' (2007, p. 27) which only a limited number can enjoy, regardless of social background. His more radical solution is to argue for a greater *contributive* justice – making opportunity to participate in work an unlimited good available to all, as society is restructured towards the social sharing of labour be it complex and rewarding, or necessary and meaningless. If opportunities are not scarce, they cease to be objects of competition, and so chances to undertake them are equalised – only then can we have true 'equality of opportunity', Gomberg argues.

6. [GapJumpers Director Peter] 'Vujosevic says the company recently analyzed data from 1,200 blind auditions and learned that 54% of those who participated were women, while 46% were men. About 58% of those selected to an interview after the blind audition round were women, and 68% of those who ended up getting hired were women' (Smith, 2015, no pagination).

7. Blind auditions work well at initial stage; as Goldin and Rouse (2000) found, partly as a consequence of the uptake of blind auditions, the percentage of women musicians in the five highest-ranked orchestras in the United States increased from 6% in 1970 to 25% by 1996. Yet, there is still plenty of scope for women (or others) to be deselected at secondary stages – such as when trialling in the orchestra (or in workplace more generally) with prospective co-workers, that is when the screen is removed.

8. See Gwyneth Mellinger (2003) for a compelling expose and critique of the ways in which quota systems (in this case, in the context of news journalism jobs in the United States) can reinforce the very systems of power they're designed to challenge, not least by institutionalising the 'difference' of recipients and leaving underlying structures of ownership and control, and the ideological presumptions that scaffold them, undisturbed.

9. https://culturalworkersorganize.org/organizations/

10. We should also acknowledge that the strategies and tactics I've used as examples here – blind auditions, quotas, fair pay – are more strongly viable in those kinds of traditional, more residually 'Fordist' cultural industries that still offer some large-scale (often unionised) employment, where workers are sufficiently organised, and systems more adequately developed to accommodate collectivised demands for parity. As we saw in chapter 6, however, most cultural work is *not* of this nature and is undertaken by freelancers and micro-enterprises operating under conditions of precarity that strongly militate against standard, across the board, solutions. A further challenge for advocates of justice in cultural work is how to bring into effect 'parity of participation' under these more opaque and (arguably) less congenial conditions for organising and collective action.

11. Nussbaum (2011, pp. 32–34) proposes ten 'central capabilities' that 'a life worthy of human dignity' minimally requires and that governments are encouraged to set thresholds to guarantee; these are

Life. Being able to live to the end of a human life of normal length; not dying prematurely, or before one's life is so reduced as to be not worth living.

Bodily Health. Being able to have good health, including reproductive health; to be adequately nourished; to have adequate shelter.

Bodily Integrity. Being able to move freely from place to place; to be secure against violent assault, including sexual assault and domestic violence; having opportunities for sexual satisfaction and for choice in matters of reproduction.

Senses, Imagination and Thought. Being able to use the senses, to imagine, think and reason – and to do these things in a 'truly human' way, a way informed and cultivated by an adequate education, including, but by no means limited to, literacy and basic mathematical and scientific training. Being able to use imagination and thought in connection with experiencing and producing works and events of one's own choice, religious, literary, musical and so forth. Being able to use one's mind in ways protected by guarantees of freedom of expression with respect to both political and artistic speech, and freedom of religious exercise. Being able to have pleasurable experiences and to avoid non-beneficial pain.

Emotions. Being able to have attachments to things and people outside ourselves; to love those who love and care for us, to grieve at their absence; in general, to love, to grieve, to experience longing, gratitude and justified anger. Not having one's emotional development blighted by fear and anxiety. (Supporting this capability means supporting forms of human association that can be shown to be crucial in their development.)

Practical Reason. Being able to form a conception of the good and to engage in critical reflection about the planning of one's life. (This entails protection for the liberty of conscience and religious observance.)

Affiliation. Being able to live with and towards others, to recognise and show concern for other humans, to engage in various forms of social interaction; to be able to imagine the situation of another. (Protecting this capability means protecting institutions that constitute and nourish such forms of affiliation, and also protecting the freedom of assembly and political speech.)

Having the social bases of self-respect and non-humiliation; being able to be treated as a dignified being whose worth is equal to that of others. This entails provisions of non-discrimination on the basis of race, sex, sexual orientation, ethnicity, caste, religion, national origin and species.

Other Species. Being able to live with concern for and in relation to animals, plants and the world of nature.

Play. Being able to laugh, to play, to enjoy recreational activities.

Control over one's Environment.

Political. Being able to participate effectively in political choices that govern one's life; having the right of political participation, protections of free speech and association.

Material. Being able to hold property (both land and movable goods), and having property rights on an equal basis with others; having the right to seek employment on an equal basis with others; having the freedom from unwarranted search and seizure.

In work, being able to work as a human, exercising practical reason and entering into meaningful relationships of mutual recognition with other workers.

12. A relativist position that sees well-being as (only) culturally determined or specific would have no grounds for objecting to (say) a regime that inflicts torture, genital mutilation, or imprisonment without trial, as this would simply be how that regime defines its own 'good' or state of well-being. A plural objectivist would oppose these practices on the grounds that while 'culturally specific' they are also objectively inimical to human flourishing and well-being, regardless of how they are discursively constructed and culturally justified. We might extend this comparison to the workplace – managers that use forced or slave labour, or violence, may very well have *ideas* about what constitutes the well-being of themselves and their workforce, but that doesn't mean to say we shouldn't oppose them on similarly objectivist grounds. By the same token, we might seek to oppose (more ordinary) forms of exploitation, inequity (and so on) on the grounds that it is damaging and degrading to those people we might regard as being objectively worthy of better kinds of treatment.

13. 'When we say something like "unemployment tends to cause suffering" we are not merely "emoting" or expressing ourselves, or offering a "subjective" opinion about a purely normative matter, but making a claim (fallible, like any other of course) about what objectively happens' (Sayer, 2011, p. 42).

14. As we saw in chapter 2, a basic presumption of fallibility is that there must be something to be wrong *about*, independent of our claims or knowledge about it; Sayer, again: 'To be a fallibilist about knowledge is to presuppose the basic claim of realism, that many objects can exists independently of particular knowledges or claims about them' (2011, p. 47).

15. Subjective in the sense of 'untrue' or merely a 'matter of opinion' (see Sayer, 2000 and Table 1 in chapter 2).

16. The Federation of Entertainment Unions is a collective body that campaigns on behalf of, and provides joint services for, members of BECTU, Equity, The Musicians Union, the National Union of Journalists, The Writers Guild of Great Britain and even the Professional Footballers Association.

17. http://www.dancersalliance.org/#!blank-2/osxns

18. http://www.equity.org.uk/documents/ten-point-code-of-conduct/

Bibliography

Abbing, Hans. 2002. *Why are Artists Poor: The Exceptional Economy of the Arts.* Amsterdam: Amsterdam University Press.

Acker, Joan. 2006. 'Inequality Regimes: Gender, Class, and Race in Organizations.' *Gender and Society* 20 4: 441–64.

Acola, Ella. 2015. 'Black Feminism is Sadly Still Necessary.' *The Daily Telegraph,* 26th August. Accessed June 2016. http://www.telegraph.co.uk/women/womens-life/11826051/Black-feminism-is-sadly-still-necessary.html

ACTT (Association of Cinematograph, Television and Allied Technicians). 1975. *Patterns of Discrimination against Women in the Film and Television Industries.* London: ACTT.

Adkins, Lisa. 1999. 'Community and Economy: A Retraditionalization of Gender?' *Theory, Culture and Society* 16 1: 119–39.

Adler, Moshe. 1985. 'Stardom and Talent.' *The American Economic Review* 75 1: 208–12.

Alacovska, Ana. 2013. 'Creativity in the Brief: Travel Guidebook Writers and Good Work.' In *Exploring Creativity: Evaluative Practices in Innovation, Design, and the Arts,* edited by Brian Moeran and Bo T. Christensen, 172–90. New York: Cambridge University Press.

Anderson, Elizabeth. 2014. Karen Blackett: 'I Haven't Been Openly Judged on Gender or Skin Colour, But I'm Sure it Goes on Behind my Back.' *The Daily Telegraph,* 17th November. Accessed May 2016. http://www.telegraph.co.uk/finance/jobs/11234164/Karen-Blackett-I-havent-been-openly-judged-on-gender-or-skin-colour-but-Im-sure-it-goes-on-behind-my-back.html

Archer, Margaret. 2000. *Being Human: The Problem of Agency.* Cambridge: Cambridge University Press.

Armstrong, Mark. 2014. *Swinging Britain: Fashion in the 1960s.* London: Shire.

Arteological. 2015. 'Getting Your Ducks in a Row at Brick Lane.' *Arteological,* 5th February. Accessed June 2016. https://artelogical.com/2015/02/05/getting-your-ducks-in-a-row-at-brick-lane/

Arts Council England. 2009. *Do It Yourself: Cultural and Creative Self-Employment in Hard Times.* June. London: ACE.

Arts Council England. 2014. *The Value of Arts and Culture to People and Society – An Evidence Review.* London: ACE. http://www.artscouncil.org.uk/advice-and-guidance/browse-advice-and-guidance/value-arts-and-culture-people-and-society-evidence-review

Arts Council England, 2015. *Contribution of the Arts and Culture Industry to the National Economy.* July. London: ACE.

Arvidsson, Adam, Giannino Malosi and Serpica Naro. 2010. 'Passionate Work? Labour Conditions in the Milan Fashion Industry.' *Journal for Cultural Research* 14 3: 231–52.

Arvidsson, Adam and Nicolai Peitersen. 2013. *The Ethical Economy: Rebuilding Value after the Crisis.* New York: Columbia.

Ashton, Daniel and Caitriona Noonan, eds. 2013. *Cultural Work and Higher Education.* Basingstoke: Palgrave Macmillan.

Atton, Chris. 2002. *Alternative Media.* London: Sage.

Ball, Vicky and Melanie Bell. 2013. 'Working Women: Women's Work: Production, History, Gender.' *The Journal of British Cinema and Television* 10 3: 547–62.

Banks, Mark. 2006. 'Moral Economy and Cultural Work.' *Sociology* 40 3: 455–72.

Banks, Mark. 2007. *The Politics of Cultural Work.* Basingstoke: Palgrave.

Banks, Mark. 2015. 'Valuing Cultural Industries.' In *The Routledge Companion to the Cultural Industries*, edited by Kate Oakley and Justin O'Connor, 35–44. London: Routledge.

Banks, Mark, Jill Ebrey and Jason Toynbee. 2014. *Working Lives in Black British Jazz.* http://www.cresc.ac.uk/sites/default/files/WLIBBJ%20NEW%20FINAL.pdf Accessed May 2016.

Banks, Mark, Rosalind Gill and Stephanie Taylor, eds. 2013. *Theorizing Cultural Work: Labour, Continuity and Change in the Cultural and Creative Industries.* London: Routledge.

Banks, Mark and Katie Milestone. 2011. 'Individualization, Gender and Cultural Work.' *Gender, Work and Organization* 18 1: 73–89.

Banks, Mark and Kate Oakley. 2016. 'The Dance Goes on Forever? Art Schools, Class and UK Higher Education.' *International Journal of Cultural Policy* 22 1: 41–57.

Barnett, Laura. 2010. 'Don't Give Up the Day Job – How Artists Make a Living.' *The Guardian,* 24th January. Accessed June 2016. https://www.theguardian.com/culture/2010/jan/24/artists-day-jobs

Beck, John and Matthew Cornford. 2012. 'The Art School in Ruins.' *Journal of Visual Culture* 11 1: 58–82.

Becker, Howard. 1982. *Art Worlds.* Berkeley: University of California Press.

BECTU. 2015. 'ITV Unions Launch Ballot for Strike Action.' BECTU News, April 22nd. Accessed June 2016. https://www.bectu.org.uk/news/2326

Bell, Matthew. 2014. 'Quotas Unfair? So is the Status Quo.' *Royal Television Society,* July. Accessed June 2016. https://rts.org.uk/article/quotas-unfair-so-status-quo

Bennett, James, Niki Strange and Andrea Medrado. 2015. 'A Moral Economy of Independent Work? Creative Freedom and Public Service in UK Digital Agencies.'

In *Media Independence: Working with Freedom or Working for Free*, edited by James Bennett and Niki Strange, 139–58. New York: Routledge.

Bentley, David. 2011. 'Advice for Young Musicians on Pay-to-Play Gigs.' *BBC News,* 1st March. Accessed June 2016. http://www.bbc.co.uk/news/uk-england-lancashire-12607737

Berardi, Franco 'Bifo'. 2009. *The Soul at Work: From Alienation to Autonomy.* Los Angeles: Semiotext(e).

Berger, Bennett. 1963. 'On the Youthfulness of Youth Cultures.' *Social Research* 30 3: 319–42.

Berliner, Paul. 1994. *Thinking in Jazz: The Infinite Art of Improvisation.* Chicago: University of Chicago Press.

Blackburn, Robin. 1967. 'Inequality and Exploitation.' *New Left Review* March-April 3–24.

Blackburn, Robert and Jennifer Jarman. 1993. 'Changing Inequalities in Access to British Universities.' *Oxford Review of Education* 19 2: 197–215.

Blumler, Jay. 1964. 'British Television: The Outline of a Research Strategy.' *British Journal of Sociology* 15 3: 223–33.

Boliver, Vikki. 2013. 'How Fair is Access to More Prestigious UK Universities?' *British Journal of Sociology* 64 2: 344–64.

Boliver, Vikki, Stephen Gorard and Nadia Siddiqui. 2015. 'Will the Use of Contextual Indicators Make UK Higher Education Admissions Fairer?' *Education Sciences* 5 4: 306–22.

Bolton, Sharon C., Maeve Houlihan and Knut Laaser. 2012. 'Contingent Work and its Contradictions: Towards a Moral Economy Framework.' *Journal of Business Ethics* 11 1: 121–32.

Booth, William. 1994. 'On the Idea of Moral Economy.' *The American Political ScienceReview* 88 3: 653–67.

Born, Georgina. 1995. *Rationalizing Culture: IRCAM, Boulez and the Institutionalization of the Musical Avant-Garde.* Berkeley: University of California Press.

Born, Georgina. 2005. *Uncertain Vision: Birt, Dyke and the Reinvention of the BBC.* London: Vintage.

Born, Georgina. 2010. 'The Social and the Aesthetic: For a Post-Bourdieuian Theory of Cultural Production.' *Cultural Sociology* 4 2: 171–208.

Bourdieu, Pierre. 1984. *Distinction: A Social Critique of the Judgment of Taste.* London: Routledge and Kegan Paul.

Bourdieu, Pierre. 1990a. *In Other Words: Essays Towards a Reflexive Sociology.* California: Stanford University Press.

Bourdieu, Pierre. 1990b. *The Logic of Practice.* Cambridge: Polity Press.

Bourdieu, Pierre. 1993. *The Field of Cultural Production: Essays on Art and Literature.* Cambridge: Polity Press.

Bourdieu, Pierre. 1996. *The Rules of Art.* Cambridge: Polity Press.

Bourdieu, Pierre. 1998. *Acts of Resistance: Against the New Myths of Our Time.* Oxford: Polity Press.

Bourdieu, Pierre and Jean-Claude Passeron. 1977. *Reproduction in Education, Society and Culture.* London: Sage.

Bracewell, Michael. 2007. *Remake/Remodel: Art, Pop, Fashion and the Making of Roxy Music, 1953–1972*. London: Faber and Faber.

Broadhead, Sam. 2014. 'Inclusion, Democracy and the Pedagogised Other in Art and Design Higher Education.' *Enhancing Learning in the Social Sciences*. 6 1: 42–55.

Brophy, Enda, Nicole S. Cohen and Greig de Peuter (2016) 'Labor Messaging: Practices of Autonomous Communication.' In *The Routledge Companion to Labor and Media*, edited by Richard Maxwell, 315–326. New York: Routledge.

Brooks, David. 2000. *Bobos in Paradise: The New Upper Class and How They Got There*. New York: Simon and Schuster.

Brouillette, Sarah. 2009. 'Creative Labour and Auteur Authorship: Reading *Somers Town*.' *Textual Practice* 25 3: 829–47.

Brouillette Sarah. 2014. *Literature and the Creative Economy*. Stanford: Stanford University Press.

Brown, Mick. 2012. 'The Diamond Decade: The 1960s.' *The Daily Telegraph*, 29th May. Accessed June 2016. http://www.telegraph.co.uk/news/uknews/the_queens_diamond_jubilee/9288411/The-Diamond-Decades-The-1960s.html

Burke, Penny Jane and Jackie McManus. 2011. 'Art for a Few: Exclusions and Misrecognitions in Higher Education Admissions Practices.' *Discourse: Studies in the Cultural Politics of Education* 32 5: 699–712.

Cabinet Office. 2009. *Unleashing Aspiration: The Final Report of the Panel on Fair Access to the Professions*. Accessed June 2016. https://www.gov.uk/search?o=unl eashin+aspiration&q=unleashing+aspiration

Caldwell, John Thornton. 2008. *Production Culture: Industrial Reflexivity and Critical Practice in Film and Television*. Durham: Duke University Press.

Carrotworkers Collective. 2009. 'On Free Labour.' Accessed June 2016. https://carrotworkers.wordpress.com/on-free-labour/

Caves, Robert E. 2000. *Creative Industries: Contracts between Art and Commerce*. Cambridge: Harvard University Press.

Chambers, Deborah, Linda Steiner and Carole Fleming. 2004. *Women and Journalism*. London: Routledge.

Chan, Jenny, Ngai Pun and Mark Selden. 2015. 'Chinese Labor Protest and Trade Unions.' In *The Routledge Companion to Labor and Media*, edited by Richard Maxwell, 290–302. New York: Routledge.

Chapple, Craig. 2015. 'Average game developer salary falls to £32,500.' *Develop*, January 30th. Accessed June 2016. http://www.develop-online.net/news/revealed-average-game-developer-salary-falls-to-32-500/0188668

CMG. 2014. 'Dangerous Work: The Reality about Reality TV.' *Canada Media Guild*, 24th April. Accessed June 2016. http://www.cmg.ca/en/2014/04/24/dangerous-work-the-reality-about-reality-tv/

Cohen, Nicole. 2012. 'Cultural Work as a Site of Struggle: Freelancers and Exploitation.' *Triple C* 10 2: 141–55.

Cole, George D.H. 1955. *Studies in Class Structure*. London: Routledge and Kegan Paul.

Collins, Marcus. 2013. '"The Age of The Beatles": Parliament and Popular Music in the 1960s.' *Contemporary British History* 27 1: 85–107.

Comunian, Roberta. Alessandra Faggian and Qian Cher Li. 2010. 'Unrewarded Careers in the Creative Class: The Strange Case of Bohemian Graduates.' *Regional Science* 89 2: 389–410.

Conor, Bridget. 2014. *Screenwriting: Creative Labour and Professional Practice.* London: Routledge.

Conor, Bridget, Rosalind Gill and Stephanie Taylor. 2015. Gender and Creative Labour. *The Sociological Review* 63 1: 1–22.

Create. 2015. 'Create Announces Findings of the Panic! Survey.' 23rd November. Accessed June 2016, http://createlondon.org/create announces-the-findings-of-the-panic-survey/

Creative Skillset. 2012. *Employment Census of the Creative Media Industries.* Accessed June 2016. https://creativeskillset.org/assets/0000/5070/2012_Employment_Census_of_the_Creative_Media_Industries.pdf

Creative Skillset. 2014. *The Creative Media Workforce Survey 2014.* Accessed June 2016. https://creativeskillset.org/assets/0001/0465/Creative_Skillset_Creative_Media_Workforce_Survey_2014.pdf

Crossick, Geoffrey and Patrycja Kaszynska. 2014. 'Under Construction: Towards a Framework for Cultural Value.' *Cultural Trends* 23 2: 120–31.

Crossick, Geoffrey and Patrycja Kaszynska. 2016. *Understanding the Value of Arts and Culture: The AHRC Cultural Value Project.* AHRC. Accessed June 2016. http://www.ahrc.ac.uk/documents/publications/cultural-value-project-final-report/

Dallman, Barry. 2011. 'The Mistake that 99% of Musicians Make...' Accessed October 2015. https://jazzofilo.blogspot.co.uk/2011/01/mistake-that-999-of-musicians-make.html

Day, Elizabeth. 2015. Geena Davis: 'After Thelma & Louise, People Said Things Would Improve for Women in Film. They Didn't.' *The Guardian,* 27th September. Accessed June 2016. https://www.theguardian.com/film/2015/sep/27/geena-davis-institute-sexism-in-film-industry

DCMS. 2008. *Creative Britain: New Talents for the New Economy.* London: DCMS.

DCMS. 2014. *Creative Industries Economic Estimates.* London: DCMS

DCMS. 2015. *Creative Industries: Focus on Employment.* London: DCMS.

DCMS. 2016. *Creative Industries Economic Estimates.* London: DCMS

DeNora, Tia. 2000. *Music in Everyday Life.* Cambridge: Cambridge University Press.

de Peuter, Greig and Nicole Cohen. 2015. 'Emerging Labor Politics in Creative Industries.' In *The Routledge Companion to the Cultural Industries,* edited by Kate Oakley and Justin O'Connor, 305–18. Routledge: London.

Deuze, Mark. 2010. *Managing Media Work.* London: Sage.

Diken, Bulent. 2015. 'Critique as Justification – and Beyond.' *The Sociological Review* 63 4: 922–39.

Directors UK. 2015. *Adjusting the Colour Balance: Black, Asian and Minority Ethnic Directors in UK Television Production.* London: Directors UK.

Dodgson, Louise. 2013. 'The Perils of Pay-to Play at the Grassroots.' *Live Music Exchange,* 14th November. Accessed June 2016. http://livemusicexchange.org/blog/the-perils-of-pay-to-play-at-the-grassroots-louise-dodgson/

Dueck, Byron. 2014. 'Standard, Advantage and Race in British Discourse about Jazz.' In *Black British Jazz: Routes, Ownership and Performance*, edited by Jason Toynbee, Catherine Tackley and Mark Doffman, 199–220. Farnham: Ashgate.

Duffy, Brooke. 2015. 'The Romance of Work: Gender and Aspirational Labour in the Digital Culture Industries.' *International Journal of Cultural Studies* 1–17.

Eccleston, Christopher. 2015. 'Christopher Eccleston Hits Out at Inequality in Acting.' *The Guardian,* 14th April. Accessed June 2016. http://www.theguardian.com/media/2015/apr/14/ex-doctor-who-christopher-ecclestone-hits-out-at-inequality-in-acting

Eikhof, Doris and Chris Warhurst. 2013. 'The Promised Land? Why Social Inequalities are Systemic in the Creative Industries.' *Employee Relations,* 35 5: 495–508.

Elan, Priya. 2015. 'Diversity in the Arts.' *The Guardian,* 17th April. Accessed May 2016. https://www.theguardian.com/membership/2015/apr/17/guardian-live-diversity-in-the-arts

Ellis-Petersen, Hannah. 2015. 'Half of Theatre Directors in Britain Earning Less than £5,000 a Year.' *The Guardian,* 8th January. Accessed June 2016. https://www.theguardian.com/stage/2015/jan/08/theatre-directors-survey-low-wages-britain

Entwistle, Joanne and Don Slater. 2014. 'Reassembling the Cultural: Fashion Models, Brands and the Meaning of "Culture" after ANT.' *Journal of Cultural Economy* 7 2: 161–77.

Faulkner, Simon, Adam Leaver, Farida Vis and Karel Williams. 2008. 'Art for Art's Sake, or Selling Up?' *European Journal of Communication* 23 3: 295–317.

Federation of Entertainment Unions. 2014. *Creating without Conflict.* Accessed June 2016. https://writersguild.org.uk/wp-content/uploads/2015/02/FINAL-CwC-Guide1.pdf

Fekete, John. 1988. *Life after Postmodernism: Essays on Value and Culture.* London: Macmillan.

Fenton, Natalie. 2016. 'Left Out? Digital Media, Radical Politics and Social Change.' *Information, Communication and Society* 19 3: 346–61.

Filer, Randall. 1986. 'The "Starving Artist" - Myth or Reality? Earnings of Artists in the United States.' *Journal of Political Economy* 94 1: 56–75.

Flood, Alison. 2014. 'Authors' Incomes Collapse to 'Abject' Levels.' *The Guardian,* 8th July. Accessed June 2016. https://www.theguardian.com/books/2014/jul/08/authors-incomes-collapse-alcs-survey

Florida, Richard. 2002. *The Rise of the Creative Class.* New York: Basic.

Forkert, Kirsten. 2014. *Artistic Lives: A Study of Creativity in Two European Cities.* Farnham: Ashgate.

Foucault, Michel. 1972. *The Archaeology of Knowledge.* New York: Pantheon.

Fox, Nick. 2015. 'Creativity, Anti-Humanism and the "New Sociology" of Art.' *Journal of Sociology* 51 3: 522–536.

Frankena, William. 1962. 'The Concept of Social Justice.' In *Social Justice,* edited by Richard Brandt, 1–29. Englewood Cliffs: NJ.

Franks, Suzanne. 2011. 'Attitudes to Women in the BBC in the 1970s: Not So Much a Glass Ceiling as one of Reinforced Concrete.' *Westminster Papers in Culture and Communication,* 8 3.

Fraser, Nancy. 2008. *Scales of Justice: Reimagining Political Space in a Globalizing World.* Cambridge: Polity.

Fraser, Nancy. 2013. *Fortunes of Feminism: From State-Managed Capitalism to Neoliberal Crisis.* London: Verso.

Frey, Bruno. 2008. 'What Values Should Count in the Arts? The Tension between Economic Effects and Cultural Value'. In *Beyond Price: Value in Culture, Economics and the Arts,* edited by Michael Hutter and David Throsby, 261–69. New York: Cambridge University Press.

Friedman, Sam, Daniel Laurison and Andrew Miles. 2015. 'Breaking the "Class" Ceiling? Social Mobility into Britain's Elite Occupations.' *The Sociological Review* 63 2: 259–89.

Frith, Simon, 1996. *Performing Rites: Evaluating Popular Music.* Oxford: Oxford University Press.

Frith, Simon and Howard Horne. 1987. *Art into Pop.* London: Methuen.

Fritz, Ben. 2016. 'Hollywood Wrestles with Diversity.' *The Wall Street Journal,* 24th February. Accessed June 2016. http://www.wsj.com/articles/hollywood-wrestles-with-diversity-1456354526

Frow, John. 1995. *Cultural Studies and Cultural Value.* Oxford: Clarendon.

Furness, Hayley. 2015. 'Daniel Craig only Brit in Forbes List of Highest Paid Actors 2015 with $27m.' *The Daily Telegraph,* 4th August. Accessed June 2016. http://www.telegraph.co.uk/news/celebritynews/11783705/Daniel-Craig-only-Brit-in-Forbes-list-of-highest-paid-actors-2015-with-27m.html

Gardner, Lyn. 2010. 'Arts Internships: Chance of a Lifetime or Cut-Price Labour'? *The Guardian,* 23 February. Accessed June 2016. https://www.theguardian.com/stage/theatreblog/2010/feb/23/arts-unpaid-interns-exploitation

Gardner, Lyn. 2015. 'Do We Need Diversity Quotas for Theatre?' *The Guardian,* 9th June. Accessed June 2016. https://www.theguardian.com/stage/theatreblog/2015/jun/09/do-we-need-diversity-quotas-for-theatre

Garnham, Nicholas. 1987. 'Concepts of Culture: Public Policy and the Cultural Industries.' *Cultural Studies* 6 1: 23–37.

Garnham, Nicholas. 1990. *Capitalism and Communication: Global Culture and the Economics of Information.* London: Sage.

Garnham, Nicholas. 2005. 'From Cultural to Creative Industries.' *International Journal of Cultural Policy* 11 1: 15–29.

Gaztambide- Fernandez, Ruben, Adam Saifer and Chandni Desai. 2013. '"Talent" and the Misrecognition of Social Advantage in Specialized Arts Education.' *The Roeper Review* 35 2: 124–35.

Gilbert, David. 2006. '"The Youngest Legend in History": Cultures of Consumption and the Mythologies of Swinging London.' *The London Journal* 31 1: 1–14.

Gilbert, David and Christopher Breward. 2008. 'Anticipations of the New Urban Cultural Economy: Fashion and the Transformation of London's West End 1955–1975.' In *Creative Urban Milieus: Historical Perspectives on Culture, Economy and the City,* edited by Martina Hessler and Clemens Zimmermann, 163–82. Frankfurt and Chicago: University of Chicago Press.

Gill, Rosalind and Andy Pratt. 2008. 'In the Social Factory? Immaterial Labour, Precariousness and Cultural Work.' *Theory, Culture and Society* 25 7–8: 1–30.

Glass, David, ed. 1954, *Social Mobility in Britain.* London: Routledge and Kegan Paul.

Goldhill, Olivia and Sarah Marsh. 2012. 'Where are the Black Ballet Dancers?' *The Guardian,* 4th September. Accessed June 2016. https://www.theguardian.com/stage/2012/sep/04/black-ballet-dancers

Goldin, Claudia and Cecilia Rouse. 2000. 'Orchestrating Impartiality: The Impact of "Blind" Auditions on Female Musicians.' *American Economic Review,* 90 4: 715–41.

Goldthorpe, John H, and Michelle Jackson. 2007. 'Intergenerational Class Mobility in Contemporary Britain: Political Concerns and Empirical Findings.' *British Journal of Sociology* 58 4: 526–46.

Goldthorpe, John and David Lockwood. 1963. 'Affluence and the British Class Structure.' *The Sociological Review* 11 3: 133–63.

Gomberg, Paul. 2007. *How to Make Opportunity Equal: Race and Contributive Justice.* Malden MA: Blackwell.

Gosling, Ray. 1960. 'Dream Boy.' *New Left Review,* May–June. 30–34.

Gray, Tim. 2016. 'Academy Nominates All White Actors for Second Year in Row.' *Variety,* 14th January. Accessed May 2016. http://variety.com/2016/biz/news/oscar-nominations-2016-diversity-white-1201674903/

Gregg, Melissa. 2009. 'Learning to (Love) Labour: Production Cultures and the Affective Turn.' *Communication and Critical/Cultural Studies* 6 2: 209–14.

Hall, Stuart. 1958. 'A Sense of Classlessness.' *Universities and Left Review* 5: 26–33.

Hall, Stuart and Tony Jefferson, eds. 1976. *Resistance through Rituals: Youth Subcultures in Post-War Britain.* London: Hutchinson.

Hamilton, Andy. 2007. *Aesthetics and Music.* London: Continuum.

Harrington, Austin. 2004. *Art and Social Theory.* Cambridge: Polity Press.

Hartley, John. 2005. *Creative Industries.* Malden MA: Blackwell.

Harvey, Alison and Stephanie Fisher. 2013. 'Making a Name in Games: Immaterial Labour, Indie Game Design, and Gendered Social Network Markets.' *Information, Communication, and Society* 16 3: 362–80.

Hayton, Annette, Polly Haste and Anne Jones. 2014. 'Promoting Diversity in Creative Art Education: The Case of Fine Art at Goldsmiths, University of London.' *British Journal of Sociology of Education* 36 8: 1258–76.

Hemley, Matthew. 2014. 'Drama Schools: 80% State School Intake Rubbishes Claims of Elitism.' *The Stage,* 9th October.

Hennion, Antoine. 2007. 'Those Things That Hold Us Together: Taste and Sociology.' *Cultural Sociology* 1: 97–114.

HESA (Higher Education Statistical Authority). 2013. 'The Gender Gap at Universities 2011–12.' Accessed June 2016. https://docs.google.com/spreadsheets/d/1M_D77jtNIQszh9fqCf3Q_Ja2dF0-VmhPdz67KYt7kEY/edit?pref=2&pli=1

Hesmondhalgh, David. 1997. 'Post-Punk's Attempt to Democratise the Music Industry: The Success and Failure of Rough Trade.' *Popular Music* 16 3: 255–74.

Hesmondhalgh, David. 2010. 'User-Generated Content, Free Labour and the Cultural Industries.' *Ephemera* 10 3–4: 267–84.

Hesmondhalgh, David. 2012. *The Cultural Industries.* London: Sage (3rd edition).

Hesmondhalgh, David. 2013. *Why Music Matters.* Chichester: Wiley.

Hesmondhalgh, David. 2016. 'Capitalism and the Media: Moral Economy, Well-Being and Capabilities.' *Media, Culture and Society* (Published Online 21st April).

Hesmondhalgh, David and Sarah Baker. 2011. *Creative Labour: Media Work in Three Cultural Industries*. London: Routledge.

Hewison, Robert. 1995. *Culture and Consensus: England, Art and Politics since 1940*. London: Methuen.

Higson, Andrew. 1984. 'Space, Place, Spectacle'. *Screen* 25 4–5: 2–21.

Hill, Kerry and Kathleen Capriotti. 2009. *A Statistical Profile of Artists in Canada Based on the 2006 Census*. Hill Strategies and Canadian Council for the Arts. Accessed June 2016 http://www.hillstrategies.com/sites/default/files/Artists_Canada2006.pdf

Horkheimer, Max. 1982. *Critical Theory*. Seabury: New York.

Howe, Michael J., Jane W. Davidson and John A. Sloboda. 1998. 'Innate Talents: Reality or Myth.' *Behavioral and Brain Sciences* 21 3:399–407.

Huffington Post. 2012. 'What are There So Few Black Ballet Dancers?' Updated 13 April 2016. Accessed May 2016. http://www.huffingtonpost.com/2012/09/11/black-ballet-dancers_n_1873760.html

Husén, Torsten. 1974. *Talent, Equality and Meritocracy*. The Hague: Martinus Nijhoff.

Ibbotson, Philippa. 2009. 'The Myth of the Maestro.' *The Guardian*, 6th October. Accessed June 2016. http://www.theguardian.com/commentisfree/2009/oct/06/orchestral-conductors-pay-cut

IDS. 2013. 'FTSE 100 Directors Total Earnings Jump by 21% in a Year.' IDS/Thomson Reuters, 13th October. Accessed June 2016. http://www.incomesdata.co.uk/wp-content/uploads/2014/10/IDS-FTSE-100-directors-pay-20141.pdf

Jackson, Jasper. 2015. 'Lenny Henry: Ringfenced Funding is needed to Boost Diversity in TV.' *The Guardian,* 25th August. Accessed June 2016. http://www.theguardian.com/media/2015/aug/25/lenny-henry-ring-fenced-funding-diversity-tv

Jaynath, Meg. 2014. '52% of Gamers are Women – But the Industry Doesn't Know It.' *The Guardian,* `18th September. Accessed June 2016. http://www.theguardian.com/commentisfree/2014/sep/18/52-percent-people-playing-games-women-industry-doesnt-know

Jeffri, Joan. 2003. 'Jazz Musicians: The Cost of the Beat.' *Journal of Arts Management, Law and Society* 33 1: 40–51.

Jenkins, Richard. 1992. *Pierre Bourdieu*. London: Routledge.

Jones, Aiden, Kevin Dowling and Helen Pidd. 2008. 'Recession Reaches Hirst's Studios.' *The Guardian*, November 22nd. Accessed June 2016. https://www.theguardian.com/artanddesign/2008/nov/22/damien-hirst-studios-job-losses

Jones, Susan. 2013. 'What Are Artists Really Worth? Funding, Friction and the Future of Art.' *The Guardian*, June 24th. Accessed June 2016. https://www.theguardian.com/culture-professionals-network/culture-professionals-blog/2013/jun/24/pay-artists-funding-friction-future

Jones, Susan. 2014. 'By Paying Artists Nothing, We Risk Severing the Pipeline of UK Talent.' *The Guardian,* 19th May. Accessed June 2016. https://www.theguardian.com/culture-professionals-network/culture-professionals-blog/2014/may/19/paying-artists-nothing-uk-talent

Joseph, Paterson. 2013. 'Why were the Baftas so White? Because There Aren't Enough Black People on TV.' *The Guardian,* 16th May. Accessed June 2016. http://www.theguardian.com/commentisfree/2013/may/16/baftas-black-actors-tv

Keat, Russell. 2000. *Cultural Goods and the Limits of the Market.* London: Palgrave Macmillan.

Keat, Russell. 2004. *Every Economy is a Moral Economy.* http://www.russellkeat.net/ethics_and_markets.php Accessed March 2016.

Keat, Russell. 2012. *Bringing Ethics Back In: Cultural Production as a Practice.* http://www.russellkeat.net/market_boundaries.php Accessed May 2016.

Kennedy, Helen. 2012. *Net-Work: Ethics and Values in Web Design.* Basingstoke: Palgrave.

Khan, Naseem. 1976. *The Arts Britain Ignores.* London: Community Relations Commission.

Kirschbaum, Charles. 2007. 'Careers in the Right Beat: US Jazz Musician's Typical and Non-typical Career Trajectories.' *Career Development International* 12 2: 187–201.

Klein, Viola. 1966. 'The Demand for Professional Womanpower.' *British Journal of Sociology* 17 2: 183–97.

Krikortz, Erik, Airi Triisberg and Minna Henriksson. 2015. *Art Workers: Material Conditions and Labour Struggles in Contemporary Art Practice.* Tartu: Nordic-Baltic Art Workers Network. Accessed June 2016. http://www.art workers.org/download/ArtWorkers.pdf

Kynaston, David. 2015. *Modernity Britain: 1957–62.* London: Bloomsbury.

Layard, Richard. 2006. *Happiness: Lessons from a New Science.* London: Penguin.

Ledbetter, Carly. 2015. 'Emma Watson says Hollywood Sexism is Right There in the Numbers.' *Huffington Post,* 30th September. Accessed June 2016. http://www.huffingtonpost.com/entry/emma-thompson-hollywood-sexism_us_560bfac3e4b076812700024f

Leung, Wing Fai, Rosalind Gill and Keith Randle. 2015. 'Getting In, Getting On, Getting Out? Women as Career Scramblers in the UK Film and Television Industries.' *The Sociological Review* 63 1: 50–65.

Little, Alan and John Westergaard. 1964. 'The Trend in Class Differentials in Educational Opportunity in England and Wales.' *British Journal of Sociology* 15 4: 301–16.

Littler, Jo. 2013. 'Meritocracy as Plutocracy: The Marketising of 'Equality' Within Neoliberalism.' *New Formations* 80–81: 52–72.

Lloyd, Richard. 2006. *Neo-Bohemia: Art and Commerce in the Post-Industrial City.* New York: Routledge.

Lopes, Paul. 2002. *The Rise of a Jazz Art World.* Cambridge: Cambridge University Press.

Lovell, Terry. 1990. 'Landscape and Stories in 1960s British Realism' *Screen* 31 4: 357–76.

Low Pay Commission. 2011. *National Minimum Wage: Low Pay Commission Report 2011.* Accessed June 2016 https://www.gov.uk/government/uploads/system/uploads/attachment_data/file/32571/8023.pdf

Luckman, Susan. 2012. *Locating Cultural Work.* Basingstoke: Palgrave Macmillan.

MacIntyre, Alasdair. 2007. *After Virtue: A Study in Moral Theory.* London: Duckworth.

Maconie, Stuart. 2015. 'The Privileged are Taking over the Arts – Without the Grit, Pop Culture is Doomed.' *New Statesman,* 4th February. Accessed June 2016. http://www.newstatesman.com/culture/2015/01/privileged-are-taking-over-arts-without-grit-pop-culture-doomed

Malik, Sarita. 2002. *Representing Black Britain: Black and Asian Images on Television.* London: Sage.

Malik, Shiv and Rajeev Syal 2011. 'Internships: The Scandal of Britain's Unpaid Army.' *The Guardian,* 4th November. Accessed March 2016 http://www.theguardian.com/money/2011/nov/04/internships-scandal-britain-unpaid-army

Mangan, Lucy. 2012. 'Don't Blame the Stink of Inequality on Oxbridge.' *The Guardian,* 10th August. Accessed June 2016. http://www.theguardian.com/lifeandstyle/2012/aug/10/mangan-inequality-dont-blame-oxbridge

Marglin, Stephen and Juliet Schlor, eds. 1992. *The Golden Age of Capitalism: Reinterpreting the Post-War Experience.* Oxford: Clarendon.

Marshall, Lee. 2011. 'The Sociology of Popular Music, Interdisciplinarity and Aesthetic Autonomy.' *The British Journal of Sociology* 62 1: 154–74.

Marwick, Arthur. 1982. *British Society since 1945.* London: Pelican.

Mayer, Vicki, Miranda J. Banks and John T. Caldwell. 2009. *Production Studies: Cultural Studies of Media Industries.* New York: Routledge.

McKinlay, Alan and Chris Smith. 2009. *Creative Labour: Working in the Creative Industries.* Basingstoke: Palgrave.

McRobbie, Angela. 1998. *British Fashion Design: Rag Trade or Image Industry?* London: Routledge.

McRobbie, Angela. 2002. 'Clubs to Companies: Notes on the Decline of Political Culture in Speeded Up Creative Worlds.' *Cultural Studies* 16 4: 516–31.

McRobbie, Angela. 2016. *Be Creative: Making a Living in the New Culture Industries.* Cambridge: Polity Press.

McRobbie, Angela and Kirsten Forkert. 2013. 'Artists and Art Schools: For or Against Innovation? A Reply to NESTA.' *Variant* 34: 3–4.

Meier, Leslie. 2015. 'Popular Music Making and Promotional Work inside the "New" Music Industry.' In *The Routledge Companion to the Cultural Industries,* edited by Kate Oakley and Justin O'Connor, 402–12. London: Routledge.

Mellinger, Gwyneth. 2003. 'Counting Color: Ambivalence and Contradiction in the American Society of Newspaper Editors' Discourse of Diversity.' *Journal of Communication Inquiry* 27 2: 129–151.

Menger, Pierre-Michel. 1999. 'Artistic Labor Markets and Careers.' *Annual Review of Sociology* 541–74.

Millar, Robert. 1966. *The New Classes.* London: Longmans.

Miller, David. 1994. 'Virtues, Practices and Justice.' In *After MacIntyre,* edited by John Horton and Susan Mendus, 245–64. Cambridge: Polity Press.

Mills, C. Wright. 1959. *The Sociological Imagination.* New York: Oxford University Press.

Mills, C. Wright. 1966. *White Collar*. New York: Galaxy.

Mohanty, Satya P. 2001. 'Can Our Values Be Objective? On Ethics, Aesthetics, and Progressive Politics. *New Literary History* 32 4: 803–33.

Muirhead, Russell. 2004. *Just Work*. Cambridge: Harvard University Press.

Murray, Gillian. 2013. 'Glamour and Aspiration: Women's Employment and the Establishment of Midlands ATV, 1956–68.' *The Journal of British Cinema and Television* 10 3: 635–49.

Musician's Union. 2012. *The Working Musician*. London: MU.

Nahai, Rebekah. 2013. 'Is Meritocracy Fair? A Qualitative Case Study of Admissions at the University of Oxford.' *Oxford Review of Education* 39 5: 681–701.

NEA (National Endowment for the Arts). 2011. *Research Note 105*. Accessed June 2016. https://www.arts.gov/sites/default/files/105.pdf

Nesta. 2013. *A Manifesto for the Creative Economy*. London; Nesta.

Nussbaum, Martha. 2003. 'Capabilities as Fundamental Entitlements: Sen and Social Justice.' *Feminist Economics* 9 2–3: 33–59.

Nussbaum, Martha. 2011 *Creating Capabilities: The Human Development Approach*. Cambridge: Harvard University Press.

Oakley, Kate. 2014. 'Good Work? Rethinking Cultural Entrepreneurship.' In *The Handbook of Management and Creativity*, edited by Chris Bilton and Stephen Cummings, 145–59. Cheltenham: Edward Elgar.

Oakley, Kate and O'Connor, Justin. 2015. 'The Cultural Industries: An Introduction'. In *The Routledge Companion to the Cultural Industries*, edited by Kate Oakley and Justin O'Connor, 1–32. London: Routledge.

O'Brien, Dave. 2010. *Measuring the Value of Culture*. London: DCMS.

O'Brien, Dave. 2015. 'Cultural Value: Empirical Perspectives.' *Cultural Trends* 24 3: 209–10.

O'Connor, Justin. 2007. *The Cultural and Creative Industries: A Review of the Literature*. London: Creative Partnerships.

O'Connor, Justin. 2016. 'After the Creative Industries: Why We Need a Cultural Economy.' *Platform Papers: Quarterly Essays on the Performing Arts*. Accessed May 2016. www.currencyhouse.org.au.

O'Connor, Steven. 1993. 'The Necessity of Value.' In *Principled Positions: Postmodernism and the Recovery of Value,* edited by Judith Squires, 31–49. London: Lawrence and Wishart.

O'Hagan, Sean. 2014. 'A Working-Class Hero is Something to be …. but not in Britain's Posh Culture.' *The Guardian,* 26th January. Accessed May 2016. https://www.the-guardian.com/culture/2014/jan/26/working-class-hero-posh-britain-public-school

Oliver and Ohlbaum Associates Ltd. 2015. *A Review of the BBC's Arrangements for Managing On-Screen and On-Air Talent*. London: Oliver and Ohlbaum Associates.

O'Reilly, Miriam. 2015. 'Sexism Thrives in the BBC and No PR Spin Will Cover That Up.' *The Daily Telegraph*, 24th June. Accessed June 2016. http://www.tele-graph.co.uk/women/womens-business/11696206/Miriam-OReilly-BBC-sexism-thrives-and-no-spin-can-cover-it-up.html

Osborn, Ben. 2014. 'The French Art World is on Strike – Why Aren't We?' *Open Democracy*, 24th October. Accessed June 2016. https://www.opendemocracy.net/transformation/ben-osborn/french-art-world-is-on-strike-why-arent-we#

Osborne, William and Abbie Conant. 2010. *A Survey of Women Orchestral Players in Major UK Orchestras as of March 1, 2010.* Accessed June 2016. http://www.osborne-conant.org/orch-uk.htm

Paying Artists. 2014. 'Gallery Case Study One' Accessed June 2016. http://www.payingartists.org.uk/wp-content/uploads/2014/05/Gallery-Case-Study-One_Fabrica-Brighton.pdf

Percival, Neil and David Hesmondhalgh. 2014. 'Unpaid Work in the UK Television and Film Industries: Resistance and Changing Attitudes.' *European Journal of Communication,* 29 2: 188–203.

Phillips, Renee. 2014. 'Beware of Vanity Galleries.' *Manhattan Arts International,* May 15th. Accessed June 2016. http://www.manhattanarts.com/beware-of-vanity-galleries/

Pinheiro, Diego L. and Timothy J. Dowd. 2009. 'All That Jazz: The Success of Jazz Musicians in Three Metropolitan Areas.' *Poetics* 37: 490–506.

Pool, Hannah. 2010. 'Black Ballet: Pointe Break.' *The Guardian,* 4th December. Accessed June 2016. https://www.theguardian.com/stage/2010/dec/04/black-ballet-cassa-pancho

Porter, Roy. 1994. *London: A Social History.* London: Hamish Hamilton.

Potts, Jason, Stuart Cunningham, John Hartley and Paul Ormerod, 2008. 'Social Network Markets: A New Definition of the Creative Industries.' *Journal of Cultural Economics,* 32 3: 167–85.

Price, Simon. 2010. 'The Low Spark of Well-Heeled Boys.' *The Word.* Accessed May 2016. http://www.simonprice.dj/thelowsparkofwellheeledboys.html

Price, Simon. 2014. 'How my Research into Pop's Posh Takeover was Hijacked.' *The Guardian,* February 23rd. Accessed June 2016. https://www.theguardian.com/music/2014/feb/23/research-pops-posh-takeover-hijacked-stars-privately-educated

Prior, Nick. 2015. 'Bourdieu and Beyond.' In *The Routledge Reader on the Sociology of Music,* edited by John Shepherd and Kyle Devine, 349–58. London: Routledge.

Qiu, Jack Linchuan. 2016. *Goodbye iSlave: A Manifesto for Digital Abolition.* Champaign, Il.: University of Illinois Press.

Quigg, Anne-Marie. 2015. *The Handbook of Dealing with Workplace Bullying.* London: Routledge.

Randle, Keith. 2015. 'Class and Exclusion at Work: The Case of UK Film and Television.' In *The Routledge Companion to the Cultural Industries,* edited by Kate Oakley and Justin O'Connor, 330–44. London: Routledge.

Randle, Keith, Cynthia Forson and Moira Calveley. 2014. 'Towards a Bourdieusian Analysis of the Social Composition of the UK Film and Television Workforce.' *Work, Employment and Society* 29 4: 590–606.

Randle, Keith and Kate Hardy. 2016. 'Macho, Mobile and Resilient? How Workers with Impairments are Doubly-Disabled in Project-based Film and Television Work.' *Work, Employment and Society,* forthcoming.

Ratcliffe, Rebecca. 2013. 'The Gender Gap at Universities: Where Are All the Men?' *The Guardian,* 29th January. Accessed June 2016. http://www.theguardian.com/education/datablog/2013/jan/29/how-many-men-and-women-are-studying-at-my-university

Reimer, Suzanne. 2015. 'It's Just a Very Male Industry': Gender and Work in UK Design Agencies.' *Gender, Place and Culture* 23 7: 1033–46.

Reynolds, Simon. 2005. *Rip It Up and Start Again: Post-Punk 1978–84*. London: Faber and Faber.

Roemer, John. 1998. *Equality of Opportunity*. Cambridge: Harvard University Press.

Rosen, Sherwin. 1981. 'The Economics of Superstars.' *The American Economic Review* 71 5: 845–58.

Ross, Andrew. 1998. *Real Love: In Pursuit of Cultural Justice*. London: Routledge.

Ross, Andrew. 2000. 'The Mental Labor Problem.' *Social Text* 18 2: 1–31.

Ross, Andrew. 2003. *No-Collar: The Humane Workplace and its Hidden Costs*. New York: Basic Books.

Ross, Andrew. 2013a. 'An Interview with the Editors.' In *Theorizing Cultural Work*, edited by Mark Banks, Rosalind Gill and Stephanie Taylor, 175–82. London: Routledge.

Ross, Andrew. 2013b. 'In Search of the Lost Paycheck.' In *Digital Labor: The Internet as Playground and Factory*, edited by Trebor Scholz, 13–32. New York: Routledge.

Ryan, Bill. 1992. *Making Capital from Culture: The Corporate Form of Capitalist-Cultural Production*. Berlin: Walter de Gruyter.

Saha, Anamik. 2013. '"Curry Tales": The Production of Race and Ethnicity in the Cultural Industries.' *Ethnicities* 13 6: 818–37.

Sampson, Anthony. 1962. *Anatomy of Britain*. London: Hodder and Stoughton.

Samuel, Raphael. 1959. 'Class and Classlessness.' In *Universities and Left Review* 6: 44–50.

Sayer, Andrew. 1999. 'Valuing Culture and Economy.' In *Culture and Economy after the Cultural Turn,* edited by Larry Ray and Andrew Sayer, 53–75. London: Sage.

Sayer, Andrew. 2000. *Realism and Social Science*. London: Sage.

Sayer, Andrew. 2003. 'Decommodification, Consumer Culture and Moral Economy.' *Environment and Planning D: Society and Space* 21 3: 341–57.

Sayer, Andrew. 2005. *The Moral Significance of Class*. Cambridge: Cambridge University Press.

Sayer, Andrew. 2007. 'Class, Moral Worth and Recognition.' In *(Mis)recognition, Social Inequality and Social Justice: Nancy Fraser and Pierre Bourdieu,* edited by Terry Lovell, 88–102. London: Routledge.

Sayer, Andrew. 2009. 'Contributive Justice and Meaningful Work.' *Res Publica* 15 1: 1–16.

Sayer, Andrew. 2010. 'Bourdieu, Ethics and Practice.' In *Cultural Analysis and Bourdieu's Legacy,* edited by Elizabeth Silva and Alan Warde, 87–101. London: Routledge.

Sayer, Andrew. 2011. *Why Things Matter to People: Social Science, Values and Ethical Life*. Cambridge: Cambridge University Press.

Scharff, Christina. 2015. *Equality and Diversity in the Classical Music Profession*. King's College London. Accessed June 2016. http://blogs.kcl.ac.uk/young-female-and-entrepreneurial/files/2014/02/Equality-and-Diversity-in-the-Classical-Music-Profession.pdf

Schlesinger, Philip. 2007. 'Creativity: From Discourse to Doctrine?' *Screen* 48 3: 377–87.

SDUK. 2015. *SDUK Report on Theatre Director's Pay.* Accessed June 2016. http://www.stagedirectorsuk.com/wp-content/uploads/2015/01/PRESS-RELEASE-THE-SDUK-REPORT-Jan-2015.pdf

Service, Tom. 2009. 'Millionaire Maestros Are Paid Too Much.' *The Guardian,* 18th May. Accessed June 2016. https://www.theguardian.com/music/tomserviceblog/2009/may/18/classical-music-conductors

Sheth, Shruti. 2015. 'The Task of Ensuring More Women Reach the Top in Journalism May Need to Start in the Classroom.' *Press Gazette*, 6th July. Accessed June 2016. http://www.pressgazette.co.uk/the-task-of-ensuring-more-women-reach-the-top-in-journalism-may-need-to-start-in-the-classroom/

Shukaitis, Stevphen. 2016. *The Composition of Movements to Come: Aesthetics and Cultural Labor after the Avant-Garde.* London: Rowman and Littlefield.

Skeggs, Bev. 2009. 'The Moral Economy of Person Production: the Class Relations of Self-Performance on 'Reality' Television.' *The Sociological Review* 57 4: 626–44.

Sibley, Robert. 2015. 'Artists Approve Historic Labour Deal with National Gallery of Canada.' *Ottawa Citizen,* February 25th. Accessed June 2016. http://ottawacitizen.com/news/local-news/artists-approve-historic-labour-deal-national-gallery-of-canada

Skillset. 2010. *Skillset Employer Survey.* Accessed June 2016. https://creativeskillset.org/assets/0000/6002/Skillset_Employer_Survey_2010.pdf

SMCPC (Social Mobility and Child Poverty Commission). 2014. *Elitist Britain.* Accessed June 2016. https://www.gov.uk/government/news/elitist-britain-report-published

Smith, Jacquelyn. 2015. 'Why Companies are Using "Blind Auditions" to Hire Top Talent.' *Business Insider UK,* 31st May. Accessed May 2016. http://uk.businessinsider.com/companies-are-using-blind-auditions-to-hire-top-talent-2015-5?r=US&IR=T

Snow, Georgia. 2015. 'Only 10% of Actors are Working-Class.' *The Stage,* 6th May.Accessed June 2016. https://www.thestage.co.uk/news/2015/10-actors-working-class-report/

SOLT (Society of London Theatre), 2016. *Agreements and Rates of Pay.* Accessed March 2016. http://solt.co.uk/what-we-do/rates-of-pay/

Sound and Music. 2014. *Commissioning Report 2014.* August. Accessed June 2016. http://soundandmusic.org/sites/default/files/projects/files/Commission%20Survey%202014v5.pdf

Srnicek, Nick and Alex Williams, 2016. *Inventing the Future: Postcapitalism and a World Without Work.* London: Verso.

Stahl, Matt. 2013. 'Specificity, Ambivalence and the Commodity Form of Creative Work.' In *Theorizing Cultural Work,* edited by Mark Banks, Rosalind Gill and Stephanie Taylor, 71–84. London: Routledge, London.

Stanley, Bob. 2015. 'Cilla Black was the Archetypal British Working-Class Pop Star.' *The Guardian*, 3rd August. Accessed June 2016. https://www.theguardian.com/music/musicblog/2015/aug/03/cilla-black-archetypal-british-working-class-pop-star

Stark, David. 2009. *The Sense of Dissonance: Accounts of Worth in Economic Life.* Princeton: Princeton University Press.

Stark, Peter, Christopher Gordon and David Powell. 2013. *Rebalancing our Cultural Capital: A Contribution to the Debate on National Policy for the Arts and Culture in England.* Accessed June 2016. http://www.gpsculture.co.uk/rocc.php

Stebbins, Robert. 1966. 'Class, Status and Power among Jazz and Commercial Musicians.' *Sociological Quarterly* 7 2: 197–213

Stern, Carly. 2015. 'They Polarize Anyone Who is Not White, Thin, Tall and Happy': Girl Meets World star Rowan Blanchard, 14, Slams Celebrity 'Squads' like Taylor Swift's For Being Too 'Exclusive.' *Mail Online.* 10th December. Accessed June 2016. http://www.dailymail.co.uk/femail/article-3354676/Girl-Meets-World-star-Rowan-Blanchard-14-slams-celebrity-squads-like-Taylor-Swift-s-exclusive.html

Stewart, Simon. 2012. 'Reflections on Sociology and Aesthetic Value.' *Distinktion: Journal of Social Theory* 13 2: 153–67.

Stewart, Simon. 2013. 'Evaluating Culture: Sociology, Aesthetics and Policy.' *Sociological Research Online* 18 1 14.

Strand, Robert. 1987. *A Good Deal of Freedom: Art and Design in the Public Sector of Higher Education, 1960–1982.* London: CNAA.

Stratton, Jon and Nabeel Zuberi. 2014. *Black Popular Music in Britain since 1945.* London: Ashgate.

Street-Porter, Janet. 2012. 'Sexual Favours Were A Way of Life at the BBC.' *The Independent,* 6th October. Accessed May 2016. http://www.independent.co.uk/voices/comment/sexual-favours-were-a-way-of-life-at-the-bbc-8200645.html

Sullivan, Alice. 2001. 'Cultural Capital and Educational Attainment.' *Sociology* 35 4: 893–912.

Sutton Trust. 2006. *The Educational Backgrounds of Leading Journalists.* London: Sutton Trust.

Sutton Trust. 2016. *Leading People.* London: Sutton Trust. Accessed June 2016. http://www.suttontrust.com/researcharchive/leading-people-2016/

Syal, Meera. 2015. 'I've Been Invisible since I Turned 50' *The Guardian,* 9th June. Accessed June 2016. https://www.theguardian.com/culture/2015/jun/09/meera-syal-invisble-television-sexism-ageism

Swartz, David. 1997. *Culture and Power: The Sociology of Pierre Bourdieu.* Chicago: University of Chicago Press.

Tatli, Abu and Mustafa Ozbilgin. 2012. 'Surprising Intersectionalities of Inequality and Privilege: the Case of the Arts and Cultural Sector.' *Equality, Diversity and Inclusion: An International Journal* 31 3: 249–65.

Taylor, Jowi. 2014. 'Music and Social Justice.' In *The Routledge International Handbook of Social Justice,* edited by Michael Reisch, 492–501. London and New York: Routledge.

Taylor, Stephanie and Karen Littleton. 2012. *Contemporary Identities of Creativity and Creative Work.* Farnham: Ashgate.

Terranova, Tiziana. 2000. 'Free Labor: Producing Culture for the Digital Economy.' *Social Text* 18 2: 33–58.

Thompson, E.P. 1971. 'The Moral Economy of the English Crowd in the Eighteenth Century.' *Past and Present* 50: 76–136.

Thorpe, Vanessa. 2012. 'Eton Spawns a New Breed of Stage and Screen Luminaries.' *The Guardian*, 21st January. Accessed June 2016. http://www.theguardian.com/education/2012/jan/21/eton-stage-screen-luminaries

Throsby, David. 2010. *The Economics of Cultural Policy*. Cambridge: Cambridge University Press.

Throsby, David and Anita Zednik. 2010. *Do You Really Expect to Get Paid? An Economic Study of Professional Artists in Australia*. Australia Council for the Arts.

Todd, Selina. 2014. *The People: The Rise and Fall of the Working-Class*. London: John Murray.

Towse, Ruth and Abdul Khakee. 1992. *Cultural Economics*. Berlin: Springer.

Toynbee, Jason. 2000. *Making Popular Music*. London: Arnold.

Toynbee, Jason. 2003. 'Fingers to the Bone or Spaced out on Creativity? Labor Process and Ideology in the Production of Pop.' In *Cultural Work: Understanding the Cultural Industries*, edited by Andrew Beck, 39–55. London: Routledge.

Toynbee, Jason. 2008. 'Media Making and Social Reality.' In *The Media and Social Theory*, edited by David Hesmondhalgh and Jason Toynbee, 265–279. London: Routledge.

Toynbee, Jason. 2013. 'How Special? Cultural Work, Copyright, Politics.' In *Theorizing Cultural Work*, edited by Mark Banks, Rosalind Gill and Stephanie Taylor, 85–98. London: Routledge.

Toynbee, Jason, Catherine Tackley and Mark Doffman. 2014. *Black British Jazz: Routes, Ownership, Performance*. Farnham: Ashgate.

Tunstall, Jeremy. 1993. *Television Producers*. London: Routledge.

Turvill, William 2013. 'Freelance Rates Survey Suggests Independent is Lowest Paying "Quality" Title.' *Press Gazette*, March 27th. Accessed June 2016. http://www.pressgazette.co.uk/freelance-rates-survey-suggests-independent-is-lowest-paying-quality-title/

Umney, Charles. 2015. 'The Labour Market for Jazz Musicians in Paris and London: Formal Regulation and Informal Norms.' *Human Relations* 69 3: 711–29.

UK Commission for Employment and Skills. 2015. 'Proportion of women in the digital and creative industries falling.' UKCES. Accessed June 2016. https://www.gov.uk/government/news/proportion-of-women-in-the-digital-and-creative-industries-falling

UNESCO. 2013. *Creative Economy Report: Special Edition*, UNDP, Paris.

W.A.G.E. 2016. *W.A.G.E. Wo/manifesto*. Accessed June 2016. http://www.wagefor-work.com/about/1/womanifesto

Wallis, Mick and Joslin McKinney. 2013. 'On Value and Necessity: The Green Book and its Others.' *Performance Research* 18 2: 67–79.

Walzer, Michael. 1983. *Spheres of Justice: A Defence of Pluralism and Equality*. Oxford: Basil Blackwell.

Warwick Commission. 2015. *Enriching Britain: Culture, Creativity and Growth: The Warwick Commission Report on the Future of Cultural Value*. University of Warwick.

Wassall, Gregory and Neal Alper. 1992. 'Towards a Unified Theory of the Determinants of the Earnings of Artists.' In *Cultural Economics*, edited by Ruth Towse and Abdul Khakee, 187–200. Berlin: Springer.

Weber, Rachel. 2012. 'Average UK Industry Salary Rises to £33,123.' Gamesin-
dustry.biz, January 12th. Accessed October 2015. http://www.gamesindustry.biz/
articles/2012-01-12-average-industry-uk-salary-now-GBP33-123pa

Weeks, Kathi. 2011. *The Problem of Work: Feminism, Marxism, Antiwork Politics,
and Postwork Imaginaries.* Durham: Duke University Press.

Westergaard, John. 1964. 'Capitalism without Classes?' *New Left Review* 26: 10–30.

Wilkinson, Richard and Kate Pickett. 2009. *The Spirit Level: Why Equality is Better
for Everyone.* London: Penguin.

Wilmer, Val. 1989. *Mama Said There'd Be Days Like This: My Life in the Jazz
World.* London: Women's Press.

Wolff, Janet. 1993. *The Social Production of Art.* London: Macmillan.

Wolff, Janet. 2008. *The Aesthetics of Uncertainty.* New York: Columbia.

Wood, Will. 2011. 'Unpaid Internships are Exploited by the Wealthiest in the
Creative Industries.' The Guardian, 30th November. Accessed May 2016. https://
www.theguardian.com/culture-professionals-network/culture-professionals-blog/
2011/nov/30/internships-unpaid-arts-culture

Woodmansee, Martha. 1994. *The Author, Art and the Market.* New York: Columbia
University Press.

Woronkowicz, Joanna. 2015. 'Artists, Employment and the Great Recession:
A Cross-Sectional Analysis Using US Current Population Survey Data.' *Cultural
Trends* 24 2: 154–64.

Wreyford, Natalie. 2015. 'Birds of a Feather: Informal Recruitment Practices and
Gendered Outcomes for Screenwriting Work in the UK Film Industry.' *The
Sociological Review* 63 1: 84–96.

Wyatt, Daisy. 2014. 'Homeland Star David Harewood Still Struggling to Find
Work as Black Actor in UK.' *The Independent,* 18th March. Accessed June
2016. http://www.independent.co.uk/arts-entertainment/tv/news/homeland-star
-david-harewood-still-struggling-to-find-work-as-black-actor-in-uk-9199504.html

Young, Michael. 1958. *The Rise of the Meritocracy.* London: Thames and Hudson.

Yudice, George. 1999. 'The Privatization of Culture.' *Social Text* 59: 17–34.

Zangwill, Nick. 2002. 'Against the Sociology of the Aesthetic' *Journal for Cultural
Research* 6 4: 443–52.

Zimdars, Anna, Alice Sullivan and Anthony Heath. 2009. 'Elite Higher Education
Admissions in the Arts and Sciences: Is Cultural Capital the Key?' *Sociology* 43 4:
448–66.

Index

About the Author

Mark Banks is professor of culture and communication in the Department of Media and Communication at the University of Leicester. His interest is in the cultural and creative industries, especially in relation to work and identity, employment, cultural policy and cultural value. He is the author of *The Politics of Cultural Work* (2007) and co-editor of *Theorizing Cultural Work* (2013), with Rosalind Gill and Stephanie Taylor. His recent writing has included work on art schools, dance and black British music. In 2016, he was appointed as the director of the new Cultural and Media Economies Institute (CAMEo) at the University of Leicester.